# The Egos
# Have Landed

# ANGUS FINNEY

## The Egos Have Landed

### The Rise and Fall of Palace Pictures

CEN 01465566

HEINEMANN : LONDON

Thanks are due to the following for providing photographs:
photo 1. © Sandie Shaw; 3. © Graham Attwood; 5. © Roger Morton; 6. © David Appleby; 7. © Clive Coote; 8, 9, 10, 11. © Tom Collins; 12. © Tom Johnston, *News of the World*; 13. © Richard Blanchard; 14. © Michael O'Neill; 15, 17. © Tom Hilton; 16. © Ph. Schiller/Dephi; 18. © François Duhamel; 19. © Alan Davidson. Thanks to Nik Powell, Stephen Woolley, Tom Cruise, *Time Out*, *Screen International*, Miramax Film, UIP

First published in Great Britain 1996
by William Heinemann Ltd
an imprint of Reed International Books Ltd
Michelin House, 81 Fulham Road, London SW3 6RB
and Auckland, Melbourne, Singapore and Toronto

A CIP catalogue record for this title
is available from the British Library
ISBN 0 434 00220 8

Typeset by Deltatype Ltd, Ellesmere Port, Cheshire
Printed and bound in Great Britain
by Clays Ltd, St Ives plc

*To Trine Piil Christensen,*
*with all my love*

'It's quite possible for good to triumph over evil, but the Angels have to be organised like the Mafia.'
Kurt Vonnegut

# Acknowledgements

There was no shortage of opinion when I came to research this story. More than 125 interviews were held, including twenty-five meetings with Nik Powell and Stephen Woolley. Both men were very helpful, and gave up considerable amounts of their time towards the research of the book. The employees at Scala Productions were also very supportive, in particular Imogen West, Polly Duval, and Pete Ogunsalu. The end result, however, remains an unauthorised, independent account of the rise and fall of Palace Pictures.

Of the people formally interviewed, the following can be thanked by name: Iain Allan, Martyn Auty, Daniel Battsek, John Battsek, Jeffrey Berg, Richard Branson, Wendy Broom, Joe Boyd, Amanda Burgess, Sue Bruce-Smith, Jenne Casarotto, Patrick Cassavetti, Michael Caton-Jones, Christopher Craib, Finola Dwyer, Jake Eberts, Angie Errigo, Tony Elliot, Mike Ewin, Stan Fishman, Susie Figgis, Christopher Fowler, Michael Garland, Linda Gamble, Terry Glinwood, Romaine Hart, Peter Hitchen, John Hogarth, Norman Humphrey, Angie Hunt, Premila Hoon, Gilles Jacob, Neil Jordan, Robert Jones, Elizabeth Karlsen, Tony Kelly, Michael Kuhn, Mary Lambert, Jack Lechner, Mike Leedham, David Leland, Colin Leventhal, Sandy Lieberson, Phil Livingstone, Allan Mckeown, Hamish McAlpine, Derek Malcolm, Maarten Melchior, Carole Myer, Katy McGuinness, Robert Mitchell, Redmond Morris, Angela Morrison, Tony Murphy, David Norris, Julia Palau, Clive Parsons, Simon Perry, Amanda Posey, Irving Rappaport, Simon Relph, Mike Ryan, Richard Stanley, Anthony Spicer,

*Acknowledgements*

Jim Sturgeon, Phil Symes, JoAnne Sellar, Anne Sheehan, Dom Shaw, George Sluizer, John Stutter, Julien Temple, Jeremy Thomas, Garth Thomas, Michael Thomas, Paul Trijbits, David Walburn, Paul Webster, Wim Wenders and Roger Wingate.

In addition to the above, there are twenty or so people who gave interviews but requested not to be mentioned by name. The author is also grateful for their time and help. Other sources which were helpful include: *Screen International* (Ralf Ludemann and Mike Goodridge in particular); *Time Out* magazine; *Empire* magazine, the British Film Institute's library staff, British Screen Finance, Smith & Williamson and Mike Ewin.

I am particularly grateful to my transcriber, Julie Farrelly, and to certain friends both inside and outside the film industry for their useful comments during the editing process. Thanks to Simon Gallant of Mishcon de Reya, whose advice was much appreciated. Trine Christensen read drafts of this book many times over, and her support was unflagging and consistently constructive. Thanks to my meticulous copy editor, Victoria Hipps; my agent, Bill Hamilton; and my very encouraging editor and publisher, Tom Weldon.

# Contents

# Principal Film Credits

|  | *Title* | *Director* |
|---|---|---|
| Palace Film Productions | *The Company of Wolves* (1984) | Neil Jordan |
|  | *Chinese Boxes* (1984) | Chris Petit |
|  | *Absolute Beginners* (1985) | Julien Temple |
|  | *A Letter to Brezhnev* (1985) | Chris Bernard |
|  | *Mona Lisa* (1986) | Neil Jordan |
|  | *Siesta* (1987) | Mary Lambert |
|  | *Shag* (1987) | Zelda Barron |
|  | *High Spirits* (1987) | Neil Jordan |
|  | *Dream Demon* (1988) | Harley Cockliss |
|  | *Scandal* (1988) | Michael Caton-Jones |
|  | *The Courier* (1989) | Frank Deasy/Joe Lee |
|  | *The Big Man* (1989) | David Leland |
|  | *Dancin' Thru' the Dark* (1989) | Mike Ockrent |
|  | *Hardware* (1990) | Richard Stanley |
|  | *A Rage in Harlem* (1990) | Bill Duke |
|  | *The Miracle* (1990) | Neil Jordan |
|  | *The Pope Must Die* (1991) | Peter Richardson |
|  | *Waterland* (1991) | Stephen Gyllenhaal |
|  | *Dust Devil* (1991) | Richard Stanley |
|  | *The Crying Game* (1991) | Neil Jordan |
| Palace Television Productions | *Lenny Live and Unleashed* (1989) |  |
|  | *Beyond the Groove* (1989) |  |
|  | *Woman at War* (1990) |  |
|  | *Red Hot and Blue* (1990) |  |

| Scala Film Productions | *Dark Blood* (Unfinished – 1993) | George Sluizer |
| | *Backbeat* (1994) | Iain Softley |
| | *The Neon Bible* (1995) | Terence Davies |
| | *The Hollow Reed* (1995) | Angela Pope |
| | *B Monkey* (1996) | Michael Caton-Jones |
| Stephen Woolley's Additional Producer Credits | *The Worst of Hollywood* (1983) | (Channel 4 series) |
| | *Interview with a Vampire* (1994) | Neil Jordan |
| | *Michael Collins* (1996) | Neil Jordan |

# Chasing
# an Oscar

Given the guarantee of world-wide publicity, demonstrations at the Academy Awards are always rigorous. On 29 March 1993, the night that Neil Jordan's *The Crying Game* was competing for six Oscars, the cardboard placards and screaming were in protest against a recent Government bill that blocked Latin immigrants' social security rights. Other signs demanding 'Justice For Janitors' protested against the venue organisers' use of non-union cleaning staff.

As the Academy's guests began to arrive at the Dorothy Chandler Pavilion, the demonstrators were pushed back by the surging paparazzi, eager to climb over the arriving black limousines to get a shot at the stars. A booming tannoy announced the arrivals as they made their way inside the Pavilion, with cheers going up for the big names.

Stephen Rea, the Irish actor and leading player in *The Crying Game*, was the first guest to win recognition; Jordan's appearance too inspired a big cheer. Stephen Woolley, *The Crying Game*'s producer, was greeted by a vague murmur, nobody quite sure who the almost diminutive, pony-tailed figure was. Yet the crowd's message seemed loud and clear. Everyone was rooting for the underdog. The little British film costing less than $4 million was being tipped for Best Picture.

As Woolley walked through the rubber-necking crowds towards the resplendent red-carpeted entrance to the Pavilion, he found himself by chance walking in step with Clint Eastwood. The Hollywood veteran was up for nine Oscars for his Western, *Unforgiven*. The two men had met at ceremonies during the previous weeks where both of their films had been picking up a slew of awards. Eastwood had always made a point of coming over to *The Crying Game* table and chatting to Jordan and Woolley, and had always been impeccably polite.

'God! It feels like I'm gate-crashing someone else's party,' Woolley remarked to Eastwood as they walked in.

'Whaddaya mean? I'm the gate-crasher! This has never happened to me in my whole life!' Eastwood shot back.

Once inside, Woolley noticed the lack of well-spaced tables, elegant bottles donated by Francis Ford Coppola's vineyard, and general civility that had embraced virtually every other American award event he'd attended in the weeks prior to the Oscars. This was different. This was like sitting down in a massive room to watch television. Strange tuxedoed figures reminiscent of a Fellini movie hovered around the edges of the auditorium, dashing into vacated seats when guests disappeared to the toilet or for a drink, turning the auditorium into a railway station during the intervals, when a quarter of the audience left the room and the stand-ins took their seats. After all, at the Oscars there could not be empty seats, glaringly vacant for the world to spy on television.

As the ceremony progressed, Woolley became aware of a strange mood in the Pavilion. A growing frustration among the majority of people connected to films that hadn't won became apparent. As the night advanced, the losers couldn't fail to outnumber the winners. More and more tuxedoed stand-ins filled vacated seats, as bitterly disappointed guests drowned their sorrows at the bar, wept in the toilets or went home.

Nik Powell, the executive producer of *The Crying Game*, was sitting next to Jaye Davidson (nominated for Best Supporting Actor) and his friend, who were both making loud, catty comments about the proceedings. Jane Fonda leaned over from a nearby row and – correctly, in Powell's opinion – told them to 'Shut up'. Davidson, dressed in riding breeches, no shirt, a riding coat and boots above his knees, was upset. He disappeared to the bar to buy four vodka-tonics, two for him and two for his friend, further irritating Powell.

Jordan was chatting away in the bar to film-maker Michael Tolkin, nominated for Best Adapted Screenplay for *The Player*, when the announcement came that that award had gone to Ruth Prawer Jhabvala for her *Howards End* screenplay. Tolkin quipped: 'There goes my prize.' A shock went through Jordan, as he realised his nomination was next. He rushed back into the auditorium, crouching down next to Woolley's chair during the announcement. In the rush, he didn't realise he'd won the Oscar for Best Original Screenplay.

Woolley explained, 'C'mon Neil, you've got to get up there.'

Ten months earlier, Nik Powell and Stephen Woolley's decade-old film empire, the Palace Group of Companies, was collapsing under debts estimated to be between £6 million and £30 million. Nobody really knew the extent of the damage, but one thing was clear: Palace had run out of money.

On the morning of 7 May 1992, Powell caught a taxi to accountants Smith & Williamson on Great Riding Street. He needed to check the final papers to be filed at the High Court seeking to put Palace into administration and to protect it from its 200-odd creditors. Despite desperate last-minute calls on his mobile phone begging for help, including one to his old Virgin partner Richard Branson, Powell recognised that the end for Palace had finally arrived.

Returning from the administrators, Powell walked into Palace's offices on Wardour Mews in the heart of Soho. His thick jet-black hair sweeping over strained red eyes, the Palace co-chairman gathered his depleted staff into the top-floor room of the offices. A crowd of around thirty people milled about in the wooden-floored space, waiting for their boss to address them. Most of them knew what was coming. Standing next to Powell was Woolley and a representative from Smith & Williamson.

'Er, I've asked you to come up here because I need to tell you that we are going into administration today,' Powell said chokingly. 'I can't offer any guarantee of employment here any longer.' After a few more words of explanation and thanks, Powell lost it. Tears began to form, his lower lip trembled and his frame began to shake with emotion. Woolley took over, saying a few words, followed by the administrator. Then it was over.

People filed out, a few in tears but most in a state of numbness, and went straight to the pub – a familiar routine in Palace's culture – and got drunk. Palace, Britain's most exciting independent film company of the past decade, was seeing its last days.

CHAPTER ONE

# The Crying Game

*The Crying Game* was conceived at Neil Jordan's and Stephen Woolley's first meeting in London in the summer of 1982. The twenty-four-year-old Palace executive had fallen in love with Jordan's début feature, *Angel*, a low-budget television film backed by Channel 4 which he'd seen at the Cannes Film Festival that May. The press at Cannes had whipped up a frenzy about *Angel*, hyping Jordan's *film noir* intricately wrapped around the IRA as a sign of great things to come. A self-described 'bad Catholic and a bad Marxist', Jordan had already established a reputation as Ireland's most promising writer of prose fiction. His short story collection *Night in Tunisia* had won the *Guardian* fiction prize in 1979, and he had gone on to write *The Past*, a novel that explored the Irish revolution of 1916.

The vigilant Woolley had spotted Jordan's mentor, the film-maker John Boorman, on the producing credits of *Angel*. Straight from his flight from Cannes, Woolley rang up Boorman and arranged to have a drink at the Ritz in Piccadilly to talk about the film and Jordan's future. The pony-tailed Woolley arrived in a suit and T-shirt, sporting a Côte d'Azur sun tan, and was promptly evicted from the hotel for not wearing a tie. The two men went round the corner to a pub. Boorman loved the newly launched Palace's risky-but-fresh approach to film distribution, and the two men nattered away about Jean-Jacques Beineix's *Diva*, a French film for which Palace had secured a British cinema release for later that year. Boorman promised to put Woolley in touch with Jordan.

A few weeks later Jordan made it to London, by which time Woolley had conscientiously bought and read all Jordan's writings. The two men met in a Camden restaurant and forged a link, talking and drinking late into the night about books, cinema, Ireland and film-making. Their friendship flowered when Palace convinced Channel 4 to allow it to release *Angel* in cinemas. Albeit modest in terms of box office success, the move was to have a far-reaching significance, pioneering the way for Channel 4's films to play at the cinema long before they reached the British living-room.

Jordan was thrilled to see his work reach the big screen. Such commitment to cinema appealed to the Irish director, who was fed up with Ireland and the eternal civil war amongst its jealous native film-makers. He was also feeling the pressure of Ireland's real war. Although *Angel* was neither pro- nor anti-IRA, Jordan had been threatened by three men who had visited his home in Dublin one night following the mass of press attention surrounding the film. 'They came in and walked through the house without saying a word,' Jordan recalled. 'My wife and children were there, and I was scared, even though I'd realised that to tackle such a political subject would be dangerous.' Jordan didn't take any chances, and promptly called in Special Branch for some protection. While the experience was sobering, it did not stop Jordan writing stories about the IRA.

*The Soldier's Wife* was just one of a number of Jordan's potential film projects that Woolley was keen to produce. It was vaguely referred to by both of them as 'The Soldier's Story', but the problem was that only half a script existed. Jordan couldn't work out a way to complete the story to his satisfaction, and it ended up on a forgotten shelf. Pushed to the back of Jordan's mind, it was rapidly replaced by *The Company Of Wolves*, which became Palace's first film production in 1984.

Nine years later, during the Berlin Film Festival of February 1991, *The Soldier's Wife* screenplay resurfaced. Woolley and Jordan were drinking in a late-night Berlin bar after a successful festival screening of *The Miracle*, Jordan's latest film. Out of the blue, Jordan brought up 'The Soldier's Story', asking Woolley: 'What do you think if Dil, the girlfriend of the black soldier who Fergus looks up in London, turned out to be a man?'

'Brilliant,' Woolley replied. 'Great twist, Neil. Just what the story needs. I promise I'll try and make it this summer.' It was a promise that Woolley was to find impossible to keep.

A few weeks later, Woolley handed Nik Powell the Jordan film script to read on one of Powell's hundreds of plane flights around Europe in search of money to make movies. For once escaping from the business paperwork that dogged him incessantly, Powell raced through the whole story in the ninety-minute plane journey from Madrid to Paris and connecting cab rides. On many occasions he startled nearby passengers as he laughed out loud at the ironic humour, admiring the way Jordan had tapped into 'some of men's darkest fears' throughout the complex but enticing plot.

Dressed in a Next suit with ink-stained pockets, Powell looked more like a used-car salesman than a top movie deal-maker. Passengers might have laughed incredulously had they known that this slight, chaotic figure with a manic laugh was co-chairman of a film company turning over nearly £24 million a year.

As Powell completed the start of the third act of *The Soldier's Wife*, his adrenalin shot up. Jordan had written a remarkable screenplay and Powell was already fired up to sell it.

His meeting in Paris was with CiBy 2000, a newly launched and cash-rich French film company set up by the conservative multi-millionaire Francis Bouygues. Bouygues's colossal empire, founded on concrete, had expanded into the media and by the mid-1980s when he took control of France's top commercial television station, TF1, Bouygues was one of France's most powerful media moguls. Making money was not Bouygues's only love in life; the man rather fancied himself as a cinema buff and patron. CiBy had consequently set about investing its money in some of the world's top film directors – including Bernardo Bertolucci, Spike Lee, Jane Campion, David Lynch and Pedro Almodóvar – in a high-profile bid to make its mark on the film world. While Palace's jungle of creaking companies back in London could not have differed more from CiBy's concrete-backed collateral, Neil Jordan would not have looked so out of place amongst CiBy's pack of prized luminaries.

Powell was supposed to be merely dropping in for a 'relationship' meeting with CiBy film executive Pierre Edelman. A laconic, husky-voiced scout whose job it was politely to fend off pitches for money from British film-makers, Edelman was used to fielding enthusiastic plugs from pushy producers. The art of pitching a project to potential backers is central to a film producer's job. It was a skill at which Powell, despite his shambolic appearance, excelled.

Correct film business protocol would normally have precluded any opportunistic pitching of new ideas for films during such an early chat, but the turbo-charged Powell rarely cared much for manners, and he was not going to start now. Fired by his enthusiasm for the script and the lure of CiBy's money staring him in the face, Powell decided to go ahead and try *The Soldier's Wife* on his host. He plunged into the pitch:

'It's about this black English soldier . . .'

'That's a negative,' Edelman interrupted, not from any racism on his part, but sensitive to the ever conservative cinema market.

But the determined Powell soldiered on: 'And he's been posted to Northern Ireland and he's at this fun fair, where he gets abducted by the IRA.'

'That's *another* negative,' Edelman said.

Undeterred, Powell cantered through the story, explaining how Jody, the black soldier, formed a relationship with Fergus, one of his IRA captors.

'Jody tells Fergus that if anything happens to him, he wants him to look up his girlfriend Dil, and he shows Fergus a picture of her. She's really attractive . . . and she's black also,' Powell explained.

'That's a *double* negative,' Edelman stated.

A few minutes later the pitch was over. The French executive slowly leant over the desk, and declared: 'But I love it.'

Minutes later, Powell was racing out of CiBy's offices into the Champs Elysées. He dashed into a nearby pay phone, rang Woolley and Jordan, and shouted: 'CiBy love it! You've gotta get over here at once.'

Virtually all serious French film business meetings are done over lunch. The French film industry collectively detests doing business on the phone, and cannot stand meeting new people. However, given Neil Jordan's and Stephen Woolley's track record, which included *The Company Of Wolves* and the award-winning *Mona Lisa*, this formidable director–producer team deserved no less than a formal lunch. A meeting was promptly set up in Paris for before the end of that week. Meanwhile, the screenplay was handed out to CiBy's top executives, all of whom read it and, without exception, admired it.

The expectant Jordan and Woolley arrived for the CiBy lunch geared up to talk about casting and production dates for shooting *The Soldier's Wife*, but as they were walking through to the dining room, Pierre Edelman took them both to one side. In a low voice, he explained: 'You have to understand that although we love this script, and we really wanted to meet you both, we cannot make this movie.'

Somewhat taken back, Jordan asked bluntly, 'Why not?'

'Because Mr Bouygues is homophobic.'

Both Jordan and Woolley were deeply puzzled by this reply. Jordan pointed out that this did not make any sense at all, given that CiBy had just financed *High Heels*, a $4 million film directed by the outrageous and openly gay Spanish film-maker, Pedro Almodóvar.

'Yes, yes, but Mr Bouygues doesn't know that,' said Edelman mysteriously. He went on to explain that at the launch party for *High Heels*, CiBy executives had deliberately surrounded Almodóvar with hordes of very attractive women. The ploy was to ensure that their boss did not have any suspicions about his star director's sexual preferences. Evidently, it worked, as CiBy later financed another Almodóvar movie, *Kika*. Bouygues was successfully kept in the dark about Almodóvar's predilections until the magnate's death in 1993.

As far as Edelman and his executives were concerned, however, there could be no pulling the wool over their boss's eyes with *The Soldier's Wife*. Yes, Jordan was a brilliantly talented director; yes, he was heterosexual; yes, they loved the script, but the answer was still no because there was no disguising the extraordinary sexual nature of the story.

Woolley and Jordan politely ate the lunch and returned to London. Thanks to Powell's resourceful foot-in-the-door introduction, they had almost managed to set the film up with one strong backer. But clearly financing this Neil Jordan film was going to take rather more than a one-stop shopping expedition on the Champs Elysées.

Woolley had whisked the screenplay over to Miramax Films, Palace's first port of call in America. Miramax Films was an aggressive New York-based distribution company run by the notoriously belligerent brothers, Bob and Harvey Weinstein. Miramax had forged a tempestuous but productive relationship with Palace during the late 1980s. The Weinsteins were regular partners on Palace productions by the time *The Soldier's Wife* landed on their desk, and Woolley and Powell were hopeful that Miramax would provide a significant proportion of the film's budget.

However, the Weinstein brothers shared two major dislikes: the thought of making a film that audiences would not understand, and the chance of losing their own money. Jordan's most recent film, *The Miracle*, had flopped for them in America. Hence, Miramax's initial response to *The Soldier's Wife* was understandably wary. Harvey Weinstein argued that there was no way Palace could cast a man as Dil, the soldier's 'girlfriend' who provided the twist to Jordan's new ending.

The relationship between Palace and Miramax was often tempestuous and there were frequent trans-Atlantic rows on the telephone, which would be brought to an abrupt halt when Weinstein would yell, 'Lose my number Nik' and slam the phone down. The office in London would go quiet.

Powell and Woolley would nervously hover around the phone. Woolley would shout at Powell not to ring back: 'Wait, Nik! Wait. Harvey'll call back . . .' Minutes later the phone would ring and Woolley, grabbing it before Powell could, would set about cooling Weinstein down.

In the case of *The Soldier's Wife*, Powell searched desperately for ways of keeping Miramax's hat in the financing ring without being bullied into casting a woman. Despite *The Soldier's Wife* being raised during many calls and meetings that spring, Miramax eventually passed on investing money upfront in the film. So too did every other American potential investor, including some of the major Hollywood studios, some of which, it appeared, barely understood the storyline. No money towards this film was going to come from North America. Time was running out if the film was to be made that summer.

Finding a cast for *The Soldier's Wife* was 'hell on earth' according to top casting agent Susie Figgis. The only certainty was that long-time Jordan collaborator Stephen Rea would play Fergus, the IRA fall guy. The early casting of US actor Forest Whitaker as Jody, the black British soldier, caused a major bust-up with British Equity. Woolley had recently worked with Whitaker on Palace's American production of *A Rage In Harlem* and was confident that the actor could pull off a British accent for *The Soldier's Wife*. He had introduced Whitaker to Jordan at Cannes that May, and the Irish director had fallen for him. 'God, Steve, he's so great,' Jordan had eulogised. 'Forest is such a wonderful actor.' As far as Woolley and Jordan were concerned, Whitaker was in from the start.

During that summer, the British actors' union used Palace's casting of a black American actor instead of a British one to argue that more domestic black actors needed lead roles in UK films. Equity's public whinging drove Woolley apoplectic. When film trade magazine *Screen International* called him about the row, he went up the wall, screaming: 'Who the fuck does Equity think it is? Palace is busting a gut to make a bloody British film, and Equity is saying in the same breath it wants more movies made here!' Following a somewhat sheepish meeting with Woolley, where Equity members found it hard to confront the fired-up producer in person, Palace agreed to pay Equity a small fee on the film and Whitaker stayed in the picture.

The part of Jude, the tough *femme fatale* IRA terrorist, also created problems for Figgis and Woolley. Although everyone wanted British actress Miranda Richardson to play Jude, Richardson had also been offered the lead part in another of Palace's productions, an adaptation of Graham Swift's novel, *Waterland*. Unfortunately, both films were scheduled to shoot simultaneously that autumn. Initially, Richardson, who was still some way from achieving the international status she enjoys today, looked a certainty for *Waterland*. She was to star opposite Jeremy Irons, hot from his recent Best Actor's Oscar for playing Claus von Bülow in the film *Reversal of Fortune*. After some weeks of heated negotiations between Woolley and the producers of *Waterland*, it was agreed that Richardson, somewhat incredibly, would find a way to play the key roles in both films. The actress was tetchy about the schedule-crunched arrangement, but was saved from performing an heroic feat of acting schizophrenia when it finally became clear that the compromise was an impossibility due to the dates. Under tremendous pressure from the producers of both productions not to let them down, Richardson – swung by her admiration for Jordan's screenplay – opted at the last minute for *The Soldier's Wife*.

It was Dil, the black 'girlfriend', who remained the most problematic character to cast. At auditions, the obvious black male actors had been rejected by Figgis: 'Most of them had either big necks, big Adam's apples, big hands, big legs, big everything. Then we tried the female impersonators – the transsexuals and transvestites – who were interesting enough but didn't work at all because they had the most horrible female characteristics.' The word had been put out to the London club scene that summer that Palace was looking for a suitable 'chick with a dick' for a unique film role. Then Figgis happened to bump into Derek Jarman's boyfriend, who told her about a late-night clubber and vaguely employed fashion assistant, Jaye Davidson.

Woolley and Jordan thought the androgenous Davidson, with his long dark hair and petite facial features, was a real possibility and tested him on video and eventually on film. Although apparently completely bored and turned-off by the entire casting process, Davidson kept calling back and turning up for numerous auditions. Despite the twenty-four-year-old's acidic asides and his abject horror at the prospect of cutting all his hair off – something he would be asked to do during the film shoot if he got the part – Davidson was clearly intrigued by the thought of playing Dil. 'Jaye was a big clubber, and we knew he'd go out dancing at really funky clubs like Kinky Gerlinky and all the trendy bars. But he only turned up late a few times,' Woolley explained. Figgis was not yet convinced, and continued to test everything in sight. Palace even brought in the actress Cathy Tyson – who, five years earlier, had played the lead role opposite Bob Hoskins in Palace's production of Jordan's *Mona Lisa* – to see how the role might work when acted by a woman.

Davidson's sanguine 'take-it-or-leave-it' demeanour and subtle attractiveness started to grow on everyone. He might not have ever acted before, but he really did seem to fit the character Jordan had envisaged in his audacious story. As Woolley put it: 'We could have cast a woman, but it would have been very dishonest. We needed a man, and yet were hoping that the audience wouldn't spot it because they'd be caught up in the drama and wouldn't be looking for it. That's the trick of the film, and Jaye offered the intrigue and secret we needed for the part.'

Symptomatic of the film industry, auditioning continued persistently throughout the summer, just in case someone had been missed. Finally, during a session at the Goldcrest screening facilities in Soho, Woolley cracked. 'This is stupid,' he said to Jordan. 'Jaye's so good and he's saying these lines so well. Can we just get on and cast him before I end up fucking him.'

The script had also been sent to the UK's government-backed film body, British Screen Finance, a regular supporter of Palace's productions and the only serious provider of film production funds left in place after a decade of Conservative government cut-backs. British Screen's chief executive was Simon Perry, a deliciously deep-voiced, smooth-talking old Etonian who had made his mark by dragging British film producers, albeit kicking and screaming, into projects with European film-makers. Perry respected Palace's proven ability to market its films to British audiences, and he greatly admired Jordan's talents both as a screenwriter and director.

Perry read the screenplay in a hotel in Ireland during July 1991. 'I remember feeling these powerfully mixed emotions, because it sent a tingle down my spine. I thought it was exactly the kind of script Hollywood would reject, but if cast correctly the film could touch gold. Then I thought, "Fuck, why did Palace have to send us this now, just when Nik and Steve are heading into a very difficult period of their relationship with us?" '

By late summer 1991, Palace owed British Screen £351,000 via a complex repayment agreement in return for previous British Screen investments in Palace productions. However, given the company's inability to maintain payments that were falling due, this debt was set to rise to £600,000 in a few months' time.

Perry was now having to reconsider all new Palace investments given that the company's financial situation was under such pressure. As if that was not enough, Perry was also hamstrung by the fact that British Screen were already committed to well over a £1 million in two other Palace productions, *Waterland*, about to be abandoned by Miranda Richardson, and Richard Stanley's next film *Dust Devil*, set to start shooting in the desert of Namibia that August.

Perry was wary of giving the ever-jealous British film industry the impression that 'Palace just had to go to a hole in the wall, put their card in, and out would come British Screen's money.' He also had to contend with his board, whose members were adamant that British Screen should not do any more 'Woolley and Powell' films for the time being. The board, like most people in the film industry, had picked up the word winging its way around Soho's bitchy gossip mill that Palace, once again, was on the edge of bankruptcy.

Nevertheless, true to his initial instinct, Perry became a committed champion of Jordan's screenplay. On his return from Ireland he had breakfast with Woolley at La Brasserie in the Fulham Road and confirmed that he would fight to help fund the film. Perry promised he would set about trying to persuade his board that it was worth making an exception for *The Soldier's Wife*. The maximum investment he could justify was £500,000, £100,000 short of the sum Palace had hoped British Screen would contribute to their patchwork budget.

In order to release the money, British Screen needed to work out an arrangement to cover its already plundered funds. In return for investing in *The Soldier's Wife*, the board insisted that Palace had to find a way of repaying the lion's share of the guarantees still outstanding. That was always going to be much easier said than done.

Wise to the ways of juggling film finance and closing deals, Powell assured Perry that if British Screen came in and the film went into production, it would trigger other monies to be raised within the Palace Group of Companies and enable him to repay the debts. It was only later, when Palace was unable fully to repay the monies due to a pile-up of cash-hungry creditors, that Powell voluntarily offered a personal guarantee. The offer was quickly accepted by the nervous board, although it ran counter to the personal wishes of Perry and his management team. Perry hated the idea of British Screen – which, after all, was supposed to support film-makers – personally going up against a film producer. More tellingly, he also suspected that Powell had been forced by this time to give out personal guarantees to other creditors around town. While Powell's offer was well intentioned, Perry had a feeling that the money simply was not there.

When Woolley and Powell arrived at the Venice Film Festival in early September 1991, they were still a long way short of the £2.8 million needed to send *The Soldier's Wife* into production. Woolley was also under increasing personal pressure from Jordan, who had been complaining about being broke and, more seriously, talking about dropping *The Soldier's Wife* altogether. This was no idle threat, and had been voiced as early as June that year when Woolley and Jordan had provided guests at the director Stephen Frears's fiftieth birthday party with some emotionally charged entertainment. Diners near the Palace table looked on with embarrassed shock as the two film-makers came to verbal blows over the timing of the film. During the dinner, Woolley pointed out how desperately hard it was to attract an American deal for the risky, albeit inspired and audacious, script. The film would almost certainly not be shot until autumn at the earliest. Jordan's reaction was loud enough for all to hear: 'I'm bust, and I'll bugger off to Hollywood to earn some real money on a movie if you don't get this film made.'

By the time Venice and autumn came round, Woolley had received an ultimatum: either he got *The Soldier's Wife* into production by the end of the year or Jordan would vanish and there would be no film.

One of Palace's crucial meetings at the Venice Film Festival was with the company's European distribution partners. At the previous Venice Film Festival, Powell, with the help of Dutch film bankers Pierson, Heldring & Pierson, had set up a complex five-partner European distribution company called Eurotrustees. The initial idea was that the companies – which included Spanish, German, Italian and French enterprises, in addition to Palace – would all agree on investing in a range of European films for distribution across the continent, providing an alternative to Hollywood's powerfully centralised distribution machines. The problems facing Eurotrustees were enormous. The original Italian and German partners had already dropped out after some thumping rows, highlighting the inherent problems within the fragmented European film industry. Although they were eventually replaced thanks to Powell's persuasive touch, the union of Euro-egos looked decidedly shaky. The biggest problem of all was that they had consistently failed to agree, with the result that they had not backed one film. With no investment, there could be no Eurotrustees movies.

Powell was determined that the imaginative financing scheme could be made to work. If the partners could be seduced into agreeing on even one film, Palace stood a good chance of putting its own future productions through the Eurotrustees pipeline. He had already contacted Eurotrustees members on the phone, yabbering on about 'what a cracking script Neil's written', and how 'we've already got British Screen in, plus Channel 4 are looking a dead cert'. Despite Powell's puffing, the Eurotrustees members were far from convinced as they flew into Venice for the pow-wow. They were aware that *The Miracle* had failed dismally for those who had released it that summer, and the thought of doing a Neil Jordan film sent a nervous shiver down their spines.

The main meeting went well enough, so Powell and Woolley decided to bring up the question of *The Soldier's Wife* during Any Other Business. Woolley, who was normally relatively quiet at these meetings, slammed his producer's hat on. This was his big chance. Here they were, all together in one room. It was time to pitch:

'Let's *do* something, for fuck's sake. If we make this movie at least we've *done* something. We've been fooling around for more than a year getting nowhere. This isn't a huge risk for you guys, and it's a terrific story, and we've already got a great star cast with Forest and everyone. If we pull this off it's going to be a bloody great film.'

'That's all very well, Steve, but what about the casting of Dil? Do you think an audience will really buy this man as a woman?' one of the partners moaned predictably. Woolley promptly yanked out a dazzling piece of artwork, showing Jaye Davidson posed convincingly in a striking pink dress, legs crossed, beneath the words *The Soldier's Wife*. The room went quiet while they contemplated Davidson's legs, leaving Powell a chance to wade in with his side of the pitch. He assured his partners that he could get Pierson, along with French and German banks to cashflow their up-front investment in the project. Powell's unorthodox but highly inventive banking deal was indeed a very attractive proposal, which left the investors with little to pay for several years. Privately, some of them later moaned to a Palace lawyer that the £250,000 to £300,000 or so invested was actually too high for the film, but as their money was to remain untouched for so long, they had been seduced into going along for the ride.

'Nik and I were being quite cheeky,' Woolley recalled later. 'We knew that Palace at that point was staring at the barrel of a gun, and that our contribution as distributors might not be a permanent one.' Cheeky was one way of putting it. The company's jewel was Palace Pictures, the theatrical distribution company. Less than two months after the Eurotrustees meeting, on 11 November, the cash-strapped Palace signed a £2 million deal with a rival UK distributor which severely reduced the role of Palace Pictures. Moreover, a long time prior to the Venice meeting, Powell had started in-depth talks with PolyGram, the Dutch music giant and newly emerging film player. The Palace co-chairman was starting to consider the unthinkable: selling the Palace Group of Companies.

The Eurotrustees crew did not have a clue that these desperate Palace deals were just around the corner. Feeling relieved to have finally agreed on a film, the partners committed just over a £1 million towards their first – and last – project.

The Venice Film Festival is normally the most relaxed and civilised of the three big cinema festivals of the year. Unlike the crazed glamour of Cannes and the business-like bustle of Berlin, Venice has no film market, where the rights for films are bought and sold, running alongside the festival. The entire event takes place on the Lido, a five-mile stretch of sand, dunes and dusty lanes that look on to the Gulf of Venice. When film business does raise its head, meetings are normally conducted over lunch-time pasta or evening glasses of champagne costing upwards of £15 in resplendent 300-year-old hotels. Rooms that normally cost £80 a night rocket to £350 or more when the festival is on. Watching films and gadding about on sun-drenched terraces are the main reasons for attending.

Powell was in Venice, however, not to watch or buy films, but to complete the financing for three of Palace's films that were supposed to be going into production before the end of that year. His hotel receptionists would marshal the bundles of little white notes with messages from around the world, awaiting the manic Powell who would dash back to pick them up every two or three hours.

That evening, straight after the Eurotrustees meeting, Powell had arranged to have a drink on the Lido with Michiyo Yoshizaki, a Japanese film financier. Despite having wooed Yoshizaki (known in the industry as 'Mitch') on previous Palace projects with little success, he was planning to try *The Soldier's Wife* out on her. Keen to give it a good shot, he kept badgering Woolley to come with him: 'C'mon, Steve, everything's worth a go. Everything's worth a try . . .'

Although buoyed up by the Eurotrustees deal, Woolley was very unhappy about certain practical aspects of his stay in Venice. The hotel where Powell and his pop-star wife, Sandie Shaw, were staying was packed out during the festival. Normally, Powell and Woolley would have shared the room and cut costs, but that was impossible given Shaw's presence. The only place for Woolley to sleep was on a fold-out bed in the hotel. He ended up kipping in the very same boardroom in which the Eurotrustees meeting had taken place that afternoon. There was not even a toilet nearby, and Woolley had to share the bathroom in Powell's and Shaw's room.

The two men, dressed in their garish, not-quite-to-the-knee Bermuda shorts and T-shirts, looked an odd pair as they walked along the Lido that evening. No one would have guessed that they were out to raise nearly half a million dollars for a movie in one fell swoop. On their way to the drink, Woolley grew increasingly pessimistic.

'You know what she's going to say, Nik: "I love Neil Jordan, but I've never made any money out of his films and I've distributed practically every one of them. And *The Miracle* was the biggest loser of the lot. Neil's great, I love him . . . but I just can't do it." '

'Steve, you know that's Japanese for "Yes",' Powell shot back. He stressed that it was going to take an incredible sales pitch to get Yoshizahi to fund the film.

After a polite and studied welcome, Powell proceeded to launch into a highly charged pitch for *The Soldier's Wife*.

'You don't want to worry about *The Miracle*. Neil's proved that he can come back and make a wonderful film from an artistic point of view. The fact that it didn't connect with Japanese audiences is neither here nor there . . . You *know* Neil can make wonderful films . . . and this is a much more "out there" script, much more universal. It's something the Japanese are *bound* to get really excited about, and [in a bizarre reference to the sexual revelation] they love shots of Western willies.'

After the third glass of champagne and an emotional dose of Woolley, Powell knew they had her. A complex Japanese tax deal was subsequently signed with Nippon Film Development & Finance, and a further £350,000 was raised.

Jack Lechner, an American-born script editor, had only been at

Channel 4 for a few months when *The Soldier's Wife* arrived on his desk in the summer of 1991. As right-hand man to the recently appointed David Aukin, Channel 4's head of drama, Lechner's support for the film was going to be vital. Aukin's background was in theatre, and he was finding his 'creative feet' within the film community. Consequently, he was relying quite a lot on Lechner's skill and experience. Throughout the 1980s, Channel 4 had taken a leading role in investing in risky film projects, leaving Powell and Woolley convinced that the company would sign up as soon as Aukin and Lechner had read the first draft. However, both men had exactly the same reactions to Jordan's script. 'We felt it was one of the best screenplays we'd ever read in our lives, and certainly the best one Neil had ever written. It kept going right up to the revelation, but from then on it was a *tremendous* anti-climax,' Lechner said.

Aukin and Lechner put these views to a distinctly unhappy Jordan and Woolley. So began a dance that was to last about three months. Channel 4's comments on the script were sent to Palace; a watchful Woolley would then filter what he thought were the best of them back to Jordan. The film-maker rewrote one or two scenes each time, which were sent back to Channel 4. 'We would read the new draft, think it was better than the last, but still not good enough,' Lechner explained. 'Each time Steve approached us with a new draft, it was very much presented as "Take it or leave it", and so we reluctantly decided to leave it. Only when Steve and Neil had come back to us three times did it dawn on us that "Take it or leave it" actually meant "Help!" '

Lechner argued that the IRA story tended to swamp the love story between Fergus and Dil, and he was also worried that the film would become a 'freak show' after the revelation. Channel 4 expressed concern over the casting of Davidson as Dil, Whitaker as Jody, and argued that Miranda Richardson was miscast.

During this period, Woolley wrote a collection of wildly impassioned letters to Channel 4. One dated 14 August 1991 and addressed to Lechner, among many other things dealt with the subject of Richardson as the IRA *femme fatale*:

'. . . Regarding your comments concerning Miranda Richardson, I am slightly at odds with the notion that because a film is Irish, or any other nationality, one has to cast according to an actor's birthplace. As you know, the dialects vary considerably in England, Ireland, Scotland and Wales from north to south in each country. Glaswegian accents are distinctly different from Edinburgh accents, which is less than an hour away by train. In Ireland itself, a Kerry accent is undoubtedly different from a Dublin or Cork accent. The list of European actors achieving considerable success in America is endless. A most recent example is Anthony Hopkins as Hannibal Lecter in *Silence of the Lambs*. Anthony Hopkins not only is not American, which is not discussed in the movie, but he is also (God forbid) Welsh. Following your comments to their logical conclusion, Anthony Hopkins should have been making only Welsh movies for the last thirty years!

This problem of casting against nationality has plagued me. I was heavily criticised for casting Bridget Fonda in *Scandal*. Bridget subsequently achieved a Golden Globe nomination for her part as Mandy Rice-Davies. Although, of course, it doesn't always turn out so happily, and, joking aside, I can sympathise with your anxieties with the additional burden of casting an American as Jody. The reasons for casting Miranda Richardson are a) Neil and I think she is a truly talented actress, b) she could play the part of Jude superbly well, and c) as we are casting the lead part of Dil with a complete unknown we really need experienced actors to support a first time movie début, and, by the way, she loves the script and I don't think her fee will be high . . .'

But Channel 4 remained unmoved, and Woolley's 'war of the letters' continued. In a final bid to convince Channel 4 to get on board, Woolley included the following lines:

'. . . If there is one shred of doubt that it *may* be a film you will later be proud of then do not pass up this opportunity. You will not be able to pass and then regret it because it will never be filmed in the near future. Neil will not be available next year. You will therefore be consigning *The Soldier's Wife* to oblivion. This letter is heartfelt and serious and if Palace has attained a clownish veneer it masks a serious and passionate desire to see good work initiated, fulfilled and applauded if appropriate. This desire traverses the world of cinema from *When Harry Met Sally* to *Hairspray*, from *Rhapsody In August* to *Evil Dead* and from *Lenny Henry Live* to *Sid and Nancy*.'

The letters provided Lechner with his first inkling that 'Stephen Woolley was the most persistent man I had ever met. Never had I seen somebody reject the word "No" to the degree he did. Steve absolutely wouldn't move until this movie was made.' The above letter was later photocopied and passed around by Colin Leventhal, Channel 4's Director of Acquisition and Michael Grade's right-hand man. It was half-jokingly branded an example of how far a film producer should debase himself before the broadcaster should commit its money to a film.

Channel 4's continuing resistance angered not only the whole Palace team, but Jordan's long-time and respected agent, Jenne Casarotto. 'I was absolutely furious with Channel 4 and Aukin, whom I really wanted to throttle. Here was a major film-maker whom they've supported before, and there they were, fiddling around with the script, saying it was this and that.'

Before Woolley left for Venice in mid-September he calmed Casarotto down, explaining that he planned to get Lechner over to Ireland to meet Neil at his home. He knew that Jordan both detested and performed badly at the nerve-wracking power meetings at Channel 4. The two of them would turn up at Channel 4's offices, which were then on Charlotte Street – ironically built on the site that the original Scala cinema had occupied – and huddle into a dull, cramped room with Aukin and Lechner. Jordan openly detested such situations, complaining that the kind of people who put money into films were unpredictable and impossible to gauge: 'Meetings are the order of the day, meetings where prevarication is generally expressed through comment on the script, or by discussion of that unpronounceable French concept, genre . . . Just at the point you think they're eating morsels from your palm, you get bitten.' In an effort at damage limitation following an uncomfortable meeting between Aukin and Jordan, Woolley wrote to Aukin early in September, stressing that 'Neil is responsive to gentle treatment'. If only he could woo Lechner over to Jordan in Ireland, Woolley thought, the three of them might be able to work their problems out quietly over some drinks.

A bemused Lechner cleared the airflight and expenses with Aukin. He packed his bags, along with a guide book, and even read some James Joyce, thinking that he was about to visit Dublin, but when he arrived at the airport he was bundled into a car and driven to Jordan's home in Bray, a few miles south of the capital.

The subsequent script conference went swimmingly well. A different animal on home ground, Jordan affably suggested that certain elements could be changed or removed altogether. 'Why don't we try this scene over there? Or perhaps we should switch these pages around?' he volunteered quietly. With Woolley patiently prodding the two men during lapses, Jordan and Lechner began to force an understanding that had previously been missing.

Woolley had hit upon the outstanding element that continued to hold Channel 4's executives back. Neither Aukin nor Lechner really knew Jordan well. As Lechner later put it: 'Neil can be very intimidating, despite himself. We only later realised that he is genuinely shy until he feels comfortable with you. It's very easy to mistake that for arrogance.' Both Aukin and Lechner breathed a sigh of relief as they finally agreed to sign on to *The Soldier's Wife*. As Lechner put it: 'When you finally say "Yes" to Steve it's great, because you're not getting five faxes and 210 phone calls every day.'

With no American up-front investment in place and little hope of any before the 4 November production start date, Woolley had long recognised that there would be a gap in the budget. The cost of Powell's complex banking deals and additional legal fees had pushed the budget well over £3 million.

Woolley proposed that a radical, across-the-board deferral – which essentially meant the majority of the people on the film working for significantly reduced fees – should be implemented. The move would mean a saving of around £700,000, bringing the budget down to a desperately tight £2.3 million. The series of deferrals were agreed by Palace, Jordan and the crew. Associate producer Paul Cowan played a vital role in persuading the crew to stay with the film. He was helped partly by the winter timing of the shoot – no other films were rolling, so alternative jobs were not around – but also by Palace's agreement to stagger the reduced payments. For example, low-paid crew members such as runners were to take smaller percentage hits than the senior production staffers. Most people went into the production on the film not expecting much pay before or after Christmas, and the balances of their wages were only going to be paid in the unlikely event that the full negative cost of the film was recouped.

Despite the combined effort of Palace, Jordan, the cast and the crew, the go-ahead still looked decidedly shaky. Powell was experiencing great difficulties pulling all the financial paperwork together in time for production money to be released for the 4 November start date. The full 'closing' of the deal had to be in place before the production finance would be made available. Part of the problem was that Powell and Palace's head of business affairs, Angela Morrison, a brilliant young lawyer, were still 'running around like lunatics' trying to close the finance on the three Palace films, *Waterland*, *Dust Devil* and *The Soldier's Wife*. Meanwhile, expensive pre-production costs such as casting and location hunting were all being shouldered by the increasingly creaky Palace, which by early November had, in Powell's words, 'stuck a million pounds into three productions, none of which were closed before principal photography had started'.

An Irish shoot was needed for the early section of Jordan's screenplay, but Woolley couldn't persuade the film's completion guarantors, Film Finances, to bond that part of the budget. Such a guarantee, which effectively acts as production insurance, is desired by banks and most other investors to guard against a film going seriously over budget. But Film Finances felt the Irish shoot was budgeted far too low, and told Woolley 'that he could go and whistle for that'.

Having already cut back the number of days in Ireland due to the high film-making costs there, Woolley decided they had to slash the Irish trip down from Jordan's initial plan of three weeks to just three days. Everything else would have to be shot in the UK. By the time Jordan and the crew arrived in Ireland, Powell still had not closed the financing of the film. There was no cash to pay anybody or to buy anything. In a desperate attempt to keep moving towards production, Woolley had already paid for many of the budget items on his American Express account and pushed his personal and company credit cards to their limit. He also borrowed money from the Palace-controlled Scala Cinema in King's Cross, and he raided the tills of Palace's video shop leaving 'I Owe You' notes behind, taking anything else he could lawfully get his hands on. By this stage, statutory demands for payments and writs were mounting in Wardour Street, while anxious creditors rang increasingly frequently. As Woolley was dragging *The Soldier's Wife* into production, the Palace Group of Companies was starting to haemorrhage cash at a violent rate.

In his desperation for money to help scrape through the first week of production, Woolley resorted to his favoured letter-writing tactic. This time he went to the top of Channel 4, targeting Colin Leventhal. In a letter dated 28 October, Woolley started with some general paperwork points, then made a heartfelt plea:

'. . . Without having to write a long tiresome sycophantic letter or creating a human pyre of myself in the lobby of Channel 4 I would beg that you provide us with the minimum funds necessary of £50,000 today. Please try and separate the three Palace movies [*The Soldier's Wife*, *Dust Devil* and *Waterland*] and regard this movie as a separate entity and accept Angela's [Morrison] security of our future feature film sales to you as a basis for the advance.

Throughout our negotiations it has been made clear to me that Channel 4 would cashflow the film. We desperately need some of that cash now. Palace are not in a position to fund a single penny more of this pre-production stage. We are planning to begin principal photography this Sunday, and we narrowly avoided a major mutiny last Friday amongst the crew. I write this letter to you with a deep sense of regret that we are faced with such an acute problem and can look only to you to solve it. However, I sincerely hope that you can salvage our movie and that you can find the funds and transfer them today . . .'

Channel 4 released £50,000. This was just enough when added to Woolley's desperate fund-raising efforts to scrape through the Irish

shoot, although the money had already been spent by the time
Channel 4's banker's order came through. By the middle of that first
week of production, Powell still hadn't completed all the financing
deals and their endless paperwork. Woolley, nervous that the movie
would collapse, went back to Leventhal for more money. This time
the Channel 4 executive was more sceptical:

7th November 1991

Dear Steve,
   You write such good letters but you know, as well as I do, that
*The Soldier's Wife* is the third in a line of films which started with
*Dust Devil* and continued with *Waterland* in which the financing
arrangements came together in a way which really would not be
tolerated in any other business. I assure you that I do appreciate
the enormous difficulties involved in financing film production in
the UK today.
   However, I am not in the business of financing film production
but in the business of helping to run a television station.
   I have really helped you as much as I can before draw-down
from the Berliner Bank, which I understand is not even
represented at your 9.30 meeting this morning. I will have another
look at our contracts on films purchased from Palace, and see what
we might do, but frankly it is not going to begin to approach the
sort of money you say you need to survive.
   It seems to me that your company has needed re-financing for a
long time and I can only hope that the necessary arrangements are
completed within days.
With kind regards.
Yours sincerely,

Colin Leventhal

By 10 November *The Soldier's Wife* was saved. Powell, greatly
aided by Morrison, came through with the signed-off financing for
the film. The nightmare jigsaw of banks, lawyers, contracts, tax
shelters, recoupment positions and guarantees was finally completed. At the start of the second week of production, monies were
all in place and *The Soldier's Wife* was at last fully bankrolled.
   The next problem to hit the production resulted from the sheer
speed at which Jordan and his crew had to work if *The Soldier's Wife*

26

was to complete photography by 22 December. Any shooting beyond Christmas was bound to unravel Powell's painstaking financing deals. Fred Elmes, an experienced American cameraman who had worked with David Lynch, was having a nightmare first week. He had brought his own gaffer – the chief lighting electrician on a film set – but used to more relaxed conditions they failed to tune in with the rest of the crew. Lighting set-ups required for fairly straightforward shots were taking too long for Jordan's and Woolley's liking. Some spectacular accidents occurred. The wrong film stock was loaded, while an unsafe rig caused a night's shoot to be lost. Another night's shooting had to be abandoned when all the film turned out black due to an exposure cock-up.

'Over an eight-week shoot this would have been fine, but in the first week it threw Neil's confidence,' Woolley explained. A decision about Elmes, prompted by an eruption from Jordan on set, had to be reached, and the cameraman left the film by the second week. Three different cameramen were lined up, but Woolley managed to replace Elmes with Ian Wilson, a British expert who had shot two former Palace movies.

Jordan worked with a furious intensity, fuelled by the realisation that if he did not pull it off, *The Soldier's Wife* would possibly be his last film for a long time. He kept striving to perfect the images and performances he had waited so long to realise. After the gentle demands of his last film shoot on *The Miracle*, this production was being run like a war. When he was not working with the actors or shooting, he demanded that everything should run like clockwork, only faster.

At times Woolley would step in, questioning certain set-ups, forcing Jordan to come up with quicker alternatives. When the schedule became stretched to its limit, Woolley and Jordan confronted the problems directly. The intense Jordan would snap back at his producer, but he would nevertheless order the crew to hustle round for the next set-up.

Despite the gruelling schedule and finger-freezing nights, Jordan managed to create the 'Irish summer' he had envisaged in his script and *The Soldier's Wife* began to find its form on film. By the time the production started at Shepperton Film Studios, the cast and crew's commitment had been effectively channelled to reach the required levels.

Even first-timer Jaye Davidson dealt with the mind-numbing boredom of hanging around waiting for the next set-up with surprising composure. To everyone's amazement, he was relatively patient and polite to those around him. However, he was still adamant about not having his hair cut off, leaving a wig the only option. Nevertheless, Woolley was relieved: 'Everyone on the set felt we were making something really special. There was something about Stephen Rea, Forest, Jaye and Miranda's attitude. It was as if everyone knew we were making a really good piece of work that they all believed in. It was how I imagine the first night of a play – everybody felt an incredibly strong spirit.'

However, although the film completed production just before Christmas, as planned, the autumn onslaught to drag Channel 4 into the film and the script changes made to please them ended up providing some costly ironies. Nobody that autumn could have known that the much debated ending was ultimately to end up on the cutting room floors.

Jordan later admitted to *Entertainment Weekly* magazine to writing 'a fake ending that I knew would make [Channel 4] happy. I had to shoot it just in order to show them that it didn't work, so I could get permission to go back and shoot my original ending.' According to one report, the unused footage involved a somewhat incredible Hollywood-style snow scene and an escape to Barbados for certain leading characters. All the actors hated the Channel 4 ending. Jordan went back to his original plan, and everyone, including Channel 4, agreed that it was a much improved option. Forty-five thousand pounds was raised from three of the film's backers to pay for a re-shoot, and *The Soldier's Wife* was in the can.

At Christmas 1992 nobody could have predicted the enormous irony of Palace's situation. Its final film was about to become one of the most successful and important films in the history of independent cinema.

CHAPTER TWO

# Virgins

'You know the way everyone has a best friend when you're a kid,' said Nikolas Powell. 'Well, Richard was mine from when we were just four years old.'

Born on 4 November 1950, Nik Powell met Richard Branson at Longacre, a small private junior school near Shamley Green, tucked away inside the Surrey stockbroker belt. It was here that the two boys grew up together, playing after school and during the holidays. They would mess around in nearby fields, climbing trees, tearing about on bikes and pushing each other in the river. Branson was a practical joker, while Powell relied on a sharper vocabulary and quick wit to keep even.

The main difference between the two homes was that Powell's family was Catholic, while Branson's was Protestant. Branson remembers his own father's passion for gardening, which he detested. At every opportunity he would sneak off by bike or on foot down a long narrow road to the Powell residence, set in the countryside. 'I was never given puddings at my house, so I'd try to arrive just before they were finishing lunch,' Branson explained. 'I'd visit partly because Nik and I were best friends, but also because his mum made great puddings.'

It was clear which of the two was more daring. Branson was constantly getting himself into scrapes from which Powell would subsequently have to rescue him. Branson even managed to ride Powell's new bike into a river, a disaster that Powell, 'in typical Nik fashion, took extremely well', Branson recalled. Apart from the odd fight, the only real cloud over the two boys' strong sense of fun was Powell's occasional epileptic fits, from which he suffers to this day.

According to Powell, his family background made his parents truly middle-class. On his mother's side, his grandfather was Sir George Weir, originally from Scotland; while his other grandfather started work as a coal miner and became a foreman in Maesteg, a mining town in South Wales. Powell never knew them. His father was the only person from their whole county in Wales to get into Oxford. Later, he became a civil servant, and went out to India.

Powell's education was traditional: a small prep school in the Malvern Hills, followed by Ampleforth, the Roman Catholic boarding school in Yorkshire, renowned as a 'public school for rebels'. Powell was a notoriously 'model' rebellious student. He would often enter into heated arguments with the monks about rules and regulations that he deemed ridiculous and old fashioned. At the same time, an old friend explained, Powell developed 'a certain work ethic and an almost puritanical streak' about wasting neither time nor money.

In the holidays he returned to Surrey, where he was a regular visitor at the Branson family home, Tanyards. As they grew older, Branson, who by this time had been sent away to the public school Stowe, began busying himself with vaguely entrepreneurial money-making schemes, none of which took off with any success.

Between the ages of ten and thirteen, Powell spent his school holidays in America, as his father had been posted to Washington by the Civil Service. The sixties were starting to swing, and a heady blaze of pop culture, including the Beatles' first tour of America, surrounded the adolescent Powell. By sixteen he had already got two A levels, although he failed French and his grades were not good enough to allow him to walk straight into Oxford or Cambridge. Instead of staying on to do the Oxbridge exams, he was infinitely more attracted to the heaving social scene. He went to

London in 1968 to join Branson and his first real business enterprise, the inter-school magazine for teenagers, *Student*.

When Branson left Stowe at fifteen to devote more time to the venture, his headmaster famously predicted that Branson would either 'go to jail or become a millionaire'. *Student* quickly became Branson's first alleged soaraway success. Youth was 'in', and the stuffy worlds of Stowe and Ampleforth were left behind as Branson and later Powell moved to *Student*'s ramshackle headquarters in Connaught Square, described by contemporaries as a squat-cum-office. The first issue of *Student* was published in January 1968, and featured a lengthy interview with Vanessa Redgrave written by Branson, a short story donated by John Le Carré and an original cover drawing of a heavily caricatured student by Peter Blake, who had just risen to fame via the Beatles' *Sgt Pepper* album cover. Branson would ring up potential advertisers, and tell them: 'I'm Richard Branson, I'm eighteen and I run a magazine that's doing something really useful for young people.' Predictably, the national press entered a tailspin of masturbatory adoration, while the magazine became a lightning rod to a growing circle of sixties groupies.

Although Powell's position was officially deputy editor, he assumed responsibility for the magazine's accounts. Like the rest of the operation, the finances were being run in a haphazard manner. Advertising was sold based on over-optimistic estimates, but, as Powell later recalled, Branson's breezy brand of brilliance-cum-bullshit succeeded in turning a 'modest failure into a perceived triumph'.

In a pattern that was to run through their early business partnership, Branson handed over most of the financial nuts and bolts to his oldest friend. Powell was the responsible one, while Branson instinctively grabbed hold of the creative mantle, flirting with risks and schemes and already starting to frustrate the more cautious Powell. As Branson put it later, 'I was always keen on the sort of grand sweep, while Nik would pick up the pieces and lead by example.'

The newly emerging Virgin – so named by Branson in a bid to emphasise its corporate naïveté – was less about business careerism than about enjoying a huge adventure. Nobody knew where it was going, and nobody gave the future much thought. As Powell later joked: 'Capital was probably just a big city in the centre of the country to Richard. He was winging it then, and he is probably still winging it now!'

When the friends were nineteen years old, a key event took place which might have changed the course of Virgin for ever. Branson owned the budding Virgin business outright, a fact that was starting to irritate his fellow workers, and Powell in particular.

One day the teenage Virgin chief happened to come across a letter on his desk which caught his attention. Written by Powell, the paper outlined a workers' takeover of Virgin. It was clear to Branson that Powell and a group of workers were going to confront him the next day and demand all his shares in the name of setting up a workers' co-operative.

'I was absolutely shell-shocked,' Branson recalled. 'I was very upset by the whole idea, so I decided to bullshit Nik.'

Branson asked Powell to come upstairs to his office, where he brazenly confronted him face-to-face about the *coup*.

'Nik, what the hell is this all about? Some of your group have come to see me about your co-operative share scheme. How could you do this behind my back?'

Powell was caught completely off guard. Instead of challenging Branson to name some of the alleged offenders, he capitulated. According to Branson, Powell apologised, and left the company.

Powell decided to take up a place at Sussex University in Brighton, to read English and American History. 'It was a lot of fun, and there were endless, wall-to-wall wonderful women at Sussex,' recalled Powell. 'I mean, that whole sixties sex thing . . .' Indeed, it was during one of his numerous scouting sessions for women that Powell happened to meet Phil Livingstone. The two of them were hanging out at The Crypt – a dark, dirty, drinking-and-jiving campus watering hole – busy fancying the same woman. They quickly hit it off, partly because Livingstone was intrigued by the 'rather unfashionable things Nik was up to. He was selling things like personal insurance and pension schemes and trying to make money.'

Livingstone was the son of Percy Livingstone, an Establishment figure in the British film distribution business. Phil had already worked as an assistant on some of the more zany, no-budget British films being made at that time. It was not long before the two students decided to set up a film company, Living Productions. The somewhat skeletal company placed an ad in *The Times* requesting film scripts. Powell's optimistic concept was that he would produce them and Livingstone would direct. 'The ad attracted hundreds of scripts from all those hopefuls out there who probably thought we were bona fide. Then we got a call from a really hard-nosed American woman who had sussed out what was going on instantly. She said: "Why should I send you my scripts when I don't know if you have anything behind you?" '

Livingstone was duly impressed by his partner's already finely tuned phone style, especially when dealing with hostile callers. Powell quickly talked his way out of the spot with a mixture of believable banter and bullish belligerence. It was a skill that Powell – by the eighties an avid fan of all electronic gadgets – later honed to great effect on mobile phones. Nothing ever happened to the scripts, although Livingstone, knowing his friend's tendency to hoard, suspected Powell had stashed them away. Meanwhile, Powell had started to drop the public school accent and affect the downwardly mobile, 'mockney' accent that became so notoriously imitated throughout the British film industry in later years. 'No' became 'Narh', while 'Fuck' turned into 'Fark'.

Powell also gave the radically left-wing Sussex University Student Union a run for its money. He decided it would be fun to stand for the Union's Treasurer position, and promptly went up to London and used his Virgin contacts to get a large sack of election flyers printed with 'VOTE POWELL'. They were duly posted all over campus, enabling Powell and Livingstone (who was running for Dance Secretary) to meet all the new students and shove leaflets around all the girls' boarding houses. Powell's subsequent election was challenged by the President of the Union, who argued, quite correctly, that he must have massively overspent the campaign limit. Not to be defeated, Powell went straight back to London, collected a stash of receipts and presented them to the Union. His total expenditure, the receipts claimed, came to just one penny short of the limit.

Living Productions was only one of numerous schemes run out of Powell's Treasurer offices during his short but hectic sojourn at Sussex University. Bursting with energy, he seemed to need to live life at a frenzied pace and this became even more pronounced when, in later years, his business interests expanded exponentially. Perhaps one of the forces driving Powell's attitude to life was his epilepsy. He took medication for his condition, though he rarely talked about it except to more serious girlfriends. This constant stress of not being in control seemed to encourage him to attack life at a cracking pace and cram in as much as possible.

Powell also loved a laugh. An excellent teller of bad jokes and amusing anecdotes, his biggest laughs invariably stem from self-denigrating banter rather than malicious gossip about other people. Like his mockney accent, his braying laugh is aped around Soho.

Meanwhile, Richard Branson was missing Powell's considerable financial skills, especially with the birth of Virgin Records, an ambitious new venture aimed at selling cut-price records through mail-order. The music industry, fuelled by the rising popularity of the Rolling Stones and the Beatles, was undergoing a revolution and Branson was there to take advantage of the new opportunities.

In need of management and financial support, Branson had offered Powell four per cent of the company before he had gone to Sussex. Powell had refused, but Branson was persistent, phoning again after a couple of terms of Powell's unconventional university career and finally he convinced his friend. 'Richard added a nought to the four, and my answer was "Yes",' said Powell. His union with Branson, Virgin and show business was sealed.

On 3 September 1956, a decade before Powell re-joined Virgin, Stephen Woolley was born in London's Marylebone hospital. His father was a building labourer, and his mother, who was just seventeen when she gave birth to Steve, later worked as a cleaner and in clubs to help support her son and two younger daughters. They lived in North Islington in what Woolley described as 'a classic Monty Pythonesque one room and half a kitchen'.

Woolley's 'Nan', three aunts and numerous cousins lived round the corner, so he grew up with an extended family. His father was self-educated, and had a voracious appetite for reading. He 'was shrouded in mystery', and it was a family rumour that he had learnt to read in prison libraries. Despite spending much of his time in the fifties and sixties gambling, Woolley senior taught his son to read well before nursery school and by the time Steve was eight years old books had become an obsession. Woolley also recalled watching his father play skilful games of poker, which gradually revealed to the young boy the art of not giving anything away to the opposition. School reports would remark on his progress in class, and praise his intense interest in his work. In fact, obsessions and obstinacy appeared to dominate Woolley's childhood. He was a Spurs fan in a family that loved Arsenal, a child who prefered to watch television rather than play in the street with other children.

He was sent to the local Greater London Council supported Thornhill Road School, which he described as 'full of middle-class brainboxes'. But his first real perspective on his self-described 'basic working class' background arose when he was ten years old. As a boy, Woolley suffered from asthma attacks and had weak lungs. In an attempt to clear the problem up, he was sent to a boarding school for asthmatics by the seaside in Margate. It was the first time Woolley had been away from his family, and although he became more healthy – 'winning all the races on the sports day' – the experience made him even more of a loner when he returned to London. 'I saw the world very differently after that summer away. It gave me the perspective that I was special.'

Woolley was clearly a smart, precocious kid. He won poetry prizes, and passed his eleven-plus at nine. By this time, his family had been re-housed in council accommodation in Archway, so Woolley started grammar school at Owens at the Angel. Until this point, his parents had given their son enormous support, encouraging him to read, write and expand his horizons, but they followed his progress less closely once he entered the grammar school circuit.

'They were working-class people who didn't know or follow the system,' Woolley explained later.

Adolescence loomed. Woolley hated all the kids on his council estate, and would steal supermarket books and break into building sites just to look at the view over London. By twelve, he was the quintessential brat. He had started experimenting with drugs, drinking, and had painted his room black. As he later described himself: 'I was an arrogant teenage rebel with a working-class chip on my shoulder.'

Fortunately, being an introspective rebel did not prevent him from discovering the cinema, and it soon became his great passion. In his early childhood, he would ask his mother for sixpence, and spend Saturday mornings at the pictures, then see the matinée performances, followed by James Bond films and other big budget commercial fare which his father or uncles took him to in the evenings. Three or four widely varying films in a day was not unusual.

'I'd start with the simple, boyish swashbuckling movies like *Zulu* and *The Great Escape*, then I'd drift off down to the West End and sit in cinemas like the Eros, which showed two-and-a-half-hour runs of Laurel and Hardy films. Then I moved on to the silent movies, and started to find Buster Keaton funny and realised the art to all that comedy.'

While most children rarely go to the cinema by themselves, Woolley became a regular, often unaccompanied customer at Mayfair's Starlight Club and the Classic in Notting Hill Gate. He also went to the National Film Theatre, where he built up an encyclopaedic knowledge of the American classics, the Nouvelle Vague and Japanese art-house cinema. He wasn't élitist in his tastes; he was hungry to sample everything that appeared on the big screen, keen to embrace all cinema rather than pick his way through the recommended masters.

'I never thought or dreamed I would work in the business. I just wanted to go to the movies. Cinema was a great escape — disappearing for three hours or more and not being worried by the social pressures of school. It was like a private world, not a world I shared with anyone else,' Woolley recalled. He became increasingly fascinated with Hollywood's 'European' films and the *Easy Rider* era, which offered up films like *Badlands*, *Five Easy Pieces* and culminated in the mid-1970s in Roman Polanski's masterpiece of the genre, *Chinatown*. He complemented his obsession with films by avidly reading American publications such as Andy Warhol's *Interview*, and spending hours in his room listening to the jazz of Charlie Parker, Charles Mingus and Nat King Cole.

Woolley's intense interest in popular culture may have been a way of compensating for his conspicuous lack of social skills. Seemingly shy and introverted, ruled by pessimism and caution, he created a protective shell to hide his vulnerable ego, and would emerge from that sanctum only when drunk or inspired by music or films, forms of release that have the same positive effect on him to this day.

Woolley left home at sixteen to move into a squat in a seedy part of Highbury with a girlfriend. He got a job three nights a week as an usher at the Screen on the Green cinema in Islington, selling tickets, ice-creams and changing the letters on the boards outside. It was almost certainly the hippest London cinema of the day. Woolley still recalls the German art-house director Rainer Werner Fassbinder 'looking massively obese, hanging out in the foyer, because it really was a hip place in those days'.

Screen on the Green owner Romaine Hart explained that the programming 'wasn't straight art-house cinema, but a mixture of the best of American independent cinema and the kinds of films I wanted to see myself. Steve picked up what we were doing, and was very enthusiastic and energetic. And he cared passionately about the films.' Woolley subsequently became an assistant manager, and started to write about cinema for the trendy London entertainment magazine *Time Out*. His relationship with the listings magazine, which smartly recognised the growth of late night entertainment and alternative culture in the capital, was later to be very valuable to Palace as Woolley made great use of his journalistic contacts and thorough understanding of how to exploit the London entertainment mouthpiece to Palace's marketing advantage.

Rock and roll quickly gave way to the anarchic safety-pin scene. In the hot summer of 1976, Woolley became a punk, shaving off all his hippy-styled hair, throwing off the Afghan and rolling along to see the Buzzcocks, the Clash and, on nine occasions, the Sex Pistols. This was a new, fresh and exhilarating sound, which made bands like The Police seem staid. Avoiding heroin, Woolley plunged himself into a world of speed and excessive drinking bouts. Yet he felt himself 'too young to be a hippy, too old to be a punk' and rather than throwing himself into the centre of frenetic punk events, he got his kicks voyeuristically. He had lengthy chats with Sex Pistols' manager Malcolm McLaren, discussing in detail the whole culture scene rather than just the music. On one occasion Woolley even begged McLaren to get Russ Meyer to make a movie about the Pistols. Although the manager had never heard of the former skin-flick director whom Hollywood had dubbed 'King of the Nudies', the idea was followed up. However, Johnny Rotten detested Meyer and succeeded in eliminating the director's involvement in the film.

Woolley's brief flirtation with the punk scene never overshadowed his steady pursuit of a career in cinema. He was hired by The Other Cinema, a radical, left-wing collective, as the token punk. The year at The Other Cinema introduced him to the art of programming a highly eclectic range of films for niche audiences, but he was not happy; the mid-seventies were failing to live up to the promise of the sixties, and Woolley grew increasingly disillusioned: 'We could do whatever we wanted, sleep around, take drugs, but I was bored with all that. I was a very frustrated guy at The Other Cinema, because everyone was so laid back. I wanted films to succeed, and I got heavily into reprogramming Hollywood Classics and music movies like Perry Henzell's *The Harder They Come*.'

Unfortunately, The Other Cinema was anything but a collective when it came to running the business and the aspiring film-makers who headed the company unilaterally decided to sacrifice the cinema in order to keep their small distribution outlet going. Woolley signed on the dole.

Once Nik Powell had re-joined Richard Branson, the two young entrepreneurs threw themselves into building Virgin. Colleagues compared their intense relationship to a marriage, a description both friends have agreed with. Branson would whiz all over the place, seeking out new ideas and opportunities, while Powell stayed at home, keeping the company running. 'Nik used to sort out the financial mess I got the company into,' recalled Branson. 'He'd sweep up the bits and sort things out.' In fact, Powell took considerable responsibility for the more tedious areas of the business. He would negotiate with local planning authorities and resistant shopkeepers, check stock-taking figures, pay crucial bills and generally deal with the day-to-day details of the business. He took his job seriously, signing up for subscriptions to Harvard Business School magazines and studies, and keeping a keen eye on the accounts. Nobody was supposed to borrow from the tills, including senior managers like Simon Draper and Branson himself. 'Nik would rankle people because if they didn't do things his way, he'd think that they were doing them the wrong way,' Branson said. 'For example, he rode a bicycle everywhere, so he'd expect everyone to ride on a bike. If he flew, then he'd take economy, and he'd expect everyone else to fly economy.' It was a *modus operandi*, a combination of close attention to detail and plain tightfistedness, that Powell was later to bring to the management of Palace.

The young Virgin, like *Student* before it, flirted with financial failure. At one particularly difficult stage, when Powell and Branson were both just twenty-two years old, they found themselves badly in need of an increase in their overdraft facility: the company was again facing bankruptcy. Catching sight of Branson, prior to their meeting with the bank manager, Powell was appalled to see his partner dressed in a pair of jeans with holes in them and a jumper. 'Richard,' he said, 'why the fuck are you dressed like that? I put on my only suit. You know we desperately need the money.'

'It's okay, Nik,' Branson soothed. 'If I go in there in a suit looking like a convicted heroin addict – which is how you look – they'll know for certain that I need the money, and banks never lend to anyone who needs it. If I go in there like this, and we talk about our expansion plans, they'll think I don't need it, and they'll offer to lend it.' The partners got the money.

Virgin's rollicking hippy image belied its business culture, which was later defined by Powell as 'a combination of liberalism and hard business sense'. It was, he felt, 'the same kind of culture shared by most successful businesses'.

The company's growth continued apace. A record shop was opened in London's Oxford Street and another planned for Liverpool, the mail–order business flourished, and the idea of establishing a recording studio and record label was hatched. Yet, despite the record orders and the London shop's healthy turnover, overheads were increasingly high and Virgin was more than £60,000 in debt.

By chance, Branson and Powell discovered a way to avoid paying customs. They filled up vans with cheap old records, while at the same time ordering a batch of new records seemingly ready to be exported to customers in Europe. The old batch, having gained an export stamp, would be dumped on rubbish tips in Holland, while the new records swiftly found their way to Virgin's stores, each vanload saving around £6,000 in duties. Approximately five 'exchange' trips were made before Her Majesty's Customs and Excise officers called in at the new Liverpool store just before its opening. When they pointed their machines at the tagged export stock 'the machine went beserk. The Customs guys were laughing out loud. We had to close the shop before it opened,' recalled Powell later, who was on the shop floor at the time. Branson was arrested that same morning, and spent the night in Dover police cells.

Six days before the case came to court, the charges were dropped in return for an immediate £15,000 payment and an agreement to pay a further £38,000 over the next three years. 'It seemed like a great adventure,' explained Powell. 'It didn't feel like we were breaking the law or a bad thing to do, but I guess it was. My first wish is that we hadn't done it, but as we did do it, I'm glad it happened then. If it had happened later in life it would have been much bigger and we would have been ruined. There are laws and you bust them at your own risk.'

At the start of 1974 Virgin moved offices to Vernon Yard, a cobbled mews off Notting Hill's Portobello Road. The building was instantly overcrowded, its tiny corridors and jumbled rooms packed with Virgin paraphernalia, mainly due to the rapid increase in the mail-order record business. A pub culture developed in the evenings, with the miserly Powell rarely buying anyone else a drink, while Branson never drank his own beer, choosing instead to take sips from other people's glasses.

Meanwhile, the music business was starting to flourish. Virgin Records had signed musician Mike Oldfield, and in May 1973 released his *Tubular Bells* album, which became one of the biggest-selling albums in the world. In a deal that was to prove hugely important for Virgin's financial growth, *Tubular Bells* and three other albums were later sold by Branson to Atlantic Records in the US for $750,000, a colossal sum for the time.

In the early and mid-1970s, Powell's management role lay in attempting to bring a semblance of financial order to the expanding businesses. Far from the glamour of US record deals, he kept his eye on the minutiae of the company. As one former Virgin staffer recalled, 'Nik was big on quality control, and would also ask staff genuinely why everyone was going through so much toilet paper at the music studios. He'd done loads of time and motion studies, and tried hard to make it a proper business; but Richard used to play games with him.'

Powell's reputation for rejecting expense claims became legendary. The worst offenders in his eyes were female PR executives. He would challenge them personally, screaming that 'the whole fuckin' point of you women being in PR is to get the blokes to buy you drinks'.

It was at Vernon Yard that he had one of his most serious epileptic fits. He walked out of the reception area, had an attack and crashed straight through a huge plate of glass. He was thrashing around with smashed glass and broken teeth in his face until some nearby builders, who fortunately knew him well, held him down and stopped him swallowing his tongue. According to Branson's biographer Mick

Brown, 'nobody but Branson knew the difficulties Nik had experienced because of his epilepsy,' but he was happy to nurse Powell with great patience and affection through awkward attacks. Branson explained that the fits 'were something that happened every four or five months rather than all the time, but Nik's had to learn to live without being able to do a lot of things that everyone else can do. To have a relationship with a woman must be a nightmare.'

Nevertheless, despite his vulnerability, Powell was successful at forging relationships with women and in 1972 he married Merrill Tomassi, the younger sister of Kristen Tomassi, who had married Branson that same year. Two years later both marriages collapsed within months of each other, heavily underlining the intense and almost incestuous nature of the two men's partnership.

However, the business marriage between Powell and Branson also had its problems and by 1981 the relationship was fraught with disagreements. Powell's influence in the group had gradually weakened over the previous five years. The music business under Simon Draper, Branson's South African cousin, was flourishing, while Powell's retailing businesses were not performing nearly so well. His efforts to stop Draper signing on the Human League were overridden by Branson, and when the group started to excite a following Powell's authority was further undermined.

Major policy disagreements over Branson's purchase of the Roof Gardens restaurant and club in Kensington and of Heaven, the gay nightclub in Charing Cross in 1981, and Powell's handling of the problematic conversion of a cinema in Victoria into The Venue, a bar, restaurant and concert hall, only served to move the men further apart. Powell's forty per cent stake in the Virgin holding company gave him considerable power of veto over projects he did not approve of, a fact that Branson began to resent. After two years of open conflict, Powell and Branson finally agreed that they should part.

'Retail was ticking along, but not really making any money,' Branson explained. 'There was a feeling that the record company, which Simon [Draper] and I were running, was starting to become the principal business. Nik was certainly out on a limb.' However, it took Branson a long time to face up to reality. 'I would fudge something for years rather than confront it,' he conceded. Finally the two partners met for dinner at the Roof Gardens, where they talked through the separation.

In the ten years that Powell had spent with Branson building Virgin, the company's sales had risen from nothing to £60 million. The main thrust driving that expansion was the will to stay in business rather than concern about profits. 'The word survival was the only word that mattered until I was about thirty-five,' Branson later said. 'If you didn't survive, all the other dreams were dashed.'

Under the influence of his new girlfriend, pop star Sandie Shaw, Powell started to study Buddhism and to practise early morning chanting, perhaps hoping that such spiritual activities would relieve his nervous disposition as well as convince Shaw that he was the right partner for her. Shaw had already filed for divorce from her husband Jeff Banks, and after a brief affair the new couple married just a month before the birth of their daughter, Amie.

Powell now wanted to start up his own business, to become his own boss. This raised the question of how much of Virgin's £60 million he was entitled to take on his departure. The problem was that the value of Powell's shareholding was based on Virgin's net assets as they appeared in the company balance sheet. This effectively excluded valuable assets such as the Virgin music list, which, boosted by artists such as Boy George who signed up after Powell's departure, was later sold for £560 million. As Branson points out today, 'Nobody could have forecast that four or five years later things were going to go so well.'

Powell and Branson both refused to discuss the eventual settlement in detail, and sources close to the deal are bound by confidentiality agreements. The received wisdom – that Powell took £1 million in cash – is certainly an over-estimate. He probably received approximately £850,000, together with a stake in the Scala cinema and the video editing facilities in Soho's Poland Street. As part of the agreement he also bought Boudisque, a Dutch-based Virgin subsidiary record company, which, he explained, would keep him in touch with the music business, although the final separation contract prohibited him from working in the UK music industry.

Just five years later the forty per cent that Powell sold back to Branson was worth £96 million. Years later, Powell's daughter was looking at a picture of her father in a book on Branson, when the caption detailing how much Powell would have been worth had he stayed with Virgin caught her eye. 'Couldn't you have kept just some of it?' she asked her father wistfully.

Nevertheless, Powell was a relatively wealthy man in 1981. He had the money to run his own business in his own way, not Branson's. Although on amicable terms with Branson, he clearly felt he had a lot to prove to his childhood friend.

Stephen Woolley did not remain on the dole for long. He took his skills to the Scala, a cinema then based in the former Other Cinema's premises in Charlotte Street, in which, in the late seventies, Branson's and Powell's Virgin group had invested. Woolley remembers the first time he met Powell: 'It was at Nik's Notting Hill house. Four or five of the Scala shareholders and myself had gone along for a meeting to ask for more money from him. He came downstairs in a bathrobe, and was very abrupt and dismissive with us. The notion of this little cinema which was losing money hand over fist and there we were wanting a new input of money wasn't taken too kindly.'

Joe Boyd, whose distribution company subleased the Scala from Virgin, convinced Powell and Branson to take Woolley on as formal manager/programmer. Powell recalled that at that stage he had 'no idea who this Steve Woolley character was, so the whole thing was a beacon of light. Two things really appealed to Richard and me. Firstly, we liked the idea of bringing in American marketing and product which had been tried and tested. Secondly, the idea of sacking old management and appointing some arrogant young know-it-all fitted in very well with Virgin's business philosophy. Especially Richard's!'

With Virgin's enthusiastic approval, Woolley drastically cut the overheads and radically altered the programming to attract the youth audience. They reinvented the programming, cutting back some of the worthy Eastern European exercises in cinema, and showing instead more accessible continental fare, together with cult American independent films such as David Lynch's *Eraserhead*. Posters from the Roxy Cinema in San Francisco and the New Art in LA were ordered. The café was funked up with some paint and a juke box, and one of London's first Space Invaders computer games was installed.

The business side of the Scala took a year to get going, but by then the New Romantic music scene had arrived in all its glitzy splendour. Spandau Ballet (whose members had been at school with Woolley) did their first gig at the cinema, and Boy George was a regular visitor. A young, new, arty and fashion-conscious audience was attracted by the eclectic programming, which ranged from double billings of John Wayne movies to early screenings of *The Untouchables*, from 'schlock horror' weeks to *Avengers* and *Prisoner* days. Other Woolley programming favourites included 'The Golden Turkeys', the best of the worst of American films. This later prompted a Woolley-produced TV show for Channel 4, *The Worst of Hollywood*, presented by the American film critic Michael Medved.

Specialised film-makers like the late Derek Jarman adored the Scala. 'Derek used to stand outside the back looking through the glass panel, grinning from ear to ear because he'd found his audience,' Woolley recalled. All-night shows became a high point, although the hectic buzz of the place resulted in some rather strange occurrences. One top Hollywood producer recently reminded Woolley of an all-night screening of *Animal Crackers* where the reels were in completely the wrong order. Woolley had shooed him away, arguing: 'What's your problem? It's five in the morning, it's *Animal Crackers*, and it's so anarchic surely it doesn't matter which way the reels are in!'

Far from operating as a subsidised, rarified, cinéaste's flea-pit, the Scala managed not only to survive the massive drop in cinema attendances which occured during the late seventies and early eighties but to turn over a healthy profit. Much of its success was due to Woolley's already well developed sense of marketing and obsession with making films reach audiences. As *Time Out* critic and long-time admirer Geoff Andrew wrote later: 'It was perhaps the Scala that first revealed Steve's interest in the American way of doing things: heavy promotion, a flippant, ostentatious accent on fun, and a disregard for traditional pigeon-holing of movies.'

Towards the end of 1980, Virgin was approached by Channel 4, who wanted to buy the Scala building back from its owners, National Car Parks. Given the late nights and effort he had put into running the cinema, Woolley was distinctly 'pissed off' about the deal and challenged Virgin directly, arguing that they could not just close the cinema without compensating him. His hustling worked. Woolley succeeded in getting £10,000 from Virgin, who, in return, took a fifteen per cent stake in his new venture and guaranteed an overdraft facility. Woolley promptly took all the old Scala equipment and moved it to a ramshackle building in King's Cross, which he refurbished with some help from his father and with the Virgin money. By early 1981 the Scala cinema had reopened.

The Scala cinema moved only weeks before Powell finally split with Branson. He took with him his lump sum, the video editing facilities and the stake in the Scala. Most importantly, in Woolley he had a potential new partner. As Powell later recalled: 'I had been really impressed by Steve, because he had an unusual combination of business savvy and creative – I don't want to overstate it, but I'd say – "brilliance". It's unusual to find that in one person.'

Nobody disagreed. Even at that early stage, Branson was hugely impressed by Woolley: 'We all just knew that Steve Woolley was a remarkable individual, with a good business head as well as being a very creative person.'

As the months following Powell's departure passed, Branson and his staff found themselves looking on in surprise as the relentlessly driven Powell threw himself both financially and creatively into launching a new company.

Palace was on its way.

# CHAPTER THREE

# Video Divas

'If the Postman only rings twice it's probably the Video Palace,' read the advertisement that ran in *Time Out* on 5 February 1982. At the foot of the page Powell boldly proclaimed that 'The Video Palace,' newly opened on Kensington High Street, was 'The World's Greatest Video Store'.

Since leaving Virgin the previous year, Powell had been dreaming up various new business schemes and video had emerged as a potentially expanding and exciting area in which to invest. Few video rental stores of notable size and stock existed in the UK at the time and the majority involved in the trade were barrow-boys out to make a quick killing. Sleaze was filling the shelves, and the horror genre was starting to make a screaming entrance into the living-room.

Powell was not going to wait for the video revolution, nor was he going to play the barrow-boys at their own game by pushing only downmarket films. He aggressively marketed his new shop and introduced 'The Palace Express', a service allowing member-customers to order videos by phone and have them delivered to their homes for just 75p. The Video Palace also stocked video recording machines, home computers, and was the first high street retailer to sell home satellite dishes. Few, however, were sold. 'The trouble was that the only available programming at that stage was Russian ice hockey matches, which weren't exactly the thing!' Powell explained later.

Powell approached Woolley, who was already running the Scala Cinema, and asked him to compile a promotional brochure for The Video Palace, listing thirty top films. A few days after the work was completed, the two men met in a pub on Charlotte Street, where Powell talked at length about his business ideas. Powell, who based himself at Soho's Poland Street, where the video editing suites were housed, had named his company The Mega Corporation, and every subsidiary was dubbed with the pre-fix 'mega'. Powell already owned Boudisque, the Dutch-based record company he had bought from Branson, and had plans for Megafoods Limited, a chain of supermarket-style health-food stores, Megavideo Limited, and for a computer software company.

In contrast with his hippy businessman image, Powell was applying a 1980s-style market-driven philosophy to his endeavours. 'Front-line experience is what these companies needed. I wanted to learn about the market and the audience through the retailing end of the business. That way you learn about the whole structure of an industry and end up knowing much more than other people who worked in just one segment. You also learn about what works and what doesn't with real people. Who would come in and fork out £3 to rent a film, and who would pay £20 to buy it? It was the same approach we'd taken at Virgin, but I wanted to apply it to my new businesses.'

Woolley and Powell's conversation in the Charlotte Street pub covered not only Powell's burgeoning empire, but his politics. Powell had been toying with the idea of standing as a Member of Parliament for the newly launched Social Democratic Party (SDP). He harboured a deep-seated liberal instinct not dissimilar to Branson's non-partisan politics, and was critical of the Tory Party. He was not greatly impressed by the alternatives, however: 'The Labour Party had all sorts of problems, and the Liberal Party was disappearing up its own arse. The launch of the SDP was the start of the process that turned the Labour Party from an old-fashioned Socialist Party into a Social Democratic Party, and I thought that could only be a good thing. It was fun to get an insight into politics, but while it has great similarities to the entertainment business – especially in terms of the marketing – politics is not really a role for bosses.' A die-hard Labour Party man himself, Woolley listened to Powell with wary bemusement. The last thing he wanted was his new business benefactor running off to pursue a career in politics, and for the wrong party at that.

Woolley need not have worried. Politics and health-food stores were quickly left on the shelf, while the video business flourished. Ramshackle rooms above the Scala Cinema in Kings Cross started to fill up with boxes of tapes ready for distribution to the High Street Kensington shop. Videos were already being sold by Scala ushers in person and on the phone between performances. If the operation was to develop, however, new titles would be needed.

Powell recognised the need to find a more senior and experienced executive to oversee key elements of the Palace operation. He had just the person in mind: Irving Rappaport, brother of the actor David, was a genial, off-beat character whom Powell, when still at Virgin, had encountered at various music markets. He approached Rappaport about joining the Palace team, telephoning him three times in an effort to convince him of the 'wonderful opportunity' and 'massive business potential' on offer.

Rappaport had just licensed and distributed throughout Europe and Australia the world's first video music album, Blondie's *Eat to the Beat*. Such experience was hugely valuable to Powell, because few people in 1982 had any idea how to handle and market video. Rappaport was also in desperate need of money to complete a small film he had started the previous year for the BBC.

'Nik was telling me how exciting it was going to be, and how they were going to do things differently,' recalled Rappaport. 'At that time, the video business was mostly sex films or straight exploitation stuff, and the people involved were not particularly interesting to me.' Rappaport, however, was intrigued by the prospect of developing a business in a new market. A formal contract was agreed between Powell and Rappaport, putting him in charge of the day-to-day management of marketing, distribution and sales, and giving him a decent commission for every cassette Palace sold. Rappaport retained the option to return to his film-making later in the year. He was struck by the fact that Powell was motivated by the desire to create innovative business opportunities, especially in video publishing, rather than by a particular interest in film. Above all, it was becoming clear to Rappaport that Powell desperately wanted to prove himself to Richard Branson.

'You can't really call something an interview when you're interviewed by somebody looking like Steve did in those days,' Robert Jones explained. 'He was wearing jeans, and he had a long pony tail. He certainly wasn't my idea of a boss.' Jones had left the London School of Economics in order to pursue a career in music, and by the age of twenty he had signed record contracts with Phonogram and Warners and was being published by Island. The band Jones played with (he was the guitarist and also wrote songs and played the trumpet) was initially quite successful, touring America as back-up to The Pretenders, playing at 10,000-seater music halls. However, typical rock-group politics led to Jones being thrown out of the band. He was selling advertising when his childhood friend, JoAnne Sellar, who was working as an assistant to Woolley at the Scala, rang him about a job vacancy at Palace.

Woolley had become frustrated by the low levels of video sales by phone, so Sellar had suggested that they approach Jones, who was selling charity advertising over the phone. The canny Jones decided to keep his options open. He took a week's holiday from the charity. If he found he liked Palace, he would stay on for good.

The twenty-one-year-old Jones was quite impressed by Palace, 'although everyone seemed to be feeling their way. My arrival happened to coincide with Palace getting some good orders from wholesalers rather than just selling ones and twos into shops, so I managed to sell a big bunch of cassettes in my first week. As it was a "suck-it-and-see" situation, we agreed to cut my commission in half by the second week. Video was a completely new market, so there was no yardstick to measure success by.'

Jones would watch a film in the Scala Cinema every lunchtime, and quickly became more interested in that side of the business than in selling videos. By now formally Palace's sales manager under Rappaport's management, Jones would spend the rest of his day selling wacky videos from the Scala, including John Waters's *Pink Flamingoes*, David Lynch's *Eraserhead*, Istvan Szabo's *Mephisto*, Werner Herzog's *Aguirre, Wrath of God*, and an off-beat Gary Numan music tape. Competitions were held to see who could shift the most difficult video title (normally a Herzog film), and all the invoicing was done by hand. The only real strain was when a big delivery of boxes packed with video cassettes was made: everyone had to help carry them up five flights of stairs.

While Jones and his growing team of telephone sales assistants remained at the Scala, the marketing operation moved across to Poland Street. Rappaport had hired a bright, pushy assistant, Angie Hunt, who quickly proved herself a gifted publicist and marketeer. However, arriving at Powell's Mega Corp centre was something of a surprise to Hunt after the cosy, chatty environment of the Scala. 'No one really liked to go to Poland Street,' Hunt recalled. 'The atmosphere changed completely when you walked in and saw Nik sprawled across his red couch.'

At the top of the video editing suites was a bar room and a small office, in which stood a desk, a chair, and a long, filthy red velvet couch, its seats stained by spilt coffee, its arms dotted with cigarette burns. Powell's secretary occupied the chair, while Powell spent the majority of his office-bound days lying in awkward positions on top of the paper-covered couch, barking into the phone. His posture became so appalling that he later developed back complications and was forced to buy a special orthopaedic chair.

Part of Powell's distinctive management style was to pay nagging attention to detail. He took a particularly critical interest in Hunt's progress, uncertain how to interpret her dedicated, never-miss-a-day approach. He would spy on her from across the room when they were working at press junkets, having warned her, 'Never let me catch you talking to a journalist you already know until you've talked to all the ones you don't.' His suspicions about her motivation and abilities were ill-founded, for each night, having put her two young children to bed, Hunt would plough through mountains of paperwork. Hunt may not have always liked Powell's manner, but to this day she pays homage to the skills he taught her.

In early 1982, Woolley embarked on a controlled buying spree, including a trip to the Berlin Film Festival, where he picked up the video rights to Chris Petit's *An Unsuitable Job for a Woman*. Soon after, Palace released David Lynch's *Eraserhead* and Derek Jarman's *The Tempest*. Foreign language videos were also seen as a major opportunity for Palace, partly due to customers' requests at The Video Palace, although the true impetus was Woolley's love of these films rather than any real profit potential. A deal was done to acquire the rights to the whole of the Fassbinder catalogue, and, later, to the films of German director Werner Herzog.

The Palace boys held a celebratory dinner at the Cannes Film Festival in honour of Herzog. However, the director, drinking copiously throughout the meal, proceeded to deride the whole exercise, proclaiming loudly what he thought of all that 'fucking video shit'. Woolley and Powell were forced to bite their tongues, muttering among their own staff and quietly trying to explain to the director that they 'weren't a complete bunch of Luddites'. Finally, the inebriated Herzog rose to leave. The great director stumbled out of the little restaurant on one of the narrow streets behind the rue d'Antibes, only to fall across a bush and into a ditch. 'He was lying there in agony, while we all just roared with laughter,' Woolley recalled. The Palace gang left him lying there, swaying back to their cheap digs near the railway station.

Rappaport, like Jones, Hunt and many other young employees who joined Palace in its early days, was to stay with the company for most of the 1980s. They were a self-motivated, close group, fired with an enthusiasm that was distinctly lacking throughout the rest of Wardour Street, which, with its tacky sex signs, film processing labs and generally grubby appearance, was a fitting centre for the British film industry.

An atmosphere of high spirits and dedication had been established at Palace that was to last a decade. 'We all had a passion for quality and a belief that there was an audience for the films we

ourselves enjoyed, despite the prejudice and "old-boys-club-busi-
ness-over-lunch-and-eighteen-holes mentality" with which we
were constantly faced,' Jones explained. 'These were the days when
video dealers thought you could catch AIDS from a box of *Prick up
your Ears.*'

With the exception of the sometimes dictatorial Powell, nobody
was telling them how to do things. As Woolley was proudly to recall,
'We just said "Fuck you! This is how you do it." ' And so the 'Us
against Them' mentality that came to depict Palace's relationship
with its film industry peers was born.

With this vigorous team in place and backed by Powell's personal
investment of £428,900, together with £221,000 invested by the
Norwich Union building society, The Mega Corporation started to
take off. Norwich Union turned out to be a perfect 'hands off'
partner, not even insisting on a seat on the board in return for its
venture capital.

Meanwhile, Powell had thought better of his company name,
which, he decided, sounded 'a bit impersonal'. (Others, given the
ease with which the adjective 'mega' could be applied to Powell's
ambitions, found this somewhat ironic.) At an extraordinary general
meeting of the board on 26 June 1983, the company's name was
formally changed to The Palace Group of Companies.

'My God, if this thing's going to continue, there have got to be some
changes around here!' Rappaport exclaimed. He had only been at
the company a few months when it became apparent to him that
Powell's accountant, whom he had brought over from Virgin, could
not cope with the rapidly increasing level of paper work. With no
systems in place to control the mounting chaos, the company was
already starting to split at the seams. It was a pattern of management
which would continue throughout Palace's history.

The picture was all too familiar to Chris Craib, a former
accounting colleague of Powell's at Virgin. Craib had left Virgin at
the end of 1980. Soon after, Powell had invited him to take a look at
his new formula for book-keeping. When the accountant tried to
explain where Powell was going wrong, he was met with an abrupt:

'It's my fucking company. If you don't like it, you can fuck off.' The prissy Craib asked: 'Could you repeat that, Nik?' Powell promptly did, and Craib walked out. He did not take Powell's calls for a while.

'It wasn't that there was anything illegal,' Craib explained. 'It was just that Nik had decided that he was going to reinvent the wheel when it came to keeping books for his company. He's basically a world expert on everything.' Craib eventually relented. 'Look, Nik, do you want to do this properly?' he asked. Powell consented, and yet another former Virgin employee was drawn into the Palace net, initially as a consultant and later as a senior manager.

Some of the early difficulties that Palace faced were due to the changing world outside as much as to the problems of rapid growth. For example, albeit slowly, the video market was starting to become more sophisticated, and it was no longer easy for the Palace telephone sales team to sell videos for £30 each. As the market expanded, the choice of films grew larger and sales of classic titles in particular became tougher.

Steps were taken to try to increase sales. One ludicrous experiment involved asking customers to send in blank and second-hand tapes, which Palace would record over, thereby allowing the public to buy films more cheaply. 'Well, blimey, what a hassle!' Rappaport exclaimed. 'We were getting all kinds of tat sent in, which the duplicator couldn't use because of the different levels of quality.' The time-consuming venture was soon abandoned. The Scala meanwhile was proving too small for the expanding video operation. Mountains of boxes and sales people were crammed into two tiny rooms at the top of five flights of stairs.

One day, Rappaport confronted Woolley. 'Steve, please do me a favour. Can you bring up a box from downstairs? Just take one box up those five flights of stairs, just to see what it's like and just to show other people you can do it, because it would make an amazing difference. You're part owner of this company, and you should be able to make decisions based upon the physical experience, as well as the intellectual.' Rappaport is convinced he saw Woolley carry a box up those stairs, at least on one subsequent occasion.

Rappaport also got into heated arguments with Powell, claiming that the whole operation needed to be more 'professional'. On hearing the word, Powell would shout Rappaport down. He believed that 'professional' simply stood for the way other people had already done business, and that was not on his agenda. But Rappaport was a shrewd operator. He realised that he had to convince Powell and Woolley that Palace needed to take a big risk by spending some money on acquiring a hit.

Sam Raimi was a classic example of the American child movie fanatic. Born in Detroit in 1960, by the time he left his local high school to go to Michigan State University, he had been involved in making nearly thirty Super-8 films. While at university, with the help of his brother Ivan and a friend, Robert Tapert, he shot a thirty-minute preview version of a horror film, *The Evil Dead*, and in 1981 presented it to potential investors and succeeded in raising $500,000. A production company, Renaissance Motion Pictures, was formed by Raimi, Tapert and the actor Bruce Campbell, who later starred in Raimi's films.

In 1982, the American Film Market – known in the business as the AFM – was held in a couple of tacky motels on Wilshire Boulevard in Los Angeles. It was the first big film market that Powell and Woolley had attended together. In an effort to save money, they initially stayed with an old girlfriend of Powell's, miles away from central LA, but when the daily cab fares amounted to nearly twice the nightly rate of a hotel, they moved to share a room in a cheap central hotel, so starting a Palace custom of accommodation cost-cutting. It was here that the fight over buying the British rights to *The Evil Dead* took place.

Woolley saw a screening of *The Evil Dead* and, while most of the audience saw it as just another awful horror flick, he thought the film 'fantastic'. The expert Woolley recognised Raimi's film as a variation on George Romero's *Night of the Living Dead* and certain Italian horror quickies, but with humorous and brilliantly gory special effects. With good reason, he was concerned about how to get the film past the British film censors, but, if this could be done, he was sure that Palace could market Raimi's roller-coaster 'splatter spoof' to great effect.

Until this trip, Powell had left nearly all acquisitions to Woolley, overseeing the video business and busying himself with his other enterprises. At the AFM Powell's attitude changed. He would roar into the little hotel rooms, chat up all the sellers and buyers, asking them a mixture of stupid and very sharp questions that confused everyone around him. 'Nik had no social graces whatsoever in those days, but he loved the parties, the people and the films. He'd really caught the buzz,' explained Woolley.

When Powell and Woolley had originally agreed to enter the video business, Woolley had insisted that they should not become involved in theatrical distribution. Having seen many cinema distributors go bankrupt, Powell had been in full agreement. However, the sales reps for *The Evil Dead* did not want to sell just the video rights. They were insisting on Palace buying everything, including the rights to release the film in UK cinemas. They were also asking for a considerable amount of money – in the region of £65,000 – which made Powell distinctly nervous.

Woolley desperately wanted *The Evil Dead* and his enthusiasm for the movie helped to change his partner's mind. Woolley now argued that Palace needed to develop a cinema distribution arm which could help drive the company's video marketing. He was also aware that Paul Webster, a rebellious but talented theatrical distributor with good contacts in Soho was looking for a new job. Initially, Powell held Woolley to the 'video only' policy, then he argued that Palace should get a sub-distributor to pay for the UK theatrical rights, thereby reducing the cost and the risk. The argument grew very heated. Woolley was the only person at Palace able to withstand Powell's ballistic bite. 'Nik used to come slamming down on people. His temper was bloody vicious,' Woolley explained. In this instance, however, it was he who finally lost control, hurling a television set across the hotel room.

Saying 'No' to Woolley was proving very difficult; and their arguments genuinely upset Powell. Despite his former protestations, the former Virgin junior partner was obviously attracted to the idea of Palace doing the whole deal on its own, and finally he relented over *The Evil Dead*. As one Palace employee commented years later, 'Giving in to Steve was a key part of Nik's behaviour pattern, and it started very early in Palace.' Raimi's horror film did not come cheap. 'We must have offered about five times more than anyone else,' Powell said, explaining that 'at that point we didn't have a clue about the prices'.

The same 'go for it' arguments were applied to the acquisition of a French thriller, *Diva*. Directed by Jean-Jacques Beineix, France's up-and-coming *enfant terrible*, *Diva* was quickly dubbed the most impressive first feature from a French director since Godard's *Breathless* in 1960. Crucially, most distributors were put off by the perceived 'foreign language problem', as at that time few subtitled films played at more than one London screen. The Palace boys adored the stylish thriller and rose to the challenge. Determined not to use jaded Wardour Street art designers, Woolley hunted down bright, young graphic artists such as Mike Sutton to work on *Diva*, while talented designer Mike Leedham was hired to work with Palace on week-long contracts. A resourceful marketing campaign, including big posters featuring a large motorbike helmet, was launched in early September 1982, and the movie played well at the Odeon Kensington and the Screen on the Hill in London.

*Diva*'s video release also offered the opportunity for some peculiarly creative touches. Aware that, at the time, a subtitled foreign language video had a very limited market, Woolley decided to bring out an edition of the film dubbed into English, alongside the French language subtitled video. The only problem was that the longer English version would not fit on one tape. 'Anyone seeing the English language version might have noticed a slightly different Godardian style,' joked Woolley. 'We had to run it a little faster to squeeze the whole thing in.'

Once more, Palace had paid well over the odds, but, together, *Diva* and *The Evil Dead* were to form the platform for the launch of a new independent British cinema distribution operation. The move was risky and audacious, for few could have guessed the huge impact Palace was to have on British cinema for the next ten years.

*The Evil Dead* opened on British cinema screens in a somewhat unorthodox manner. The newly hired head of theatrical distribution, Paul Webster, decided to release the film initially in Scotland, with a tour of Glasgow, Edinburgh and Stirling, and then gradually move it south and across England on a regional basis. The twenty-one-year-old Raimi, who made his living shooting second-hand car commercials, came over to support the film's release, and insisted on calling his distributor, the twenty-six-year-old Woolley 'sir': after all, Woolley was co-chairman of a company prepared to throw everything into his first feature film release in the UK.

Webster, hugely encouraged by Powell and Woolley, took a showman's attitude to promoting Palace's first big film. He organised a late-night sneak preview and special effects demonstration for the Friday before the Sunday opening in a poky little cinema in Glasgow's Hillhead. The place was packed with 700 drunk Glaswegians, Raimi, an assistant and Webster.

'Everyone in the cinema was absolutely smashed,' Webster recalled. 'I was up on the stage all dressed up in this ridiculous horror make-up. Sam [Raimi] was wonderful value while the audience was screaming and shouting. A really tacky mock dismemberment was performed on the assistant, and blood was pouring and squirting all over the stage. Then the big end moment came, when my own hand burst out of my stomach. I don't know how Sam did it, because I was completely drunk too. After that we nipped backstage and the movie began.' With appetites whetted, the audience loved the film.

In order to maximise publicity and takings, the film was released simultaneously on video and at the cinema. The move was guaranteed to incite the wrath of the rest of the British film industry, who were fearful that video was going to 'finish off cinema for good'. Adding insult to injury, *The Evil Dead* posters shouted 'AVAILABLE ON VIDEO NOW'. As Woolley put it: 'Rank and the rest of them went bonkers.'

The general rule at the time was that films should not reach the video rentals shelves until at least nine months after their cinema release. Cinema attendance was at a distinctly low ebb in 1983, having dropped to fewer than 60 million admissions per year, less than half today's attendance levels. The business was haunted by badly situated, disintegrating facilities, and the sight of an arrogant upstart distributor apparently furthering cinema's decline infuriated the industry.

Woolley, meanwhile, had already experienced a bruising encounter with the then-named British Board of Film Censorship (BBFC). According to Tom Dewe Mathews's book, *Censored*, James Ferman, the Secretary of the BBFC, had originally liked *The Evil Dead*, and told Woolley that it had been made with 'a great deal of talent', and that it was 'almost a parody of horror'. He had indicated that it could probably go through uncut. At the examination screening, Ferman and a fellow examiner roared with laughter but unfortunately a colleague was less amused. She said the film had left her 'nauseated', and she felt that her 'bodily integrity had been attacked'. Ferman decided to 'take it down a bit'.

'Much of the cutting was done in-house by Jim "Creative Surgeon" Ferman, who stayed up late at night actually chinagraphing the print,' said a former Board examiner. Around forty seconds of the film were removed. Ferman cut back scenes such as those showing a pencil being twisted in a leg; Bruce Campbell's lead character being repeatedly hit over the head by an iron girder wielded by a female zombie; and a man being assaulted by a tree. The notorious sequence where a woman is raped by a tree remained surprisingly almost untouched. 'I think that probably says quite a lot about the British,' Raimi told *Time Out* later. 'I was very aware that a lot of those films are very unfair in how they portray women, so I worked quite hard to avoid that.'

Webster, who was a self-described anarchist in those days, by mistake released the uncensored print in the cinemas. Nobody noticed for a few weeks, but horror enthusiasts who saw the film more than a dozen times spotted the difference on the censored video version. 'I just apologised all round, palming it off as a cock-up,' Webster explained, laughing.

The real shock of *The Evil Dead* was how much money it was taking. The film entered the London circuit in February 1983, and in six weeks grossed more than £50,000 at the Prince Charles cinema alone. At other cinemas around the UK it took just over £100,000. However, the serious profit was made on the video, which was the best-selling title that year. The old timers on Wardour Street were in apoplexy over Palace's success, but Romaine Hart, Woolley's former cinema boss, was not that surprised to see Palace thrive: 'I thought from day one that they'd either do incredibly well or they'd go broke. There was no middle ground because they always took far greater risks than anyone else.'

With success came certain associated problems. During the summer of 1983, Mary Whitehouse, the housewife and moral crusader, screened a show of horror highlights to Tory MPs at their annual party conference. *The Evil Dead* was billed by Whitehouse as 'The No. 1 Nasty', despite the fact that the film censor had passed it earlier that year and that even the video release was properly certified, which could not be said for hundreds of other films on the video market at that time. Egged on by a rampant right-wing press, crusading against 'video nasties', the Tories decided to act.

The Police, empowered by the Obscene Publications Act, initially decided to raid video retailers, but soon changed their line of attack to distributors, and brash Palace was the perfect prey. Fortunately, a call came in to the Scala, tipping Rappaport off about the forthcoming raids. A bunch of *Evil Dead* cassettes were swiftly removed to a local church, but the police then went to the main warehouse, from where they took the master tapes. A lengthy prosecution case was prepared by the Director of Public Prosecutions, and Raimi, Powell and others gave testimony at Snaresbrook Crown Court. A verdict of not guilty was returned in Palace's favour on 7 November 1983, with the court supporting the Censor's certificate judgement in full. The surrounding publicity simply assured *The Evil Dead*'s rise to the top of the video charts, where it was to remain for a record-breaking number of weeks.

Flying halfway round the world to buy a film was Woolley's idea of an incredible experience. To Powell, it was a nightmare: to his mind Palace could hardly afford to pay the air fare to Japan, never mind spend a six figure sum on a film screening at the Tokyo International Film Festival. After much debate, a flight was booked for Woolley, and he left to meet the British producer, Jeremy Thomas, and his sales agent, Terry Glinwood, with a view to seeing the first-ever showing of Nagisa Oshima's *Merry Christmas Mr Lawrence*. The film starred David Bowie, who was hot from his recently released *Let's Dance* album, and the relaxed Glinwood was sitting back and waiting for the bids to come tumbling in. Not leaving anything to chance, Woolley had already held a meeting with Thomas in London, where he made it clear that he wanted to go to Japan to see the film before any other British distributors had a chance to place offers.

After the screening, a nervous Woolley rang Powell insisting that they should buy the film. The deal cost the company £225,000, of which £175,000 was payable up front. This was at least four times the amount Palace had paid for any film up to that point. Exhilarated after closing the deal, the three men went out for a big sushi meal that evening, but the combination of rice wine, raw fish and paying all that money was too much for Woolley, and the boy from Islington spent most of the evening being sick in the plush Tokyo restaurant's toilets. 'Steve was incredibly brave,' Thomas recalled. 'To fly round the world to get a film showed incredible enthusiasm and guts. We immediately decided not to even bother trying to sell the film to anyone else in the UK.'

*Merry Christmas* had been eagerly accepted for the official competition at the Cannes Film Festival in May 1983. Woolley watched admiringly as Thomas energetically marketed the film. The music sound-track was vigorously exploited through Virgin Records; the Laurens van der Post novel, *The Seed and the Sower*, on which the film was based, was re-released by Penguin; and coveted black and white T-shirts bearing the words 'The Oshima Gang' were paraded round Cannes. Bowie and his co-star Tom Conti flew in for the screening, and everyone was praying for a prize. On the night, however, the award fell to the festival's other Japanese film.

Palace milked the media frenzy and, three months after the festival, released the film to fine critical acclaim. Tony Elliot, publisher of *Time Out* magazine, recalls the young distributors taking him out for lunch at Graeme's on Poland Street, explaining that 'they'd bet everything on the deal, and that they hoped they could count on my support. To which I replied: "That depends on the film standing up, and on whether the film department thinks it's any good." '

'It wasn't exactly *Jurassic Park*,' Powell later said, 'but it did do very well on video and we just about got away with paying all that money for it.'

Other leading European film-makers were also caught by Palace's web, which was mainly spun by Woolley. While away in Germany in 1983 working on a small Chris Petit film, Woolley grabbed a chance to see an early cut of Wim Wenders's *Paris Texas*. When the film's screening was over, Chris Sievernich, the film's producer, turned round to Woolley and said, 'Christ, it's got some real problems, eh?' To which Woolley replied, 'Palace must have this film. How much do you want?'

'It was a little crazy to give them the film for a cinema release, because they didn't have much experience at that stage, but Nik and Steve were so young and enthusiastic we couldn't say no,' Wim Wenders explained later. 'They had the energy and marketing initiative to bring the film out at a time when foreign-language movies were having a terrible period in Britain. The one time I visited the Palace office I remember being so impressed by the creative culture they had surrounded themselves with. And the film did really well for all of us.'

By the end of 1983, Palace had grown and its workforce expanded. Employees' friends would be asked to come in to cover for absent secretaries, and end up staying for five or more years. Sue Bruce-Smith, a former French teacher and friend of Rappaport's, joined Palace in exactly that way. Rappaport rang her up one day, saying his secretary had disappeared on holiday for two weeks, despite having joined only a few days earlier. 'Sue, we both know you'll be useless, because you can't spell or type,' said Rappaport encouragingly, 'but can you catch the 73 bus into Soho anyway?'

After a few weeks, Bruce-Smith was taken out to Le Tire-Bouchon for a lunch interview with Woolley and Webster. The only question they asked about her qualifications was whether she had passed her 11-plus. 'They weren't interested in degrees or post-graduate diplomas, and I didn't own up to having one until later. Steve really hated the Oxbridge syndrome, and later it became clear to me that Nik was sold on the "University of Life". It wasn't a snobbish thing, he just thought that those three or four years were wasted, and that you were better off experiencing real work.' Bruce-Smith was taken on to handle cinema bookings and print dispatch for a salary of £6,600, although when she realised that her previous job had paid better, she asked Webster for a twenty-five per cent pay rise, and 'amazingly, it was forthcoming'.

The Palace offices, crammed with precariously stacked boxes of publicity material, were rarely calm. 'There'd often be a row going on; someone would be quietly working away in a corner, touching up a marketing poster; while an accountant would be prevaricating to a creditor about not being able to pay a bill that week. Everyone answered the phone, including Nik, Steve, Daniel [Battsek] and Paul [Webster]. It was frenetic but also very democratic. We all just pitched in,' Bruce-Smith recalled.

Powell and Woolley's overall sense of purpose was often disguised by the superficially casual approach taken to internal meetings. 'A serious part of the Palace philosophy was going round at the end of the day to The George [which in those days was referred to as 'The Independent Producer'] and getting legless. We needed to do that,' explained Bruce-Smith, 'because we had to come down from the high.'

Marketing meetings had originally taken place in the back room of the Scala, but were continually interrupted because Palace was trying to develop its computer games company in the same room. The meetings moved to a local restaurant with rotten food, deliberately chosen because Palace could have the place to themselves, but passions flared too high for the waiters and manager, and Palace was soon kicked out. In the end, the meetings were held at The Coach and Horses in Poland Street, at first on

Monday nights, but later, when the workload had increased, on Tuesday evenings as well. Advertising campaigns, poster ideas and proofs, press coverage and forthcoming releases were discussed heatedly and in detail. Posters would be handed round the pub and comments from nearby punters noted, while Powell or Woolley invariably criticised colours, copy and lettering, demanding to know who was responsible for the design. One particular row errupted over the colouring of the advertisements for *Merry Christmas Mr Lawrence*.

'Who the fuck decided to do the pink and grey?' Powell yelled.

'What? I did,' replied Rappaport. 'It's not grey, it's silver.'

'I wanted this poster red and black.'

'But pink and silver's completely distinctive. It's classy.'

'Fucking change it back.'

'Well, you can fire me if you want, but it's going to be pink and silver, and if it doesn't work, you can blame me,' Rappaport retorted.

Despite Powell's remonstrations, the advertisements and video duly went out pink and silver.

Taking on Palace's press coverage was a heavy responsibility. Phil Symes, a young PR executive who had started in music and moved across to film, and his assistant Angie Errigo, would attend the marketing meetings. 'There was always a lot of screaming between Steve, Nik and Paul,' Symes recalled. 'Poor Nik always got the rough end of it, because he was always trying to do the right thing by those they employed, and was more considerate of people than Steve. He'd scream, but only when he felt that his message wasn't getting through. Often Nik really wouldn't be getting through because Steve was totally dominating and wouldn't even listen to him. You could see Steve's ego manifesting itself and growing, and although Nik was the boss, he appeared to be the underdog.'

Others saw Powell less sympathetically. While Webster was close to Woolley, he often found Powell's abrasive approach too much to handle. Pub meetings would often start with a blunt criticism from Powell, so incensing Webster that he would pick up his newspaper, whack his boss forcefully over the head and storm out of the pub.

Following such outbursts, an embarrassed Woolley would smooth things over, quickly moving the meeting on. Powell's jocular sociability with people outside the work place was often but not always matched when inside the office jungle. Woolley even trained his personal assistants to tell Powell, when he behaved badly: 'Fuck off and never talk to me in that way again.'

Nevertheless, talented people could not help finding Palace attractive. Errigo, an over-the-top American-born film fanatic, had come to Woolley's and Powell's attention during a preview screening of *The Evil Dead*, when a volley of screams and uncontrolled laughter had erupted from the back of the cinema.

'Who *is* that woman?' Powell had asked Woolley. Woolley tracked her down and decreed that she should sit at the back of all Palace screenings, especially at film festivals, because her noisy enjoyment encouraged the audience. Errigo loved it, finding the whole thing madly exasperating but always exciting.

Given that Palace had few resources to buy advertising in newspapers, let alone on prohibitively expensive television, a guerrilla-style campaign for free press coverage was esssential to each film's success. Above all, the British film critics – quick to slap down Palace as video barrow-boys – needed to be circumvented. 'They always had a plan of attack for every film. Nik would explain what he had in mind, but whatever film he was talking about, he'd want it to be the biggest thing since *Gone with the Wind*. In reality, we had to get *Time Out*, the *Standard*, and the *Guardian* for a film to open in London just for starters. There was no such thing as a small film for Palace. To Nik and Steve, it was always a matter of life and death. We had to bludgeon every single paper in every town and every possible outlet, but it was never enough for them,' Errigo recalled.

Cutting costs wherever conceivable was intrinsic to Powell's method of business. Even when Palace did celebrate its numerous early triumphs, Powell kept a firm hold of the purse-strings. 'Nik and Steve's idea of a party was a few baked beans on a Ritz cracker, and some crap deal on beer that they could get free,' Errigo said. 'They just blustered their way along, and were the most insensitive people in the world. Even Steve used to describe Nik as "capable of being the rudest man on earth".'

During Palace's hectic first two years of business, it became clear to both Powell and Woolley that they were losing key films to stronger financed opposition. Woolley would fly to the film markets, search out interesting films, offer up to about £75,000 only to find himself outbid by a richer rival. Virgin Vision, Branson's newly launched film and video distribution operation, was a particular thorn in Palace's side, snapping up films which fitted perfectly with Palace's profile.

The answer to Palace's problems seemed to lie in an organic move towards production. Woolley, in particular, was keen to realise this option. He had already been developing material with Neil Jordan, and had started reading screenplays and cementing links with the talented people he had met through Palace's distribution activities. Powell and Woolley were accustomed to work closely with film-makers when releasing their films, openly sharing their ideas and energetic marketing plans. As a result friendships developed and luminaries such as Sam Raimi, Jean-Jacques Beineix and the Coen brothers could be seen shooting pool with Palace staff over a few beers in the pub. While the staff were enjoying themselves, working and playing hard into the early hours, Powell and Woolley were firmly in the centre of the action, revelling in their company's energy and strong sense of fun.

Powell recognised that, by forming Palace Productions, they would make the company less dependent on competitively acquiring films. With their own films, Palace would hold UK rights and exploit their creative endeavours abroad.

CHAPTER FOUR

# The
# Company
# of Wolves

In 1982, in Dublin's grand Shelbourne Hotel on St Stephen's Green, Neil Jordan found himself talking to the writer and feminist Angela Carter. They were both attending a week of festivities and drinking for writers and artists, including such luminaries as Anthony Burgess and Dennis Potter, to mark the centenary of James Joyce's birth. It was not long before their conversation moved to a shared obsession: film. Jordan recalled how he used to go to the cinema as a child every Friday, Saturday and Sunday, trading a ticket for two empty jam jars when he had no money. He discovered that Carter had been commissioned by Channel 4 to write a thirty-minute script based on her short story, 'The Company of Wolves', which had already been broadcast as a radio play. Their conversation was interrupted when Jorge Luis Borges, the celebrated South American writer, began to make a keynote speech, but his words were drowned out when a local ceilidh band struck up next door. Jordan complained to the head of the Irish Tourist Board about the din, only to find himself thrown out of the party and on to the street.

Jordan and Carter continued drinking that night, joining an Irish university lecturer in mediaeval philosophy and a gay priest in a pub argument. 'Most of the conversation consisted of a discourse about farting and the problem of erections on buses,' Jordan recalled in a subsequent *Time Out* article. 'But Angela proved herself to be a model of tact in the face of these and other manifestations of the national temperament.'

Less than a week later, Carter's script arrived on Jordan's doorstep. He was impressed by the series of tales told to a small girl by a wicked granny, which culminated in an imaginative version of the legend of Little Red Riding Hood. He got the script to Woolley, who liked the story but felt it needed to be longer. Palace managed to raise some money from Mamoun Hassan, an executive at the then-titled National Film Development Fund (NFDF), and Channel 4 (which at that time was not co-producing or heavily financing films) provided development finance for the screen-writing process.

Each morning Jordan would cycle to Carter's home in Clapham, where they would spend the entire morning working together on the screenplay. Drinking enormous quantities of tea, they worked their way through the script in a very businesslike manner, and in the afternoon Carter wrote up the scenes. Her demeanour reminded Jordan of the surrealist painter, Magritte, 'who would dress impeccably every morning, pack his briefcase, kiss his wife goodbye, then walk around the block, return home and begin to work'. Jordan was quite taken by her streak of Scottish puritanism, which belied the wilder elements of her work. He also appreciated the company of a co-writer, which helped him escape the painful, almost alienating experience of working alone.

'After a while, though the pattern of the day maintained the same order, the script lost all touch with common decency. It became gothic and sensual, acquiring a special kind of horror. Images began to come from nowhere, lurid and illogical, but somehow perfect for the tale,' Jordan wrote later, adding that every scene had somehow included a pregnancy, though he had not realised that Carter was with child until after the first draft had been completed. Clearly some cuts were required. After a bout of birth control via the editing pen, the ambitiously expanded script was delivered to Woolley, who was eager to start the game of finding the finance.

Christopher Hambley Brown was an unlikely person for Woolley to choose as a producing partner. The son of George Hambley Brown, a big British film production executive in the busy 1950s, Chris Brown – who dropped the 'Hambley' family prefix – had grown up not only under the shadow of his father's success but competing with his sister's, Tina Brown's, precocious achievements as she started her meteoric rise to media fame, becoming editor of *Tatler* in 1979, and five years later taking charge of the American monthly glossy, *Vanity Fair*. Chris Brown had public school and privilege stamped across his forehead, but somehow Woolley took a liking to him. 'Chris was this incredibly nice guy who wore bow ties and sounded like he was just out of the Coldstream Guards,' he explained.

Brown had produced a short film which Woolley had screened at the Scala. The two had then gone on to co-produce the Channel 4 show, *The Worst of Hollywood*, so when Palace started to prepare the production strategy for *The Company of Wolves* Brown was a natural choice as producing partner.

Channel 4's film executives experienced something of a shock on reading Jordan's and Carter's first draft. 'I think they were horrified, to be honest,' Woolley said. 'Channel 4 had no idea how violent it would be, and Neil had filled it chock-a-block with crazy special effects that were clearly going to be very difficult to achieve.' A budget was put together that far exceeded Channel 4's £1 million maximum investment ceiling. Forced to look elsewhere, Woolley decided to approach every potential backer he could think of, pitching the ambitious project to all of them within a few days. Verity Lambert, the television producer unfairly slated in later years for *Eldorado*, the BBC's £10 million 'sunshine and sangria' soap, was working at Thorn EMI's Screen Entertainment in 1983. Like other British backers, she had admired Jordan's début, *Angel*, but failed to envision how *The Company of Wolves* would work on the screen. Woolley also tried Universal Studios and Orion in Hollywood, meeting rejections but making excellent contacts for future projects.

Woolley and Powell had been told by the NFDF's Hassan that the one place they should not send the script was Lew Grade's former company, ITC, which had changed hands following the disastrous failure of *Raise the Titanic*. Powell promptly sent it to ITC. Bernie Kingham, the key ITC executive whom Palace needed on board if the film was to be made, was enthusiastic about the project. Powell's and Woolley's banter persuaded him that they were the new kids on the block, and that Jordan had an incredible directing career in front of him.

Palace had struck lucky. ITC was one of the few British companies at that time that would provide a hundred per cent finance for a feature film. Kingham set about persuading ITC that the company should finance the film's estimated £2 million budget. The cost reflected the array of special effects, the most striking of which was the transformation of a man into a wolf. This was no easy task on a non-Hollywood budget. Three years earlier, it had taken the special effects team on *An American Werewolf in London* nine months to prepare such sequences. Woolley and Jordan discussed in detail how they were going to deal with human flesh being removed and fur showing underneath the skin. Anatomical drawings of the muscular structures of dogs and wolves were studied, as were Francis Bacon's portraits of screaming heads. Christopher Tucker, a rising special effects star, was hired to make the most of the limited money available.

The production's three major transformation sequences were crucial to Jordan. 'The imagery in films like *Alien* and *The Thing* conveyed a very deep hatred of sexuality, a pathological disgust with the human form. This is possibly because the most obvious use of anamotronic effects – a term which basically means the building of articulated dolls and models to simulate real actors – is to tear the human shape to shreds, to have heads burst like melons and chests explode, releasing the gore which covers a multitude. *The Company of Wolves* was to be about sex, not about hating it. A wolf that crawls out of the skin of a man covered in various red and yellow liquids wouldn't hold much attraction for a thirteen-year-old girl.'

In the autumn of 1983 the decision was taken to shoot the entire film in Shepperton Studios, just outside London. Live locations and a sense of realism were abandoned in favour of a fabricated landscape constructed from polystyrene, plaster and wood. The hand-built sets included a forest, a village, a graveyard and an extraordinary well, which acquired strange hydraulic arms and shafts that appeared to run miles into the earth.

Anton Furst, an eccentric but technically brilliant designer, whose work ranged from creating the eggs in Ridley Scott's *Alien* to staging rock concerts and London's first hologram shows, was faced with the problem of finding a fantastic, gothic look without recreating a predictable Disney-style fairy-tale setting. Furst, who went on to win an Academy Award for *Batman*, was hugely encouraged by Woolley, whose passion for the project was partly rooted in his desire to recreate Michael Powell and Emeric Pressburger's exuberant film-making of the 1940s and '50s. Films such as *The Red Shoes*, *A Matter of Life and Death*, and *Black Narcissus* showed a visual sensibility that Woolley felt was sorely missing from British film-making in the early 1980s. Reinvention and experimentation underlined Powell and Pressburger's work – elements that for Woolley represented the true meaning of cinema – and their strong sense of eroticism and the supernatural celebrated the themes that Woolley felt so strongly about in *The Company of Wolves*. In his eyes, Jordan's and Carter's imaginative screenplay provided an inspired opportunity to take ground-breaking creative risks. It was not just the multi-layered tale that excited Woolley: here was the chance to combine story and music, electronic gadgets and animal 'acting', to create something new and exciting. Woolley was pleased with the idea that Palace was trying to create something different, unlike the rest of the British film industry, most of whose exponents, in his opinion, were born with silver spoons in their mouths and insisted on producing over-literary films with too much dialogue, failing utterly to grasp the power that the big screen offers.

Fired by Woolley's enthusiasm, Furst set about assembling a team of experienced and less experienced specialists happy to give the risky project a go. Much of his budget was spent on eight three-dimensional model trees, with assorted stumps and root structures, which were designed to create the illusion that they soared to a sky that could rarely be seen. The trees were built on rollers, so that they could be shifted around the set to produce different kinds of space.

In January 1984 *The Company of Wolves* went into production, led by a gang of enthusiastic but inexperienced producers and directed by Jordan, who had only one film to his name. The schedule was tight and nobody had any real experience of shooting in a studio. Because each episode of the script demanded its own fresh environment, sets had to be turned round at desperate speed. Every camera move had to be meticulously checked, or one of the countless holes and missing props in the set would make the shot useless. Live props, including snakes, cockroaches, ducks and doves, only added to the problems of continuity and cinematic coherence.

Finding actors for *The Company of Wolves* had been relatively straightforward. Angela Lansbury took the role of the grandmother, Stephen Rea – the lead in Jordan's *Angel* – turned into a wolf and a new young actress, twelve-year-old Sarah Patterson, played the sexually awakened young girl. The most troublesome 'actors' proved to be the wolves, which had been hired from a gypsy in Nottingham, and Jordan soon found himself becoming increasingly impatient with his star beasts. Coaxing just one wolf out of a well, over a bridge, or on to the bough of a tree seemed to take days. Many hours were wasted trying to make a wolf appear from its hillside lair. They were also capable of turning nasty. The first time the animals were transported down to Shepperton, the production crew found that one of the wolves had been attacked and eaten by the others. A curious *Time Out* journalist visiting the set in early 1984 was warned: 'Careful, they're liable to forget that they're tamed and snap your hand off.'

Preparations for a key scene that involved thirteen wolves dressed in immaculate eighteenth-century costumes seated inside a pink marquee proved particularly problematic. Somebody came up with the idea of tranquillising some of the wolves so that they could be dressed while drugged and then filmed as they awoke, tore off their clothes and bounded away to freedom. Unfortunately, after the crew had waited for twelve hours, the wolves merely shifted, yawned and went straight back to sleep.

During the shooting of the film, Woolley and Jordan shared a dingy flat in Maida Vale. 'It was a very shitty place, completely filthy,' recalled Woolley. This was the base where he and Jordan 'screamed and fought their way through eight weeks of hell'. The two of them would normally return late at night, deeply exhausted, down a couple of drinks and collapse. On other nights their disagreements would escalate. 'We'd be drinking whisky, screaming at each other, fighting in restaurants, and generally arguing and consoling,' Woolley explained. 'The next morning we'd go back to the set, meet with Chris Brown, and implement agreed decisions.'

Despite their arguments, Woolley and Jordan became close friends. While Chris Brown was dealing with the line producing, which included managing the daily schedules and budget reports, Woolley would spend his entire time on set, and soon learned how to balance his personal relationship with Jordan with his role as the producer.

'A lot of producing during a film comes down to how important a scene is. For example, I would be asking Neil whether we should spend four hours on these two scenes, or spend some of that time on something else. The result was that we argued a lot,' Woolley admitted.

The film came together in a haphazard but exciting manner and the distribution staff back at Wardour Street soon had to address the question of how to market the film. Aware that the film needed to appeal to a wider audience than the average arty fairy-tale, they began to prepare a host of images ranging from horror movie to teenage fantasy. One member of the team had only just arrived at Palace, but was to stay with Powell's and Woolley's company until its demise.

Daniel Battsek was desperate to work in the film industry. A short, dark, curly-haired young man in his early twenties, Battsek had left Oxford Polytechnic in 1981 and trawled Wardour Street for three months in search of a job. 'I got about as far as the reception desk. If I did manage to see anybody, they said I should come back when I'd got some experience. I promptly asked them: "But how can I get any experience if you don't give me a job?" It clearly wasn't going to happen to me in London.' Battsek left for Australia, where some supportive government tax legislation had led to a relative boom in film-making. Resourceful and pushy, he managed to get a job in early 1982 as a runner – 'well, less than a runner, actually I was making tea for the runner' – on a Gillian Armstrong movie, *Starstruck*. He soon talked his way into a junior job with Hoyts, an Australian cinema chain, where he learnt the basic rules of film distribution. 'It was fantastic grounding. Because I had to get film prints across several territories miles away from each other, it quickly got into my head that a distributor is a link in a chain. The people who are sitting in a cinema are at the end of that chain, and they're not going to take too kindly to a blank screen.'

Nearly four years after his six-month visa had expired Battsek was kicked out of Australia and found himself back on the Wardour Street trail, where a Virgin Vision film executive suggested he approach Palace. After his many stuffy interviews with vaguely bored film distributors, Palace seemed a wonderfully exciting place for Battsek. A casual chat with Powell, on his infamous red stained couch, was followed by a more cagey interview with Webster, who examined in considerable detail what Battsek really knew about film distribution and marketing. Battsek got on well with Powell and Woolley, enjoying their different characters while sharing their enthusiasm and passion for films. 'Steve is as proud of his working-class upbringing as I'm apathetic about my middle-class roots. I'm sure he sneered at my Highgate public school, although one of my saving graces as far as he's concerned is that I got kicked out. We have prejudices about each other's entire view of life, but they're reduced to nothing when it comes down to films, books and football, the three things that really matter.'

Webster marshalled his new recruit towards Palace's press and marketing department, where Battsek worked closely with Phil Symes and Angie Errigo on the release plans for *The Company of Wolves*. Battsek was amazed at the amount of time and effort that Woolley put into Palace's first film production: 'I could see what making movies did to Steve. It was almost like he was a vampire's victim, because the film seemed to be sucking the blood out of him quite literally. It was an image I couldn't get out of my mind when it came to trying to find audiences for his films, and it made it that much harder to say "no" to Steve.'

A key question facing Palace was how to launch *The Company of Wolves*. As the film still had to be sold to North America, Palace needed a big UK splash for its first production. Consequently, much of the press campaign had been devised with the American sale in mind. The hype began in May at the Cannes Film Festival, where Symes launched the film to the international press with a ten-minute show reel. The cleverly cut footage created a classic Cannes-style furore. The international film industry, far from harbouring the narrow attitude of Wardour Street, was demanding to know who these new guys were.

Symes, Webster and Battsek worked hard on every conceivable marketing element, including a cover story in *Time Out* that May, T-shirts distributed at Cannes, and the production of about ten different posters, with detailed florid images and sensational quotes from the script, such as 'Hairy on the Inside' and 'Sharpest Tongue'. One of the inspired posters showed a wolf's head coming out of a large mouth. Palace even stretched its budgets to cover an unusual advertising deal with ITV and Channel 4 for Wim Wenders's *Paris, Texas*, Stephen Frears's *The Hit* and Jordan's film. The advertisement reflected the same sophisticated strategy of appealing to both art-house and general cinema goers, as well as, in the case of *The Company of Wolves*, the horror fans.

Woolley decided that the film should have a platform release, showing only at the Odeon Leicester Square in its opening weeks, and then moving to other cinemas at a later date.

The Odeon Leicester Square is the biggest cinema in London, seating 2,000. It is owned by the Rank chain, whom Palace had come up against when it had released *The Evil Dead* on video at the same time as the film played in cinemas. Webster approached Stan Fishman, the managing director of Odeon, about the chances of *The Company of Wolves* opening in Leicester Square. Fishman was bemused by the proposal, and politely suggested to Webster that Jordan's film was too specialised and arty to fill such a big cinema –

besides which, no booking could be confirmed until Odeon's management had seen the completed film.

Woolley and Powell began to woo Fishman over cups of coffee in Soho cafés. They would debate film industry trends, such as the growing importance of video, and the Rank executive could not help but admire the new company's pluck. Fishman pencilled in *The Company of Wolves* for a September release, but the booking confirmation was still strictly 'subject to viewing'.

In June 1984, Webster and Battsek reluctantly decided that they ought to go down to the sleepy Devon town of Torquay to attend the annual Cinema Exhibitors Association Conference. British film distributors and cinema managers come together every year to discuss the state of the film industry, and screen forthcoming films to exhibitors. The majority of attendants are well past fifty years of age, and the traditional event feels like a cross between a freemasons' meeting and an old people's outing. It was to this grey-haired gathering that Webster and Battsek distributed Palace's splashy brochure promoting the company's new films. Late one night they went round all the conference guests' hotel rooms and pushed the leaflet under the doors. Splashed across the front was the banner announcement:

## THE COMPANY OF WOLVES
### Exclusive presentation – Odeon Leicester Square, September 21 1984.

'I now know why this was such an extraordinary *faux pas*,' Battsek explained. 'When you deal with the Odeon Leicester Square, you don't even write it on a piece of paper in your own office unless you have an absolute agreement. Every other distributor in Torquay thought they had that date pencilled in. It was like putting a time bomb under everybody's door. We woke up the next day thinking that we'd really arrived, only to be met with universal outrage. Paul and I played snooker throughout the rest of the entire conference.'

Fishman and the Rank old guard were predictably incensed, but to Battsek the episode summed up the entire culture clash that was about to grab Wardour Street by the throat. 'That was my first understanding of why Palace had to be Palace, and had to always remain separate from everything else going on in the film industry. We were swimming against the tide and the Establishment, but using everything around us in a hip, spot-on way. This was my family. I felt I was never going to let it down, and that I'd never want to leave it.'

Fishman and his Odeon staff finally agreed to see a completed print of *The Company of Wolves* at Wardour Street's Bijou theatre in August. Despite liking the film, Fishman was very concerned about its commercial appeal. A subsequent meeting was fixed up with Powell and Webster, where Fishman asked them for the estimated box office takings for the first week of the play at the Odeon. Powell suggested £60,000, some £20,000 higher than Fishman's best expectations. A deal was offered to Powell, whereby Odeon would take the first £20,000 of box office earnings, with Palace receiving ninety per cent of all subsequent takings. Powell and Woolley debated the merits of the risky deal for two days before committing to it. *The Company of Wolves* was finally fully booked into the Odeon Leicester Square and news of the deal quickly travelled throughout Wardour Street.

Proud of their first production, Woolley and Powell organised an industry screening at BAFTA's cinema on Piccadilly. The British film Establishment came to turn its cynical glare on the film and barely managed to clap when the closing credits rolled. 'It was very badly received, and deeply depressing for us,' Woolley recalled. 'We really felt the film was a watershed for the industry, but it simply turned round and poured water over it.'

In early September 1984, some three weeks before *The Company of Wolves* release date, Woolley received a call from film producer David Puttnam, with whom he had spoken only a few times previously. Although clearly well intentioned, the call was viewed by younger Palace staff as patronising. 'David was very polite and nice, but he did say that we were absolutely mad to go out in the

Odeon. We'd never fill those seats, and the movie would die in front of our eyes,' Woolley recalled.

Whatever the relative merits of *The Company of Wolves*, the UK industry deeply resented Palace's happy-go-arrogant approach to getting things done. Malicious gossip suggested that Powell was 'a music man who doesn't have a film brain; while that Steve Woolley has no idea about the business. He should stick to running cinemas.' Many jealous observers hoped that Palace could be written off as a doomed bunch of lightweights. Inevitably, such attitudes merely strengthened Palace's resolve to prove everyone wrong. Powell and Woolley had surrounded themselves with a strong, animated group of young people who would not be shouted down, and who remained intensely loyal to the company. As one employee later explained: 'It was like being a Millwall football fan, who sing on the terraces every week, "No one likes us, we don't care." '

Palace also met a negative reaction from James Ferman at the British Board of Film Censors. As Jordan later explained: 'When we showed the finished film to the censors, we found the absence of a moral lesson created some outrage. A film with little nudity and less sex was seen as an erotic enticement to teenage girls. Image after image from the film was banned by the London Transport Authority [which has to approve all film posters]. We had to content ourselves with an 18 certificate, though the film was made with a teenage audience in mind.'

As the release date approached, Palace's marketing drive did not diminish. Launch parties, although traditional in show business, tend to have no effect on subsequent box-office takings. Powell, however, recognised that the party was a further marketing opportunity and asked Phil Symes to organise a suitable affair on a tight, £2,000 budget. The resourceful Symes booked Jubilee Gardens on the Thames Embankment, where a huge pink marquee was erected.

On the night, celebrity gate-crashers attracted to the Palace-induced buzz included Robert De Niro, Christopher Walken and Mikhail Baryshnikov. Dozens of photographers snapped pictures of De Niro and Walken racing across the lawns and over a wall in a desperate attempt to escape publicity. Sarah Patterson, the teenage star of the film, was caught drinking from a bottle of wine. The newspapers the following day were splattered with photos and gossip, bringing the film to the public's attention, just as Powell, Woolley and Symes had planned.

During the nervous last weeks before the movie's release, the Palace staff organised a £5 sweepstake to be won by whoever made the best estimate of the opening week's box-office takings. Cinema booking veteran Mike Ewin, who was helping Webster select the right cinemas for the film to play in across the country, asked him:

'What's the highest estimate to date?'

'£45,000 is the biggest so far,' Webster replied.

'Okay then, I'll bet £50,000,'

Ewin went on to raise his bet to £60,000 after a late punter bid above him. When the takings were finally counted on 28 September, Ewin won hands down. Proclaimed by the *News of the World* 'A Howling Success', *The Company of Wolves* took £69,000 in its first seven days.

As the film took off in the UK, Palace, in close consultation with ITC, started to make headway with a sale to North America. *The Company of Wolves* had already been shown to all the Hollywood studios in the hope that one of them would distribute the film in North America. 'The only guy to call back was Disney's Jeffrey Katzenberg,' Woolley recalled. 'He loved it, but didn't want to distribute it. It may have seemed brash to show it out in LA, but it was a good idea to keep building contacts there.'

A month after *The Company of Wolves* successful UK opening, Powell and Woolley flew to Italy to attend MIFED, the annual international film market. Held in the heart of Milan, in a grey, stuffy building with endless halls and pocket-sized rooms, MIFED reflects some of the less glamorous aspects of the film business.

Undeterred by the grim surroundings, Powell entered negotiations on behalf of ITC with the Cannon Film Group, run by the two Hollywood film moguls, Menahem Golan and Yoram Globus. Infamous for their distinctive brand of sex-and-horror films, including the 1970s *Happy Hooker* series, and films such as *Maid in Sweden*, *Cauldron of Blood*, *Invasion of the Blood Farmers*, *Blood Legacy* and, later, Michael Winner's *Death Wish* films, the unconventional cousins took up much of Powell's patience and time trying to hammer out a distribution deal. 'It was very complex, but finally we got it all together and agreed it,' Powell said. However, late one evening, just as the deal looked set, Globus turned to Golan and, out of the blue, announced, 'Menahem, before you sign this, I think you should see the film.'

'Shit!' thought Powell, 'Menahem's going to hate it.' Publicly keeping his cool, Powell pointed out that there was a market screening of the film at 9 o'clock the next morning. Golan grudgingly agreed to come along.

The next morning Powell happened to be passing the Cannon office at around 9.05. He peeped through the open door, only to see Golan's considerable bulk behind his desk.

'What the hell are you doing here? I thought you were at the screening!' Powell exclaimed.

'I've seen it,' Golan replied bluntly.

'What do you mean you've seen it? It's only been running for five minutes.'

'Look, Nik, I only see a frame of my own films. Yours, I saw five minutes.'

Powell was quietly astonished, and came away thinking how lucky he had been to sell a film for distribution after the buyers had seen just five minutes of footage.

By the time Woolley and Powell flew out to Los Angeles for the American Film Market in February 1985, Cannon had begun to prepare some extraordinarily aggressive marketing material.

Although Woolley was impressed by Cannon's energy and commitment to *The Company of Wolves*, he sometimes found their method of business difficult to brook. In a meeting with Cannon's head of distribution, Woolley suggested that the US campaign could capitalise on Angela Lansbury, who at that point was appearing on American television in the *Murder She Wrote* drama series. Woolley thought that American chat shows in particular would be interested in Lansbury.

'Why would you use some prissy pensioner to promote this movie?' the executive shot back.

'I'm sorry . . . ?' Woolley stammered.

'We don't send Chuck Norris on chat shows. Don't come over here and tell me how to fucking promote movies.'

Woolley shut up. A moment later the executive again shouted out. 'What's this shit?' he screamed, turning to confront a red-headed female assistant responsible for some sample posters. Woolley watched, astounded, as the marketing assistant was reduced to tears. So this is how they do things at Cannon, Woolley thought to himself.

*The Company of Wolves* was badly released in North America with a launch that made Neil Jordan's delicately constructed allegorical fantasy appear a *Friday the 13th* blood-and-guts offering. Instead of gathering the support of film critics, and showing the film at specially selected cinemas where specialist audiences might have enjoyed the film, Cannon booked *The Company of Wolves* into 800 American cinemas for the March 1985 release.

Jordan, whose fears had been aroused by Cannon's gory trailer, flew over to New York for the film's opening night. He joined a packed audience on 42nd Street, tucking himself in quietly at the back of the cinema. He quickly realised that his film had been badly mishandled. Unlike Palace's imaginative UK campaign, which had marketed the film to a range of audiences, Cannon had treated *The Company of Wolves* as nothing more than its usual brand of 'horror fodder'.

Completely misled, the highly vocal audience was soon seething with frustration and booing loudly at the screen. Finally, with twenty minutes to go, one inspired wag shouted out: 'Yo man, this is *Little Red Riding Hood*.' In an emotionally charged scene where the Wolfman seduces the heroine, one noisy section of the audience started to scream: 'Fuck the wolf!' only to be answered by another group shouting, 'Shoot him!' 'Fuck him!' 'Shoot him!' 'Fuck him!' 'Shoot him!' rose the chorus.

Jordan, who had never seen a horror film in the US, had no idea of the vocal commotion they inspire. He quietly left the cinema hoping that nobody would recognise him. He, like all the Palace staff, was bitterly disappointed by Cannon's folly. While *The Company of Wolves* grossed more than £1.6 million in the UK, the film took a paltry $4.3 million in North America, failing to cover Cannon's excessive print costs and horrific advertising bill.

While Palace was cutting its teeth in the film business, the British film industry was starting to run out of bright new ideas. The so-called 'British Film Year' of 1985, presided over by Richard Attenborough, was followed by a major U-turn in Conservative government support for film. The Eady levy, a film support system whereby a proportion of box-office receipts was channelled back into British productions, was abandoned following a July 1984 White Paper on Film Policy and the subsequent free market-obsessed Films Act.

Channel 4's arrival in 1982 and its subsequent early investments in film production, including Jordan's *Angel* and Peter Greenaway's *The Draughtsman's Contract*, had certainly boosted domestic pro-ducer's opportunities. However, Palace had not yet benefited directly from the new television station's production support, although it was managing to sell foreign language films and other distribution fare to Channel 4 on a regular basis by the end of 1984.

While Palace was edging into the production business, in spring 1984 Goldcrest Films and Television, the apparent jewel in the somewhat paltry British cinema crown, was building up a capital fund of £12 million, plus a £10 million line of bank credit in a high-risk pursuit of a larger share of potential profits.

Founded by the Canadian-born Jake Eberts during the early 1980s, and backed by the established film-making services of David Puttnam, Richard Attenborough and a host of highly paid executives, the Pearson-supported company had produced a flurry of hits and Oscar-winners such as *Gandhi*, *Chariots of Fire* and *The Killing Fields*. Goldcrest's executive squabbling and uncertain production line-up, however, were starting to take their toll and the company began to flounder. Eberts, who had become physically and mentally tired of running the high profile company by the end of 1983, left to join Embassy International, a wealthy American film company. As he and film journalist Terry Ilott later explained, in *My Indecision is Final*, a lengthy tome on the Goldcrest saga, 'When James Lee took over as chief executive of Goldcrest in December 1983, he did so in circumstances and in an atmosphere that were far from happy'. Lee, an American-born Harvard Business School graduate and previous non-executive chairman of Goldcrest, offered excellent credentials for running a company, but had little experience of developing, producing and making money out of films. With frank alacrity, Lee himself recalled that the scene in early 1984 'was set for disaster almost from the beginning'.

Goldcrest was detested by up-and-coming Wardour Street film-makers. Woolley in particular would make constant digs at the so-called saviour of the British film industry whenever interviewed by the press and Palace staff and young film-makers, over pints in The George, would mock Goldcrest's opulent offices and pompous press announcements. Everything about the cash-rich company smelt of 'the old way of doing things'. As one young Turk recalled, 'Everyone else working in British film production had one major ambition – to outlast Goldcrest.'

This creature of the Establishment could not have differed more radically from Palace and yet the two companies were soon to form an alliance. It was out of this marriage that one of Britain's most notorious film productions was born.

# CHAPTER FIVE

---

# Absolute Beginners

---

One evening during the heatwave summer of 1976, Julien Temple was walking down Oxford Street on his way to the 100 Club. The sun was setting behind Marble Arch and sweaty office workers in their crumpled dresses, suits and ties struggled on to buses or dragged themselves down to the relative cool of the London Underground. Out of this humid English city setting appeared a vivid image that for Temple summed up the entire punk experience.

The girl coming down Oxford Street was wearing a plastic see-through raincoat, splattered with polka dots. Beneath it, she was completely naked. Her shaven scalp had dyed blond stubble on top, and two black clumps of hair spiked upwards above her ears. Her eyebrows were arched in feline fashion, and almost every facial feature was lacerated with jewellery. Pedestrians were so freaked out by this vision that a path was cleared before her, and Sue 'Catwoman' – as she was known on the punk social circuit – in all her anarchic glory, was left free to cut a swathe through the evening commuters.

'At that moment, I had an epic feeling of why punk could *do* something,' Temple recalled. 'The fifties summer setting of the story of *Absolute Beginners* was supposed to be hot like that. The heat was supposed to have a wonderful effect on the uptightness of

British morality, to loosen its cold Victorian moral freeze that I so hate about England.' Having a go at conservative Britain was nothing new to the Cambridge- and National Film School-educated Temple. Radicalism ran in his family: his father had been a leading light of the British Communist Party.

In the seventies, Temple threw himself headlong into the frenetic punk scene, working closely with Sex Pistols' manager Malcolm McLaren. He used his directing skills (developed through the rapid rise of the pop promotional film, which provided the young film-maker with access to a wide range of music stars who greatly admired his energy and innovation on video) to make short films which would screen on concrete walls before the Pistols' music gigs, culminating in 1979 in *The Great Rock 'n' Roll Swindle*, a powerful final chapter in the Sex Pistols' saga, starring McLaren, the Pistols' Ronnie Biggs and Sex Pistols' groupie Sue 'Catwoman'. Three years later, at the age of twenty-nine, Temple directed *The Secret Policeman's Other Ball*, starring comics such as John Cleese, Rowan Atkinson, Alan Bennett and Billy Connolly.

Temple clearly enjoyed the trappings of his success. As Woolley commented pointedly in his diary (subsequently published by *Time Out*): 'Julien [made] promos for the likes of David Bowie, Jagger, Sade and Boy George . . . He's given huge budgets by the record companies, he gets what he wants, maybe he's even encouraged to behave like a rock 'n' roll star.' Temple's tall, slim frame was regularly adorned with designer clothes, and he mixed with the stars of his video creations with ease. He was not brash or cocky, but instead communicated with a quiet concentration that those who did not know how emotional he was mistook for arrogance. However, by 1983 Temple's ambition was to apply his talents to larger projects.

*Absolute Beginners* was definitely going to be a 'large project'. Colin MacInnes's loose, free-wheeling narrative about London's vigorous 1950s Soho life was based on the writer's magazine articles of the time. The book endorsed the teenage spirit of revolution – epitomised by its scenes of the Notting Hill race riots in 1958 – and won revived interest following a 1979 reprint. The book was not an obvious subject for film, and would certainly have stayed on the shelf had it not been for Temple's emotional commitment to the project.

In the young director's view the novel depicted one of Britain's greatest exportable assets: a vibrant youth culture summed up by the words, 'Attitude, Music and Fashion'. As the *The Face*'s Paul Rambali explained later, Temple 'became obsessed, like all those who wrote sparkling reviews or pressed [the book] on their friends. Except that, as an aspiring film-maker whose hero was Orson Welles, his obsession grew till it became a fully-fledged motion picture.'

Rambali was not exaggerating. Temple's determination even extended to projecting an imaginary film set on to a Notting Hill street, Lambeth Crescent. He went so far as to spend £50,000 of his own earnings on a house there. Temple later explained that he thought it would improve the film's chances of being produced if he made it 'dead cheap' to shoot.

Despite emotional efforts to woo the Eberts-run Goldcrest, Channel 4 and other possible backers, the project found no financial support. 'After having several doors slammed in our faces on Wardour Street, it became clear that we needed to make more investors aware of the saleability of the subject,' explained Temple. 'So we embarked on a press campaign for MacInnes's novel, and drew on everyone in the press to maximise publicity. In a way this was the beginning of our undoing. By needing to get this level of publicity to validate *Absolute Beginners* as a film, we created this monster that by the time we had finished was out of control.'

Bored with rejection and worried that his project was not going anywhere, Temple encouraged a mutual friend, *Time Out* journalist Don MacPherson to approach Woolley about making the film. Woolley and Temple had first bumped into each other at punk gigs and cinemas when Woolley had been an usher at Islington's Screen on the Green. 'I'd always find myself like the other guy in the cinema on a wet Thursday night at Notting Hill's Electric, watching a Nick Ray double bill in the days before video, when people sought out the flea pits to watch movies on the big screen,' Temple explained. 'All the films I was interested in, Steve would seem to be at. We both came out of that punk ethos, and were both very committed to the spirit of cinema and trying to do something with films in England.' Despite Woolley's claims a decade later that he was not very taken by the book's prospects as a film, the fledgling producer could not resist the spectre of stars, songs, jazz and a shoot that would showcase London's most alternative locations through sexy sets.

Temple's personal standing also played its part in seducing Woolley. The young director was a high-profile, glamorous figure in London's media scene, and his tremendous talent behind the pop-promo camera clearly helped convince Woolley of the project's potential. Moreover, the hip buzz surrounding *Absolute Beginners* dovetailed perfectly with Palace's image. Surely Palace's black leather jacket brigade was made to produce films such as this?

The main reason for Palace's commitment to Temple's film, however, was the tremendous depth of Powell's and Woolley's shared ambition. Here was a film that was clearly going to be a huge event, and Palace's partners were equally determined to be at the forefront of such a national spectacle. To say 'No' to *Absolute Beginners* was unthinkable.

Becoming involved in the project was the easy part. Financing Temple's musical vision was quite another matter. In a complex and contorted financing journey, Palace succeeded in bringing Virgin and Goldcrest – which Jake Eberts had by now left – into the picture. Goldcrest's newly appointed head of production, Sandy Lieberson, became a major supporter of the project, while Virgin Vision was attracted to the project's youth appeal and musical dimension. In a manner that was to be seen as typical of Palace, in spring 1984 *Absolute Beginners* hurtled into pre-production – the stage of a film when casting, locations, set preparations and final touches to the script are normally tackled. The script required far more than 'final touches', however. Rolling in at a whopping 160 pages – when the average length of a screenplay is closer to 100 – this script was horribly out of control. Initially written by MacPherson, the script had been rewritten by Richard Burridge, but Woolley was still not particularly happy with it. Some of the difficulties originated with the source material that had so inspired Temple. The director admitted that 'MacInnes's book has a very flawed narrative to my mind, and is very hard to adapt. It lacks drive in terms of plot, and largely concerns the central characters views on the world, about jazz, pop stars, television, advertising and so on.' Unfortunately, Temple made this frank assessment to *Time Out*'s Geoff Andrew two months *after* the film shoot had wrapped. Such a candid understanding of the script's shortcomings was absent prior to, and during, the film's production. Despite Woolley's and others' efforts to control the monster script, the screenplay stubbornly refused to be hammered into shape.

Nevertheless, a buzzy momentum propelled *Absolute Beginners* on, and the film was scheduled to go into production on 30 July 1984. Dancers were hired to start rehearsals, and a slate of famous names from the music world was bandied about. In May 1984, *Time Out* reported that Gil Evans had been hired to arrange the music, using his own original score and with the help of jazz greats such as Coltrane, Mingus, Slim Gaillard, Charlie Parker and Miles Davis. Also commissioned (or, in some cases informally asked) to write small pieces were Elvis Costello, Paul Weller, Ray Davies, Mick Jagger and Keith Richards, as well as, at a later stage, David Bowie and Sade. Stages were booked at Shepperton, and art and set designers were signed up for the summer shoot. Woolley described the film to *Time Out* as 'something like a Vincente Minnelli musical', adding that 'it's all a big risk'.

It was also big money. When a film production company enters pre-production, thousands of pounds are signed away on a daily basis. Palace soon notched up costs of £300,000, much of which went on securing soundtrack rights and paying the famous artists, and all of which was the company's own exposure.

Woolley, revealing much of Palace's *modus operandum*, explained exactly why he rushed *Absolute Beginners* into pre-production: 'It's the only way. If you want to get a film made, you have to start, because if you don't start, nobody else will. So we'd started, basically.' It was a line that Powell was later to elaborate: 'Steve starts, while I and everyone else have to catch up.' The two comments drive to the heart of independent film financing and its precarious nature. One way of defining a producer's job is to see him as a seducer of financiers. The key is to make the people with the money grow pregnant with the film, while at the same time lining up the creative talent. As Powell explained, 'The assembling of the creative talent comes together at a certain point. At that point, you've got to make sure your finance package comes together. So often, movie projects fall apart because the talent has come together but the money hasn't, or the money comes together but the talent hasn't. One of the skills required by a producer is the ability to keep those two groups in play until they can both be signed off.' Woolley, aided by Powell on the financial side, was catching on quickly, but that first summer with *Absolute Beginners* it did not work quite to plan.

In June 1984, financing for *Absolute Beginners* suddenly collapsed. An increasingly wary Virgin and Goldcrest conceded that the film was not ready, and that the original budget of £4 million (already rapidly rising) was unrealistically low, especially given Temple's ambitious intentions and a script that was both over-long and suffering from conspicuous structural problems. When Woolley and Powell apologetically broke the news to Temple, he burst into tears.

After further wheeling and dealing by Palace, a new deal was cut between Virgin, Goldcrest and Palace, which reduced Palace's exposure to around £100,000 and kept the project moving towards an early-1985 production date. The deal also stipulated that if Palace could raise forty per cent of the budget from the US, then Virgin and Goldcrest had to come up with the rest.

Tempers ran high during this period of preparation. A row broke out over the suggested casting of David Bowie, with the perfectionist Temple initially objecting to the pop star on the grounds that Bowie was not 'pure jazz'. By now, Woolley was growing used to Temple's polemical posturing. As far as the producer was concerned, Bowie was precisely the kind of star who would attract American financing for the ever-rising budget.

Woolley, Powell and Temple made two trips to Hollywood in an effort to complete the financing triangle. By October 1984, Woolley and Powell had convinced Mike Medavoy, the head of production at Orion Pictures, to come up with some money. Medavoy felt confident enough to commit to an investment of forty per cent of a newly enlarged £6 million budget (although Goldcrest was still arguing that this budget figure should have been £5.5 million). Orion was slipping the production into a package of ten films required to fulfil the studio's Home Box Office pay-television deal. In order for *Absolute Beginners* to be included in the package, some of the film's scenes had to be shot in January 1985, before the HBO deal expired, which put further pressure on the already harassed project. In November, it became clear that the definition of 'some scenes' meant that a week of principal photography had to be shot (i.e. with principal cast). That must have sounded reasonable to the other investors, but there were two key problems. The first was blatantly apparent: neither of the two main parts – Colin and Crêpe Suzette – had been cast. The second problem only raised its head later: When Orion's forty per cent advance was fixed to the exchange rate (then at $1.06 to the pound) and the agreed budget, it came to an unswerving $2.5 million. During the film's shooting the pound's worth rose from $1.06 to $1.56, effectively reducing Orion's contribution from forty per cent to less than thirty per cent of the rising budget.

Woolley ensured that Goldcrest remained behind the project by constantly charming Lieberson and Lee. The young producer was very successful. Lee subsequently signed documents agreeing to Goldcrest covering the contingency and giving a guarantee of completion on the film. Although Goldcrest had a partner, Entertainment Completions Inc., on the completion side, Lee's company was first in line to cover any eventual over-expenditure on the film's budget. This was an exceptional move for an independent company, especially as its partners' contributions to the budget were now fixed.

In August 1984, a new version of the screenplay was completed by yet another writer, Chris Wicking. However, it was still far too long, and the central love story between Crèpe Suzette and Colin was subjected to much criticism. Woolley, unhappy with the script, asked the celebrated playwright Terry Johnson to do an uncredited edit of the rambling draft. As Goldcrest's Lieberson was to concede: 'It was never nailed down, and it kept being edited and *not* edited during the whole run-up to production and during the production itself.'

Nevertheless, by this stage, Woolley had really got the bit between his teeth. One Palace employee recalls the producer turning up nearly two hours late for supper, and proceeding to talk about nothing but *Absolute Beginners*. 'Steve loved the film, loved its bigness, and sure enough, the film got bigger.' Woolley's intensity was also due in part to some ominous problems that still needed to be ironed out. As he was to write in his diary, in addition to the breakneck casting requirements there was a real problem with the cost. 'The money has been secured on a budget that is optimistic,' he wrote. 'The screenplay has to be cut. I have to get the script down.' When the film went in front of the cameras, however, in early June 1985, the script was still far too long and the film's production costs were already spinning out of control.

On 27 June 1985 Woolley wrote:

The costume people are spending money like it's going out of fashion. It's always the same on a big-budget movie. Nobody's guilty, everyone gets inspired by the director and wants to make his vision. And spend a lot of money. It's worse here, because there's a feeling 'This is a big movie, it's got David Bowie, we can spend money'. Silly things are happening: I walk on the set and see a fucking horse and cart. I know we're not going to shoot it. So who ordered the horse and cart? We struggle through one of the worst summers in recent history, going radically over budget. In addition, construction figures are far higher than anticipated.

Garth Thomas was Goldcrest's executive in charge of production. A sizeable character in terms of both his sharp wit and his bulky physique, Thomas is the British film industry's 'hard man' when it comes to crunching numbers on a film set. He had earned considerable respect from the film production community while working on Ridley Scott's and Alan Parker's films, including, in 1982, the complex *Pink Floyd – The Wall*. As one friend put it: 'Garth has a big belly, a bald head, a considerable bark and a huge bloody bite. But he really knows what's going on on a movie set. The trick is that Garth is everybody's mate. Within twenty minutes of walking around a set he can spot if the director's screwing the lead actress.'

Knowing that he needed a strong line producer, Woolley had telephoned Thomas to offer him the job. 'Woolley asked me to dinner upstairs at L'Escargot to meet him and the gang,' Thomas recalled. 'I was nervous right from the start about the sort of attitude that was coming across about the "divine right of the director". Having been wooed by the producers to work on the film, I was somewhat surprised that I still had to earn Temple's stamp of approval to be a line producer. Frankly, that's not the way the business works. It's of little consequence if the director likes me or not, because we are hardly likely to run into each other a great deal. I'd never override the producer and start talking straight to the director on the set about why we're so slow, and why he doesn't do this and that. Basically, I fill in the cracks for the producer, who might tell the director that the film is behind, and I'll say "Yes, by three days and forty-three minutes, and you can get ahead if you cut this and that, saving two hours and twenty-two minutes." That kind of thing, you know.'

Thomas had immediately identified Woolley as a 'whizz kid' similar to Alan Parker, whose career had kick-started some fifteen years previously. There were however some differences. 'I mean, Steve Woolley really was a barrow boy, while Alan Parker was never one.'

Thomas took an instant liking to Woolley. The young producer's passion and commitment held great appeal, and Thomas loved the idea of the Scala being run as a cinema, office and virtually a home. 'Woolley saw every film. He knew who was in every film. Nothing came into this town that he didn't know about in terms of viewing and assessing it. And it was infectious.

'At that stage, and all the way through *Absolute Beginners*, I had no such feeling about Mr Sandie Shaw [Powell], whom I never held in any very high regard. I always felt that the word "deal" came up too often. I'm fortunate to be in a job where I don't do deals. And people who do put me on edge.'

In the end, Thomas could not accept Woolley's job offer. Ironically, shortly after the Palace meeting he was approached by Goldcrest, who wanted him to take responsibility for the company's productions, and in particular, *Absolute Beginners*. So the big man ended up dealing with the film anyway, but from a notably different perspective. He was Goldcrest's man on the set, not Woolley's, and a key part of his job was to handle the guarantee of completion that Goldcrest had so unwisely offered.

For Temple, the elaborate sets at Shepperton Studios represented the 'ultimate trip' – an opportunity to create an intricate, surreal vision of Notting Hill and Soho in the 1950s. 'We took these bits of clubs and Soho, and we mixed them up to create this one magical world. It was very sad when they knocked that set down because it was a phenomenal creation.' Yet he also frankly conceded that the cost of the sets was a major reason for the film's ultimate overspend. The production staff went to extraordinary lengths to find authentic props. Period cars, scooters and bikes filled the time-warped streets; posters, paintings, genuine shop signs and 1950s knick-knacks lovingly adorned the walls and window shelves. Looming in the background of a wonderful replica of Old Compton Street was a repositioned Piccadilly Circus, with Eros, a large neon sign for Bovril and the Guinness clock. 'The visual side of the film was very close to my heart and I was really involved in that side of the whole thing,' Temple explained. (Months later, during the *Absolute Beginners* royal première, Powell – Princess Anne's escort that evening – whispered to Her Royal Highness how good the film's period detail was. During the screening, Princess Anne objected to a small bridge in St James's Park, stating that it was definitely *not* built by 1958. Powell protested, politely backing the film's designers. To his surprise, Princess Anne stuck to her guns, finally saying abruptly: 'I'm sorry but I should know. I opened it!')

The first change Thomas made to the sets was to cut a building, literally, in half. 'I had to stop them building the unforgivable: a circle, with green in the middle and the intention of shooting right the way round.'

'That's going to be far too expensive, boys, let me tell you now,' Thomas exclaimed. 'You only build half of it. Then you change your curtains, paint a door and chuck some grafitti up, and – bang! – you come back the other way with the camera.'

The production staff could not help but see the logic of this simple cost-saving move. Builders swivelled round quickly to cut the planned circle into a semi-circle, and the sets continued to go up.

'It's basic film-making,' Thomas explained later with a laugh. 'You know, left to right, then revamp the furniture and track back, right to left.'

Thomas, with his acerbic advice, was whisked away before he could really make a mark on the young producers. Goldcrest needed him to deal with Hugh Hudson's *Revolution*, which, with cranes falling off cliffs, was clocking up its own spectacular overspend, and was even more problematic than *Absolute Beginners*. *The Mission* was later to add to Goldcrest's difficulties, missing its original delivery date by many months due to an extended shoot in Argentina. By the time Thomas returned to *Absolute Beginners* to pick up the pieces, it had become apparent that the politics at Goldcrest would have a significant impact on the financial and creative elements surrounding Temple's musical baby.

A twenty-seven-year-old National Film School student, Michael Caton-Jones, looked on proceedings with a mixture of amazement and disgust. He and a film-school friend had happened to overhear Palace's Irving Rappaport at the school asking around for a film crew to shoot the making of *Absolute Beginners*. The ambitious Scottish-born Caton-Jones was not going to miss seeing such a film being shot. He quickly got a few friends together, and they trooped down to Shepperton with a camera to check out the scene.

'I was frankly quite appalled by the whole palaver, because we were at school trying to shoot films on nothing,' Caton-Jones recalled. 'We'd stroll through Shepperton and watch all this conspicuous waste going on. Steve, Chris Brown and Julien were the best dressed people I'd ever come across – really tasteful – and there was an aura of self-declared hipness which was faintly disgusting to anybody outside it. Steve was fascinating because he was such an arrogant son of a bitch. They epitomised the whole kind of well-hung-young-buck syndrome, which stemmed from all these people from pop promos trying to get through.'

Caton-Jones and his mini-crew would turn up on set, only to be told, 'You can't film today. Sade doesn't feel very well.' Creeping round, quietly shooting the chaos, the students witnessed a spectacularly incoherent film shoot. 'They were doing stuff that I'd watch and think, "Well, that'll never make it in the film. And why are they doing that?" ' Caton-Jones recalled. 'And Palace ripped us off something drastic, offering us two thousand quid for twelve weeks' work. Rappaport would complain about some fucking little stickers, saying, "Do you know how much these cost?" while of course back at the movie money was bombing everywhere. There were piles and piles of cash just smouldering away.'

By early August 1985 – nine weeks into the shoot – Woolley pointed out that the producers 'were in a state of terror, day in, day out, because the money was running out'. Thomas, back from the *Revolution* nightmare (which was getting worse by the day), had been instructed to take over *Absolute Beginners* as the completion guarantor's representative on set. This effectively gave him full financial control over the production. No cheques or orders could be executed without Thomas's approval.

Predictably, the press had begun to react to all the hype, and, in turn, Temple became obsessed with the media attention the film was attracting. At the express encouragement of Goldcrest, he held numerous press conferences, especially for foreign journalists. He even modelled clothes in magazines at one point.

Thomas found himself increasingly worried by Temple's self-indulgent posturing, and felt that Woolley held Temple too much in awe to curb the director's more imaginative cravings.

'Julien was absolutely right with his wandering shot at the start of the film, because that was what he was good at,' Thomas explained.

'But the trouble was that nobody knew what was landing up on film. There were no shot lists, because that wasn't the way Julien worked. It was all instinctive stuff.'

Temple would suddenly demand a steadicam for a shot.

'We haven't got one,' a crew member would reply.

'Well go out and get one. We've got to have one for this.'

The morning would be spent practising the shot, waiting for the steadicam. By lunchtime the special camera would not have turned up.

'Where the fuck's the steadicam?' Temple would rage.

One department would blame its non-appearance on another department, and then it would transpire that there was only one available in the country, and it was winging its way down from Leeds.

'Why didn't someone do something about this before?' Temple would demand.

'Because you never said you'd need one.'

'Well it's obvious I was going to need one.'

Thomas, irritated by the director's ability to waste time, later remarked that 'David Lean never needed a fucking steadicam, but he made some bloody good films, eh?'

For Thomas, the steadicam saga illustrated once again how important it is to have a director who wants to work *with* the production team. 'But if anything didn't work on this film, that would quickly become another reason for going over budget, not a reason for quickly finding a workable alternative.'

Woolley, who had been asked by Thomas on numerous occasions to dump Temple and take over the film as director, continued to shield Temple from the anger and tension. At the same time he pleaded with Temple to cut back his precious script, but when it came to his cherished scenes, painstakingly drawn on storyboards, the director had scant interest in budget problems. A wedding sequence spurred a huge row, when Temple demanded an enormous spectacle. Woolley scaled it back, with the result that the director childishly refused to shoot the scene. Woolley wrote in his diary that Temple '*is* paranoid and suspicious, very careful of how much of the film is his . . . *He gets antagonised about how much you're affecting his vision.*'

Woolley, under fierce questioning from journalists, managed both to irritate and to amuse Thomas by telling the press that the producers were very happy to have Thomas around, and that everything was under control. Privately, Woolley and Powell felt that Thomas represented the old school of line management, where it is always 'easier to say no than yes, because you don't have to care about the creative side of the film. We were facing an impossible task,' Woolley explained. 'I was trying to contain Julien – who was trying to make three movies at the same time – and a script that should never have been put into production. Unlike Neil [Jordan], who can rewrite scenes the night before, Julien isn't a writer. That said, I don't think Julien was any more indulgent than Roland Joffe or Hugh Hudson.'

Woolley's diary entry of 10 August 1985 showed how inventive he was in trying to keep the film moving:

This is the most disastrous day so far. One of the oldest stars we're using, Slim Gaillard, just doesn't turn up. He came in last night, thinking we were shooting then. I should have realised that there was something odd. I asked him if he wanted a car to drive home the next day. He said he'd make it himself. So: eight o'clock this morning, the party sequence. We've got James Fox, we've got Bowie, we've got Kensit. Everybody's in it. But no Slim. He's not there. We freak, ring his agent, anybody I think of who knows Slim and find out that he's on the set of another film, *Gun Bus*. This seventy-year-old jazz performer who's been going for years with nothing to do with movies is suddenly in two films on the same day. He's so excited, he doesn't even bother to tell his agent. He needs the money. And we're fucked. I figure that *Gun Bus* is probably in better shape than we are, so I find out where it's shooting, we go down to the set and during the lunch break kidnap Slim, just bundle him into the car. The people from *Gun Bus* quite rightly go crazy, but we finish a day's work. From now on, we'll make sure we have a car outside Slim's house every morning.

The numerous and costly mistakes were due to underlying poor accounting that started before *Absolute Beginners* was shot, but only became evident weeks into the film's production. Tracking the practical costs of a film is essential if a budget is to be realised. In the case of *Absolute Beginners*, the cost of the sets was woefully underestimated and poorly recorded. Most studio films are more straightforward to budget accurately than those shot on location. Building costs can be checked by finding out how many days and workers it will take to build a set. The answer will come back: 'A dozen carpenters for six weeks, six riggers for four weeks, ten painters for three weeks, and twenty further painters for one week.' The labour and material costs will be calculated and it is rare to be more than a few hundred pounds out at the end of a twelve-week shot.

The sets on *Absolute Beginners* were enormous and built as if they were to last for ever. Large sets not only cost more money to build but are more expensive to light and most costly in terms of props required to fill them. This, coupled with the production team's unwillingness to face bad news and a director whom Woolley increasingly regarded as paranoid about keeping creative control over the shoot, meant that it was hardly surprising when things started to go wrong. It was the manner in which things went wrong and the way the bad news was explained that so infuriated Thomas.

Under considerable pressure from the Goldcrest board, Thomas used his most tried and tested production accountant to work out how much the film was likely to go over budget. Entertainment Completions Inc. and Thomas also calculated the overspend and all three came to within £50,000 of each other's estimates of a final budgeted cost. Yet costs continued to rise almost on a daily basis.

During the last three weeks of August, Woolley would regularly seek out Thomas:

'Look Garth. We'll be absolutely honest with you. This is the new costing. It's six seven fifty [£6.75 million], and I promise you not a penny more. We've spent all day on it, and I'm being upfront with you. I'm going to need that much to finish this film.'

'Is that it? Is that really it?' Thomas would retort.

'It really is, Garth. There's no way it can go above that, no way.'

A week later Woolley would start again: 'Garth, we need to talk.

There's a bit of a problem. I can't work out why, but it's gone up again.'

'What! Why?'

'We just don't know Garth. But it's six eight fifty.'

'How am I going to tell that to the board?'

'Garth, it's better that you should have it for the truth. I don't think you're going to get this film for less now.'

For Thomas there was almost a temporary relief in knowing the so-called truth. He would return to the board and say to the anxious Goldcrest executives: 'Look chaps, it's going to cost a bit more. We all knew it was going to cost a bit more, didn't we? I mean, Woolley's got Julien under control now, he's stopped farting about on set and posing, he's in there with the accountants and Wimbury [Goldcrest's associate producer], and my two assistants. I mean, he's really on top of the case . . .'

Four days later, Woolley would be back: 'Garth, I don't know how this has happened. There's one or two things that were missing from the last costing, for which I apologise profusely. I'll write to the board myself, but now they're in, there's nothing else.'

Thomas had to take such news to the board on at least three occasions during those last tumultuous weeks of August, until, in Thomas's words, 'It became a screamingly funny joke and yet desperately embarrassing at the same time.'

Thomas did not think Woolley knew that much more about why there was such a heaving overspend than the rest of the film's producers or accountants (all of whom had been hired by Goldcrest and approved by Thomas). The real problem lay in the level of experience and professionalism of the production's financial staff, who regularly demonstrated what Thomas calls 'the bottom drawer syndrome'. Instead of keeping an accurate budget statement, with a daily recording of the cost of building work for the film, expenses were forgotten and bills thrown into 'the bottom drawer'. In many cases costs were entered on the budget statement not days but weeks late. It is not surprising, therefore, that a flurry of unpaid and forgotten bills appeared towards the end of the production, causing the overspend to balloon and a cash-flow crisis.

An increasingly nervous Entertainment Completions Inc. watched the budget, by mid-August, rise above £7 million, nearing the level at which it would be liable for the over-spend, following the completion guarantee it had signed together with Goldcrest. Its response was simple: it instructed Thomas to sack Woolley. Thomas, mindful of the damage such a move could inflict – including possibly losing the director and David Bowie in one fell swoop – decided not to implement ECI's order. As it was, Bowie's arrival on the set towards the end of the shoot gave rise to a major showdown between Thomas and the producers. Temple and Woolley wanted five days to complete the Bowie 'Motivation' song and dance sequence. Thomas insisted that the most they could have was three days, after which the sets would be taken down. 'The problem is, what they don't appreciate or want to appreciate is that the sets – the globe, the typewriter – need building and we just cannot do it with the time,' Woolley wrote in his diary.

Bowie, who knew Temple from his work as a music video director and wanted to help him, asked his agent Duncan Heath (also known as 'Sunken Teeth') to insist on his client having more time to perform the dance routine.

'I do have a dislike of all agents, although I like Duncan,' Thomas explained. 'But the problem is that they start with the premise that there is a deal. For me, it was always zero. I was under firm instructions from Goldcrest, and I wasn't going to budge an inch.' A heated, lengthy meeting between Thomas, Chris Brown, David Wimbury and Duncan Heath ensued. Heath argued that the guarantors had to find more time for Bowie, or his client would have no alternative but to walk off the film. Thomas explained in his inimitable style that any indication that Heath's client might not perform would be interpreted as a breach of the £15,000 rock-bottom contract Bowie had generously signed.

'A contract is a contract, dear, regardless of the figures,' Thomas carped. 'That's why we have them.'

Heath doggedly continued to insist that there had to be a way of finding more time for the shots, while Wimbury and Brown, knowing that the film could not survive losing its star asset, twisted uncomfortably in their seats. The meeting went on and on, and Thomas still did not budge.

'Just tell me to which house you want me to mail the writ,' Thomas boomed. 'I'll go wherever he likes to avoid the disturbance of the neighbours.'

An embarrassed silence lingered. Then Heath suddenly said, 'Oh, come on chaps! There's got to be an answer there somewhere! We should be able to get this thing sorted out. After all,' he said, looking round at the room's exhausted occupants, 'we're all public school here.'

Not surprisingly, given this confounding logic, no deal was done. Heath returned to his client armed with the impression (given by Thomas) that the producers were at fault for wasting Bowie's time: he was on set at 8.30 a.m. but was rarely used until hours later. Heath strongly berated Woolley's crew. The problem remained unsolved until Palace decided to spend approximately £50,000 of its own money to cover the two extra days.

Woolley later explained that the 'official' Goldcrest line – that the producers 'massaged the figures and hid the overages' – was one that he 'would stick to if I was them. We knew that the film was budgeted too low from the start, and we were always going to go over. It wasn't a conscious thing to keep quiet about the money, but we were making an effort to get the film made and keep everything going.'

When Jake Eberts returned in mid-summer 1985 to run Goldcrest for the second time in his career, he was immediately confronted with *Absolute Beginners* and *Revolution*, both of which were in deep trouble. In the case of *Absolute Beginners*, 'It seemed to me that neither Steve nor Nik had a true grasp of the extent of the problem, nor did they seem to be expressing the kind of concern that I thought was appropriate in the circumstances. It was overwhelming, and I know what the problem is – it [the budget] gets away from you. It's happened to me, and you can't do much about it, especially if you don't know what's going on because the purchase ordering and accounting systems aren't functioning.'

Eberts first saw a compilation of the film on videotape at his home one night, not the best way to view Temple's visual efforts, and was soon convinced that Goldcrest was 'in deep deep trouble. I saw very little that was good in the movie except maybe that opening tracking shot, and that was the sum total of the movie.'

He promptly rang his old friend, producer Alan Marshall, 'who was a real pro at getting these things under control', and agreed to pay him £50,000 to oversee the editing and finish the film. Marshall, a thick-set Londoner, then in his late forties, belonged to the tough, sock-it-to-them school of film producing. He had just completed *Another Country*, having produced Alan Parker's *Birdy* the previous year, and the job suited his schedule.

His availability certainly did not suit Woolley and Temple. 'Steve did resent it, there's no question about that,' Eberts said. 'That's entirely natural. He thought I was old fashioned and passé, but what was I to do? The fact is, it was Goldcrest's money, and my job was to protect it, and certainly what I'd seen on film didn't convince me that we had a hit. At that stage it was damage control.' Eberts was not exaggerating. Cutting a script on paper may be creatively difficult, but it is many thousands of pounds cheaper than cutting a film in the post-production labs, an area of film production where costs can spiral.

Marshall's arrival to supervise the editing caused Woolley and Temple a great deal of consternation. Woolley was on his way to Corsica for a holiday with his girlfriend, Palace employee JoAnne Sellar, when he heard the news about Marshall. Sellar recalls the intense stress the producer was under at the time: 'After two days on holiday he had to fly back because he was worried about Julien being fired and him losing his job. Steve's a very private person when he's under pressure. He bottles it up inside, and I just remember that there was always some real emergency that he was having to cope with.'

Nevertheless, Woolley wrote in his diary in late August: 'I respect Alan Marshall. He's a North Londoner, another terrace boy from the same part of town as me. His problem with the film seems to stem from the fact that it is very stylised . . . the kind of cinema he's into is not the kind of cinema that Julien is trying to achieve with *Absolute Beginners*.'

'You're never going to like a guy who locks the director out of the cutting room of a film that you've lived and breathed for three years and was almost as precious as life,' Temple admits. 'I should have done what Mickey Rourke did with him [on Parker's *Angel Heart*] and just fought him, and then it probably would have had more effect. It was like having a savage Rottweiler set on us to fuck us up.'

Woolley used his producer's contractual position to gain access to the cutting rooms, and throughout this traumatic period remained an emotional ally and conduit of information for Temple. The news he had was not encouraging to report: neither the cutting nor the social politics were progressing smoothly. Three editors were working with Marshall – one on the beginning, one on the middle and one on the end – and none of them was familiar with the many miles of footage that Temple had shot.

Tempers came to a head on 12 October, when Goldcrest organised a big press screening of all their productions, including approximately thirty minutes of footage from *Revolution*, *A Room with a View*, *The Mission*, *Smooth Talk* and *Absolute Beginners*. Woolley recalls the show reel going down very well, although their 'rough presentation' was criticised by Marshall.

Lunch was held at Maxim's for all the guests who had flown in from around the world for the typically high-profile Goldcrest junket. Everybody at Goldcrest was made to wear a badge, except the somewhat rebellious Thomas, who busied himself managing the stage and tried to avoid the corporate side of the event. After the lunch most of the guests left to do their business, leaving the *Absolute Beginners* table in deep discussion.

'It was going full pelt,' Thomas recalled. 'It was one of those classic scenes where the bottles of wine are piled up all round the table, and there's a lot of "fucking this and fucking that . . ." Fortunately we were the only ones left when it got leery.'

Marshall turned to Chris Brown, who had been having a rough time trying to tie up the endless outstanding music contracts on the film, and, ever suspicious of Brown's public school accent, said provocatively, 'You don't know anything about fucking London. You're not a real Londoner.'

'How dare you say that! I live in Brixton. You're not the only person that has a copyright on London,' Brown retorted indignantly.

'Yeah, but not real Brixton, not with the blacks and all that.'

'Yes, I do. I'm as much a Londoner as you are. You're a fucking liar.' With those words, Brown took a wild, drunken swing at Marshall, missing him completely. Thomas stumbled to his feet in an effort to calm the men down, but was quickly pushed out of the way, first by Brown and then by Marshall.

'This can't go on,' Temple exclaimed to Woolley. 'It's got to stop.'

The table collapsed. Everyone staggered up to encounter a furious manager ordering them to all leave. Marshall had already made an exit. Thomas had lost his watch and was bleeding from cuts made by his broken glasses.

Brown and Thomas disappeared into Soho to clean themselves up and recover over something to eat, although Brown was still muttering about how he was going to 'fucking kill' Marshall. They had ordered a meal, when Brown said, 'Hold on Garth, I'm just going to the loo.' Thomas waited. Two meals turned up, but Brown failed to reappear. The producer had gone off in a daze around the streets of Soho, leaving the cashless Thomas to eat and pay for two meals.

Marshall finally left *Absolute Beginners* at the end of the year, and Temple and Woolley started to work more closely with the editors, trying to make some sense of the celluloid carnage. The first fruits of their efforts became apparent in January 1986, when a sneak preview screening was held in the San Fernando Valley by Orion's Mike Medavoy. Even Eberts flew out for the trial. It was held in mid-afternoon, and Woolley and Temple sat at the back of the cinema nervously waiting to see how the audience would respond. When people wanted to walk out of the cinema, they had to open an exit door next to the big screen. Temple remembered 'incredible blasts of light every time someone went out. It was probably only twenty-odd people out of a 100, but nevertheless it was a major event every time they left the cinema.'

In late March 1986, Powell and Daniel Battsek, together with other Palace staff and friends, were sitting in a pub talking over potential marketing angles on *Absolute Beginners*. A former Virgin executive interrupted their talk: 'For God's sake, Nik,' she said, laughing, 'people in outer space have heard of this film.' The comment was later aped in *Spitting Image*, when a spaceship sailed across the television screen with the words *Absolute Beginners* plastered across its side.

*Absolute Beginners* is perhaps best remembered as an extraordinary British marketing phenomenon. An enormous party was held by Palace inside the railings of Leicester Square. Newspapers, magazines, cartoons, radio chat shows, a South Bank television special, and all other ways of promoting the movie were pursued relentlessly. Phil Symes and Angie Errigo worked long hours to ensure the film maximum publicity coverage.

The one thing the PR team could not control was the critics' reaction to the film, and, almost without exception, they panned it. Battsek admitted later, 'I was too filled with the fever to accept that people couldn't be made to like it. I got really excited when I watched it, and I always did word-of-mouth exit polls after all our movies, hanging around in the cinema catching what people were saying about the film. But there were so many slag-offs of the film. When they came out of the cinema they were scared to say they liked it, for disagreeing with *Time Out* and the rest of them. They just couldn't swim against the tide.'

Much has been written about the alleged 'over-hyping' of the film, but according to Mike Ewin, who booked the film into cinemas, the initial public awareness was so high that the film's box office takings were top of the range for two weeks. 'And then it went. It was the quickest film to die that I ever handled.'

The fact was, for all its brash energy and ambition, the film was deeply flawed. Three weeks after the film's UK opening, when the cinemas had already emptied, Phil Symes was called into a meeting with Woolley and Powell, where he was told by Woolley that the film had not performed as well as expected because 'Palace definitely over-hyped it to the press. Our effort went overboard.' Although

Woolley now takes full responsibility for the débâcle, explaining that he personally orchestrated the massive campaign; at the time Symes and his assistant felt that they were being rather unfairly blamed – after all, was it not Woolley who was famous for saying: 'There's no such thing as too much hype'?

That Julien Temple chose not to talk about the film for many years afterwards is hardly surprising. Remembering the events and emotions of those months was difficult even ten years later. 'This whole period is hard to describe because it was like being one of those people who have a fly in their ear. They end up going mad because of this noise buzzing in their head. I do think we learned very heavily from the experience. One of the reasons why I haven't talked about it since is because it now seems silly to have said so much before we had actually done it. I don't think there's any need for a director to model clothes, so I haven't done that since.'

Temple's main complaint about the film's production concerned his exclusion from the cutting rooms. 'It was edited by three editors under the control of someone who really didn't like not just the film but the reasons behind the film. When they finally brought us back, the editors had cut things up to such an extent that putting it back together again was very hard. We couldn't find all the missing bits.'

Even Woolley, so strongly supportive of the film, disappointed Temple. His *Absolute Nightmare* diary article published by *Time Out* in April 1986, just days before the film's opening, seemed to Temple to be highly critical of the director. When Temple later challenged Woolley about the article, it was the producer's turn to vent his spleen. 'I went into print because Julien never appeared to appreciate my support throughout the entire film. I was angry and frustrated, especially because Julien failed to grasp the reasons for the so-called betrayal.'

Woolley's feelings about the film remain highly charged and emotional to this day. 'Palace were the new boys, who I admit did have a reputation for being arrogant sods. But there's no doubt that Goldcrest used us as whipping boys for their problems. We learned an awful lot on this film, and I don't feel ashamed or embarrassed: I didn't do anything that was outrageously irresponsible.'

The critical reaction to *Absolute Beginners* was considerably less hostile on the Continent and in America, where the film performed far better than in the UK. Nevertheless, Temple still feels deeply sensitive about his experience with it. 'There was a feeling in the industry at that time that we should be spanked,' he recalled. 'By the end of the film, I was aware that a long dark cloud had come down.' Two years later, despite the set-back, Temple directed *Earth Girls Are Easy*, a successful sci-fi rock 'n' roll musical starring Geena Davis, Jeff Goldblum and which introduced Jim Carrey and Damon Wayans to Hollywood.

The final cost of *Absolute Beginners* was £8.6 million, a great deal more than the 1984 £4 million budget and the £6 million budget established in the spring of 1985. Palace had risked more than £500,000 of its own money on Temple's film, but managed to recoup the majority of it through the cinema release. Virgin, making the most of its music contract, also did not suffer too badly. Goldcrest, however, was forced to write off £3.2 million of its £5 million investment and almost ended up in court over a £2 million claim that it made against its joint completion partner, Entertainment Completions Inc. In the end the case was settled on the steps of the court, with Goldcrest accepting £800,000, plus costs. As Eberts later pointed out, Goldcrest, Virgin, Orion and Palace were jointly to blame for the poor script. Goldcrest's decision to guarantee the film's completion, however, was a mistake for which only they could take responsibility.

# CHAPTER SIX

# Wardour Mews Meets the Riviera

The film industry is, above all, a relationship business, and Powell recognised that Palace's future depended in large measure on his ability to form contacts within the industry around the world, particularly if Palace were to overcome perceived failures such as *Absolute Beginners*. The packed calendar of industry meetings, festivals and parties provided him with the opportunity to make such contacts, to sell film rights and generally cut deals. There was no better place for such networking than the Cannes Film Festival.

The festival is a mirror of the industry it serves: more than 23,000 delegates, together with thousands of journalists and tourists indulge themselves in hype, glamour, stars, parties, élitism and ego for twelve days each summer, creating an intoxicating cocktail which Woolley and Powell eagerly imbibed each year.

Late April and early May, just prior to the festival mayhem on the Côte d'Azur, always induced a manic atmosphere in the Palace offices as the team rushed to complete posters and compile information on films that were either premiering in the festival competition or were to be sold at the market. Year after year the overworked PR and marketing teams missed the trade magazine deadlines for announcing which films Palace was to sell that year at Cannes.

Despite all their hard work, the staff had to fight to be allowed to attend the festival. 'First of all, there was this battle as to who should go. People would be in tears, and I had to fight with Nik every single year to actually go, and yet other companies would bring everyone,' Daniel Battsek explained. Once Powell had picked a crew of around seven to eight key employees, including himself and Woolley, economy class aeroplane tickets would be booked. Hardly would they have left Heathrow airport, when Powell, sitting on the edge of his seat, legs tapping in nervous excitement, would begin barking instructions to the team. The rest of the plane would be filled with half the evening pub crowd from The George, as Wardour Street temporarily moved to the Côte d'Azur.

Powell and Woolley left behind them their early Cannes days, when they had lived in an 'unspeakable dump' of a hotel behind the railway station, with no phones and limp showers that trickled out of mouldy plaster. At first the team spent the festival fortnight in a tiny apartment which could hardly hold the staff, let alone extras such as Neil Jordan, who would turn up unexpectedly and sleep on a mattress on the floor.

For Battsek, the way Powell and Woolley organised the Palace flock at Cannes was deeply frustrating. Unable to hang his clothes up or to use the bathroom when he needed it, Battsek often wondered what he was doing in this chaos. Clothes were a secondary issue for Powell. During his second year at Cannes, he had been given a new suit by his wife, and had been firmly instructed to wear it. It had looked pretty good for a few days, but by the fifth day he had obviously not taken it off.

Woolley, who was obsessed with washing his hair, would wander round the place with his long hair soaking in a towel, while the little balcony which they used for meetings would be decorated by everyone's clothes drying in the sun.

Woolley's and Jordan's dress sense occasionally inhibited their film-viewing especially at official evening screenings where black tie was often required. On one rainy evening when the two film-makers wanted to attend a screening of Peter Greenaway's *Drowning by Numbers*, in which Palace owned the UK distribution rights, Jordan was barred by an officious festival guard from entering the Palais

Theatre's screening rooms because he was wearing training shoes. Woolley, who was allowed to enter, spied John Stephenson, an Irish acquaintance, and explained that he needed to borrow his shoes. 'Neil's outside, and they won't let him in without decent shoes,' Woolley explained to the bemused man. Woolley ran out to give Jordan the shoes, but the festival guard had spied their trick. This time he barred Woolley on the grounds that he too was wearing (previously unnoticed) black trainers. Fed up, the two men went for a drink at the Majestic, later moving on to a restaurant, Jordan all the while carrying his trainers in a plastic bag, completely forgetting that he was still wearing the Irishman's shoes. A sodden and barefoot Stephenson finally found them after midnight.

Powell pushed himself and his staff into overdrive during the festival. He viewed Cannes as a superb opportunity to meet the world's buyers and sellers. Moreover, as Powell saw it, Palace had a unique franchise to protect and the only way to hold on to its distinctive place in the market was aggressively to cover every corner of the festival.

Morning meetings at Cannes would be held at 8.30, while everyone nursed stinking hangovers from the celebratory parties and subsequent carousing at Le Petit Carlton, a notorious watering hole on the rue d'Antibes, where many attending the festival would gather to exchange film gossip, most of which would be forgotten by the following day.

Drink, and the excessive consumption of it, is a large part of the Cannes experience, yet this did not prevent Powell from picking on Symes's PR staff about their expenses. He would spot them talking to people in the bar of the Majestic or the Carlton, two of the big – and massively overpriced – hotels on the sea-front and then take them to task later. Angie Errigo remembers Powell ordering her to one side, and warning her, 'I hope you're not buying journalists any drinks in these places, because it's far too expensive.'

'Sometimes it's sort of difficult if you've fixed up a quick meeting, Nik,' Errigo explained.

'Yeah, well, if you have to, then take them round the corner to the ones down the back streets, they're much cheaper.'

Powell was not the only British producer worrying about the cost of the £5 orange juices on the Majestic terrace. Other producers would walk on to the hotel's terrace with an empty bottle of Perrier water and some glasses, so the waiters would assume that they had already ordered and let them get on with their meeting.

One of Palace's most notable strengths was its ability to discover and buy small films that often ended up providing hits for the company. During one memorable Cannes Festival, Woolley and the writer/director David Leland caught a screening of the Italian film *Cinema Paradiso* many months before the film had become a hit. 'There were just three people in the cinema, and there was David – the "hard man" of the British film industry – sitting next to me,' Woolley recalled. 'By the time we're halfway through the movie, I'm quietly sobbing into the side of my hand, shielding myself from David's steely eyes. Then I caught a glimpse of his face, and the tears were just streaming down his cheeks.' Naturally they bought the movie, which was later to become one of the most successful foreign language films in the history of British cinema.

In the early days, Woolley, Powell, Rappaport and Webster all played major roles in seeking out new acquisitions, with Powell especially quick at moving in to close the deals. Later, Robert Jones, who was to become director of acquisitions, and Daniel Battsek built upon this powerful platform. The two young men started to form a strong axis on the film-buying side in the mid-1980s, working together and exchanging notes on films they had viewed.

Jones's job was to provide films for Palace Pictures and Palace Video, the two companies that were consistently proving to be Palace's major source of cash and which were providing the money to support Palace's productions. 'Those early years at Cannes were tremendously exciting,' Jones explained. 'To be any good at acquiring films, you have to think that in the next cinema you go into you'll discover something wonderful. I would be watching at least seven or eight movies a day, because Palace relied on our searching out the gems before our competitors. We didn't have the depth of resources or relationships with larger companies to rely on in those early days.' Above all, Palace was showing the way by taking risks on foreign language and arthouse films that most of Wardour Street continued to steer clear of.

The rest of the film industry viewed Palace's buying operation with some scepticism, arguing that the company paid far too much for UK rights and threw money around in an irresponsible fashion. As one rival distributor explained, 'Palace might pick up four or five films at Cannes, and we'd just buy one. But Nik would give his boys hell that we'd got that picture and Palace hadn't. It was a stupid ego thing because Nik just couldn't bear to be one down.'

In Palace's defence, Battsek argued that the company deliberately never set a budget for Cannes, 'which everyone else used to criticise. But so what? If there was no budget then we didn't have to spend it either, so we were free to buy a lot, a little or nothing. It was just pure envy on the part of our competitors.'

Some of the competitors' envy was provoked by Powell's and more notably Woolley's clout and connections with talented people on the creative side of the film industry. An annual Palace dinner would be held at some venue in the back streets of Cannes, and the company also regularly organised a festival supper in honour of the BBC film critic Barry Norman. The event was tactically astute, given that Norman had a far greater impact on potential cinema-goers than most of the print critics put together. Norman, like many film critics, enjoyed discussing films with Woolley, and admired the producer's informed and passionate views on each year's Cannes offerings. Woolley would always criticise Puttnam and the rest of the Establishment, while Norman would defend them to the hilt. 'It wasn't personal, it was just that they had very different views on what films should be made,' Battsek explained.

Given that the rest of the UK industry rarely made a splash at Cannes, Palace parties were high-profile events which many people would try to gatecrash. Powell and Phil Symes would invite the main British film critics and film-makers, as well as the stars they knew who happened to be at Cannes that year. Critics such as the *Standard*'s Alexander Walker and the *Guardian*'s Derek Malcolm enjoyed the Palace dinners. Malcolm, an Old Etonian and former racehorse jockey who has never been scared of cracking the whip over what he thought to be a bad film, would trundle along to the Palace parties in 'Vietnamese restaurants, something always pretty cheap'. He admired the cheerful confidence and enthusiasm Palace exuded. 'You never knew what they'd come up with. One film would be marvellous, and then there'd be a frightful disaster like *Absolute Beginners*. It was a devil-maker operation that tried plenty of different things, but I had more faith in Nik and Steve than I did in their choice of directors. There was always a sense that the bubble might burst any minute with Palace.'

Highlights of the Palace Cannes parties included the time when Jordan bumped into and invited Oliver Stone, who ended up squeezing on to a table next to a thrilled Errigo. Another time Palace held a party for its prized acquisition *Kiss of the Spider Woman* (a deal Woolley had secured by signing the agreement on a napkin in Rio), and Raul Julia and William Hurt attended, bringing with them Christopher Walken. The festival screening was the first time anyone from Palace had seen the completed film, and its rapturous festival reception gave the company a huge boost. At the end of the screening in the Palais Theatre, the audience had sprung to their feet, clapping and cheering all the way through the film's closing credits. After the beach-side party, Julia started singing opera extracts at a little bar at the Carlton that happened to have a piano, while Hurt sang Country and Western and played the guitar. To Battsek it felt as if 'we were the kings of the world and it was brilliant'.

As Palace grew the Cannes team moved to a big apartment overlooking the Festival Palais on the Croisette. Everyone still mucked in, but the headquarters, smack in the middle of the festival action, were distinctly glamorous. Due to everyone's hectic schedules, impromptu meetings were often held in the early morning hours. Acquisitions meetings to discuss which films to buy occurred at three a.m., partly because Woolley could never be raised in the morning and nobody could be found anyway. Woolley recalls one occasion when a member of staff called to fetch him for a nine a.m. meeting. Hearing him coming, Woolley climbed out onto the window ledge before he entered the room, only to return to bed when the coast was clear. Jones remembers Powell sitting in the apartment in nothing but his boxer shorts and 'having to stare at his bollocks peeping out, and not having the heart to tell him'.

Late one night in Cannes, Jones and Battsek had one of the most heated rows with Powell in the history of Palace. The Coen brothers had been invited to the Palace dinner that year, for the company had previously handled their wacky film, *Blood Simple* in 1984. The party was a big event, held in an Arabic restaurant that resembled the inside of a mosque, to which Palace had invited a selection of bankers, backers, critics and film-makers. The Powell-conceived rule for all Palace staff at such dinners was that each person had a designated seat at a table, and they were instructed to charm everyone around them because, in spite of the dinner, they were still at work. 'At a certain point, Robert and I made the dreadful mistake of moving from our allotted places, and going over to join the Coen brothers, whom we both knew anyway. When we got back to the Palace apartment at about three o'clock, Nik went mad and turned on us: "What the fuck were you doing? You come down to Cannes and you know how important it is to us, and you have the temerity to sit next to each other. You know this is a business thing, and you should be working." '

'Okay, Nik, fucking fire me then,' Jones screamed, while an alarmed Battsek warned his colleague not to rise to the bait.

The row did not stop there, however. As in many family arguments, a small disagreement escalated into a broad argument about what Palace stood for and whether the company was going in the right direction. It went on and on into the morning. At various intervals, one of the three would fall asleep but when he awoke he would get straight back into the argument. Every now and again they would burst into laughter and be friendly, but Powell would not let the argument die. 'After all we've done for you, how could you do this to me?' he would moan, incensing Jones. Battsek later explained why the row was so painful: 'Our working lives at Palace, whether at Cannes or anywhere else, were twenty-three out of twenty-four hours in the day, so to say that we weren't working was like a knife in the heart. Robert took it even worse than me, and got really upset. Having been with them right from the start he was really sensitive to such stuff, whereas I had more distance.

'Sometimes Nik showed so little understanding of the way Palace worked. He failed to see that we knew how to use our knowledge and ability to help the company.'

From 1989 Woolley decided to stay in an apartment behind the Carlton Hotel rather than muck in with the Palace team. 'I couldn't bear the lack of privacy and it didn't seem wonderful any more. In the first few years I was seeing so many films I never saw the sun, but I became increasingly disenchanted with buying and selling films.' Woolley's change in attitude was partly due to his growing older but it also marked the fact that he was beginning to want to distance himself, both in his private and public life, from Palace's 'boys' club' attitude.

Although Palace bought many films at Cannes, the deals would often not be completed for many months. Powell, Webster, Woolley and later Robert Jones would normally agree a deal memo at the festival, but Palace (like every other company) would never sign contracts at that stage. 'The distribution contract would be sent out as late as possible so that Palace didn't have to pay the signature fee [normally at ten per cent of the overall cost]', explained a Palace lawyer. Piles of contracts would sit in Palace's offices for months before distributors would start chasing up their missing down-payments. Nik would then say, 'But we haven't signed the contract yet. Let's get it closed!'

By the late-1980s, Palace's success in selecting and promoting films had made it a model to admirers both at home and abroad. Unlike so much of the British film industry, Palace was innovative and daring. 'Cinema is not just about process,' Woolley explained. 'It's about realising dreams. Film needs to be pushed out there to the public and beyond. Palace engaged with and realised those dreams at every opportunity.'

By 1986 Palace had moved the heart of its operation to Wardour Mews, a narrow alleyway in the centre of Soho. While numerous film companies' offices in the mid-eighties were the size of

Goldcrest's self-described 'Wembley Stadium', furnished in high-tech style with plants, leather seating and glass tables, Palace's Wardour Mews offices were small, cramped and chaotic – rather like Palace itself. The cobbled mews was littered with used condoms from the neighbouring prostitution racket and decorated at night by blinking red lights and hand-painted signs for sexual services. Inside the office, a maze of corridors and small rooms with creaking wooden floorboards and lowish ceilings was packed with posters, tapes, desks and chairs, leaving small pockets of space with telephones, but little else, where people worked. Bits of the building would fall off on to the floor, quickly to be absorbed into the general mess.

Powell adored these offices. To him they were physical proof that Palace was not profligate. He continued to apply his 'lean and mean' philosophy to the daily running of the company, not permitting employees to pass on the responsibilities of their old jobs when they were promoted to more senior and tougher positions. This ensured that the staff felt personally responsible for any mistakes, and it also effectively held salaries down.

For all Powell's cantankerous bark, certain people did gradually learn how to handle him. Sue Bruce-Smith made a point of pushing her way into his office and taking him to task on personal matters when she felt that Palace was not doing enough for its employees. For example, she believed that the accounting staff should get free tickets to the première of *Absolute Beginners*, so that they were involved in the more glamorous elements of the business, but Powell refused point blank. 'What the fark are you trying to start? All these tickets cost money, Sue!'

'I got used to the level of swearing and realised that he did listen to people . . . not at the point of verbal contact, but somehow things would sink in later,' Bruce-Smith recalled. She found herself screaming at Powell to buy a new chair for an accountant, to have the photocopier mended and to handle the ever-vigilant fire inspectors, whose arrival would always cause havoc in the potential death-trap offices. When they appeared, Daniel Battsek would helpfully tell Bruce-Smith to say, somewhat incredibly, that 'nobody was in', and leave her to greet them politely and to show them around the rabbit warren. Later she would confront Powell with the required changes, and he would instantly ask, 'How much? Because if it's more than fifty quid you can forget it.'

'Nik was so busy doing multi-million film deals that you'd sort of understand why he'd react like I was a stupid woman hassling him over a fire drill. It was like swatting a fly for him,' Bruce-Smith recalled. Nevertheless, after a while, Powell would come back to Bruce-Smith, saying that she was right about the tickets for the accountants, who would also find themselves awarded a new chair, and the fire hazards too would be dealt with in the end. Powell, more than anyone else, felt responsible for the Palace family. When Bruce-Smith wanted a lazy runner fired, Nik would take pity on the guy, telling her: 'Aw Sue, he's all right really. Give him another week.'

Powell would always support his staff once outside the building, criticising them only to their faces. If he did drop his guard and was prodded about it, he would immediately return to his original position of unconditional public support. When Bruce-Smith finally left Palace to head up the British Film Institute's sales operation in 1989, Powell gave her a big send-off and a firm offer of support for the future.

As Powell got to know the film business better, he started to take a keen interest in which films Palace bought to distribute. Often his more commercially orientated suggestions would attract healthy debate amongst the staff, but no one movie created more friction than *Nine ½ Weeks*. Robert Jones, Daniel Battsek and Powell went to an early screening of Adrian Lyne's controversial pop-sex offering, starring Mickey Rourke and Kim Basinger. According to Battsek, he and Jones realised its box-office potential and were keen to pick up the film, 'but Nik really had his tongue hanging out. He absolutely loved it.'

The problem was Woolley. Woolley wanted to buy only films he could be proud of or films which had a certain quality that distinguished them from others in the market. Integrity, quality,

quirky and challenging were Woolley's buzz words, and exploitation and soft-porn were not things he wanted Palace or himself to be
associated with.

Powell was less interested in Palace's cultural image than in the
amount of money the film might generate. *Nine ½ Weeks* fitted
perfectly into Powell's plan for the company's distribution operation to grow through expansion into more commercial fare.

'Steve desperately didn't want to handle this film,' Battsek
recalled. 'Then he did that thing he always does. He went into a
huge tirade, and when it was over, he said, "Well, if you really want
to do it, then go ahead."

'He made you feel guilty for buying it, guilty that there was a good
campaign, and guilty that it all went well. That didn't stop him
slagging off the film to the film editor at *Time Out*, even if that meant
getting bad reviews. Neither did it stop him telling us that it was
always going to do well.'

Woolley was not alone in his distaste for *Nine ½ Weeks*. Palace's
women staff were deeply hostile to the film. Bruce-Smith agreed
with Woolley that in no way was this a classic Palace film: 'It was a
sleazy, soft-porn movie with nothing arty whatsoever. Daniel
wanted to experiment with some artistic licence on the ad poster. It
was a picture of Basinger going down on Rourke, but Daniel added
the touch of a black blindfold. It was clever marketing because it
hinted at S&M, but I saw it as flagrant doctoring, and threatened to
resign.'

Although Powell let Bruce-Smith take a back seat on the film's
release, he would later constantly remind her how successful it had
been, carping: 'Well, Sue, good job we didn't take your advice on
*Nine ½ Weeks*, eh?'

The film's release attracted angry student and feminist demonstrations and a national press debate regarding it's dubious sexual
politics. Battsek was fully aware of the flak coming Palace's way, and
decided to release the film in the middle of May, subsequently
moving it back a week to coincide with the Cannes Film Festival.
Webster bravely stuck it out in London, while most of the senior
staff ducked the opening from the safety of the Côte d'Azur.

\*

It was not only certain Palace staff who grew genuinely fond of Powell. Carole Myer, a razor-sharp, short-haired, American-born sales agent, developed a close business relationship and friendship with the Palace chief. She had known Woolley for more than a decade, and first met Powell in 1984 when she sold David Hare's Channel 4-backed début feature film, *Wetherby*, to Palace. There was an embarrassing moment when it was discovered that Palace, in a cheeky effort to capitalise on the impact of the story's early suicide, had, with no authority, retitled the film *Violent Stranger* for video. David Hare and the producer Simon Relph were livid about the new title, under which appeared in tiny letters *Wetherby*. Hare even wrote a letter to Woolley explaining that he would have 'understood if the film had been called *Big Cocks* or *Huge Tremulous Buttocks*', indeed, anything was better than *Violent Stranger*. The row was smoothed over, and once again Palace scraped through on the back of its cheeky charm.

Myer's next major encounter with Powell was over *A Letter to Brezhnev*. Palace, and in particular Paul Webster, had been helping the producers of Chris Bernard's film to complete their low budget production in return for the UK theatrical rights. The production was in a terrible mess financially, but somehow the footage was put together for a rough cut of the film to be shown. The footage still needed a sound mix, but Myer loved it and ended up sharing with Powell the job of selling the film.

*A Letter to Brezhnev* was booked to play at the midnight screenings at the Venice Film Festival, and the Italian press adored the film. 'It was a fairly hilarious operation,' Myer explained. 'Nik had never been to Venice at that stage, and he was expecting to go around the Lido and get buyers right up against a wall. Once he'd let them down, they were supposed to be left to me to pick up the pieces and sell them the movie. The trouble was, Nik couldn't find anyone on the street or get hold of anyone even on the phone. He hadn't worked out that they were all at the swimming pool.'

Powell's relationship with Myer and Relph was to crystallise into a serious business operation by the autumn of 1986. Relph was at that stage the chief executive of British Screen, the government-backed body that invested in UK films; while Myer had recently resigned from her job as film sales manager at Film Four International, the sales wing of Channel 4. Together with Zenith Productions, producer of some Palace releases, such as Stephen Frears's *The Hit* and David Leland's *Wish You Were Here*, the three partners established The Sales Company, to be headed up by Myer.

The new company was to represent the film output of the three companies – Palace, Zenith and British Screen – who all wanted more control over the sales of their films around the world and a closer relationship between producers and sales agents. In a structure close to Powell's heart, it was also designed to overcome what they perceived to be the high cost of being represented by outside sales agents.

Setting up a new company with two other partners and an independently minded manager was not easy for Powell. Myer's previous experience at the British Film Institute and Channel 4 had taught her how to prepare and control meetings with ruthless vigour. The early meetings dealt with everything from the landlord's latest bill to the hotel booked for Cannes and the copy and posters for individual movies. Relph and the managers at Zenith were keen to listen to Myer's experienced views on sales and marketing tactics for smaller films, but Powell would argue that Palace's films had to be hyped 'the Palace way'. The result was that, at the early meetings, the two of them would regularly resign. When Myer sent artwork round to Palace, Powell would throw a fit, demanding to know who had approved the images. Myer was smart enough to check her work with Woolley, and her reply of 'Steve' would silence Powell.

Myer was renowned amongst distributors for being tough but honest in her dealings. She would sometimes take lower offers on the films she was selling because the distributors had a good track record in that territory. She knew that they would be honest about their earnings, which was quite an advantage given the 'grab-it-and-run' nature of most international film distributors. She was convinced that smaller independent films required first-class promotional materials if they were to have any chance of making an impact and chose whom she dealt with accordingly.

Powell constantly queried how much was being spent at The Sales Company, but he had finally met his match. 'There's no one cheaper than I am,' Myer explained. 'Steve finally came to a Sales Company board meeting, and told him: "Nik, if you want to go through how much Carole is spending on stationery, can we do it another time? I'd like to talk about the movies." '

Myer also had to contend with Powell when Palace owed The Sales Company money from films it had bought from her. 'Every time Nik owed me money, I'd be on the phone in the morning saying that if the cheque wasn't here in half an hour, I'd come up the street myself. What the hell he thought I would do to them, given my size, I don't know, but Nik didn't want me coming up the street screaming for my money, so I was always paid. You owe me money and you're in dead shit.'

Part of the difficulty facing Myer in sales meetings was holding Powell back. 'He was always desperate for the deal to go through. He always needed the money for the productions so badly.' Invariably this desperation was the result of Powell playing 'catch-up' with Woolley, who would start Palace productions without all the finance being in the bank. It was a pattern that was to have serious repercussions as Palace came to produce more and more films, closer and closer together.

Powell's eagerness to close deals could lead Myer into difficult situations such as when she and he were selling *Scandal*. Powell had set up a screening of the promo reel for Michael Williams-Jones, head of UIP, the powerful Hollywood distribution company which handled film marketing and releases for Paramount, MGM and Universal. On the day of the meeting, Myer had taken some penicillin by mistake, and an allergic red rash was visible around her neck. As they were about to leave for the big meeting, Powell told Myer she could not go with him because she looked 'funny'.

'I'm not looking funny! I've just got this rash all over my body,' Myer screamed. Powell relented, and they made it to the meeting to discover that Williams-Jones was not in charge of one of the most powerful distributors in Europe for nothing. He knew everything that was bought and sold in every country, and he was informed about even the most minuscule outfits in the smallest territories.

'While I'm sitting there, Nik tries to sell Sweden twice. We've already sold Sweden to another distributor. Nik suddenly realises, and asks Michael if we could take it out of the deal without explaining why, but he refuses to budge. So we come out of the meeting and I say:

' "Nik, you've just sold Sweden twice!"

' "Argh, Carole, don't worry. I'll fix it." '

Powell promised to fix it for months, but it did not happen. There was no way Myer was going back to Williams-Jones to explain what had happened, so in the end she phoned the Swedish distributor to ask it to cancel the deal, thereby getting Powell off the hook. 'It was the only time Nik went this far to my knowledge. One other time he suggested we should try so-and-so, and I had to remind him that we'd already sold that territory and he just said: "Argh, yeah, Carole, I forgot." '

CHAPTER SEVEN

# 'Fast Cars, Loud Music and Blow Jobs'

When the *Sunday Correspondent*'s film critic Adrian Turner wrote in 1990 that a typical Palace film contained 'fast cars, loud music and blow jobs', Stephen Woolley was incensed. According to Woolley, by 1990 the critics were 'sharpening their knives and going for a pound of Palace flesh'. Part of the reason for this, he believed, was that most British film critics are male, well over fifty years of age, and often astonishingly ignorant of the industry that produces the films they write about. Woolley deeply despised the way certain critics set themselves up as the intellectual and cultural arbiters of the day. As one Palace collaborator explained, 'Critics saw Nik and Steve as wide boys who were flogging brown nylon shirts off the back of a truck somewhere in Chapel Street market. They just didn't see them as legitimate traders.'

Palace's taste for working with new writers and directors might also in part have been to blame for this problematic relationship. Woolley had a penchant for taking on creative challenges, and developing film scripts that tackled political scandal and the social iniquities of the Thatcher era. To take risks on new talent was admirable, but the way Palace developed and prepared its scripts for production was the subject of some debate both inside and outside the company. As one senior employee admitted, 'Palace didn't develop their scripts enough. The consequence was that some of its projects went into production with flaws that remained all too present in the final film.' The company's determination to move forwards and make its films happen was also sometimes its weakness.

Woolley and Powell make much of the fact that Palace had a very high conversion rate for selected scripts to finished films. Over a ten-year period, just three projects were abandoned by Palace, while sums of between £100,000 and £300,000 were spent on nearly all their films at the development and pre-production stage. However, sometimes a decision *not* to make a film can be more profitable in the long run than going ahead. Given the problems that had surrounded the numerous drafts of the *Absolute Beginners* screenplay, Palace should have been very aware of the potential pitfalls of pushing a project into production without a finalised script. Yet even now Powell warns against the dangers of 'over-development', when a script is re-written so many times that it loses its initial strength and appeal. The partners' reasoned talk about the importance of development a decade later is a far cry from their manic drive to get some of their films into production in the mid- to late-eighties.

Although Palace was not damaged financially by *Absolute Beginners* (according to the company's reliable cinema booker, Mike Ewin, the film took around £1.8 million at the UK box office) the film did threaten the creative credibility of the company. With the exception of the co-production *A Letter to Brezhnev*, (which Palace successfully released in the UK), the company had not produced an acclaimed film. If Powell's and Woolley's ambitions were to keep charging forwards, Palace needed to produce a film which the industry and the critics would have to take seriously.

It was a Jordan–Woolley collaboration that came to Palace's rescue. Typical of the extended life of a film in preparation, *Mona Lisa* was conceived well before *The Company of Wolves*, but only went into pre-production in October 1985 on the heels of *Absolute Beginners*. The story was inspired by a short article, which Chris Brown had read in a newspaper, about a heavy in court on a charge of 'grievous bodily harm'. This thug claimed that he was protecting the prostitutes from their pimps, and, according to Jordan, 'had this wonderful vision of himself as a knight in shining armour. He was obviously a totally inarticulate man and probably a very dangerous criminal, too. I just thought what a wonderful situation, and I just made up the story.'

Woolley loved the idea, and saw this 'George' character as a criminal product of the King's Road sheepskin-jacketed wide boys of the sixties, whose brand of thuggery had gradually matured into the mafia-style respectability of property and drugs dealing in the Thatcherite eighties. 'My father had been on the shady side of things in the fifties. My mum loved Nat King Cole, and the references, love story and the subversion of the idea really appealed to me,' admitted Woolley.

Due to Jordan's busy schedule, David Leland, an English writer who was researching what was to become his début feature, *Wish You Were Here*, was called in by Woolley to write a first draft of the screenplay. 'I was given a brief which was like a third of a page, and ended up writing something that was very hard and violent, and then gave it back to Steve. The idea was that Neil would then do a draft, which would come back to me, but the screenplay disappeared for ages.' The reason for the project losing momentum was that ITC pulled the finance after its new owner Robert Holmes à Court saw *The Company of Wolves* and hated it. When this news was relayed to Jordan, he moved on to other work. Woolley kept hawking the idea around, only to collect a batch of rejection letters from suspicious financiers, including Channel 4, who kept complaining that the 'drugs and prostitution' were too much for them to stomach.

Jordan had wanted to make a very different film to Leland's initial draft. 'I was a bit upset that we had asked him to write the first draft of the script, because David's very talented but he was not quite appropriate for the story I had in mind. He wrote a very realistic script, and I came in and made it something else. It's about a criminal trying to invent a sense of morality out of a world that has none. It's really about very vulgar things that are only elevated by a certain sense of romanticism.'

During a visit to Hollywood to see Orion's Mike Medavoy about *Absolute Beginners*, Woolley by chance bumped into Sean Connery in a lift. Seizing the opportunity to pitch *Mona Lisa* to the star, Woolley blustered, 'Hello, Sean, I'm Stephen Woolley. I believe we have a mutual friend, John Boorman?'

'That's right,' said Connery convivially.

'Well, Palace have this great new script which will be directed by Neil Jordan. I think you'd be really interested in the lead part.'

The often taciturn Connery was charmed by the producer's enthusiasm, and suggested he send him the script. Unfortunately, Connery's agent was less charmed by the sum Palace could afford to pay the actor. He stubbornly refused to reduce Connery's fee, which at that time was £400,000 a film, while the actor prevaricated. Bob Hoskins was approached to play the part and, after some negotiating about the character with Jordan, the cockney star of *The Long Good Friday* came on board for considerably less than Connery's agent was insisting on. Hoskins in turn showed the script to his friend Michael Caine, who signed up for seven days' work on set at a generously low price.

Leland did not come back to help with the script until just before the film started shooting in November 1985. By this time it had the full backing of George Harrison's company, HandMade Films, which was managed by Dennis O'Brien. 'I acted as a devil's advocate really,' says Leland, 'because the ultimate débâcle of that film was that there was no ending. Neil has a wonderful tone and imagination, but he gradually realised the story was too soft. Very late in the day he brought in the vicious pimp and some of the more bruising elements that were really from my draft . . . I thought there were so many holes in the film's construction and it had no resolution. But I was always being pedantic and wanting to see life through modern terms, and that's where I learned from Neil. He would turn left when I turned right, and it taught me a lot about the illogicality of film and image.' Leland's version of events is backed up by Woolley, who stressed that the co-writer 'did things which helped Neil wrestle with in the script'.

Woolley realised that he would not be able to produce *Mona Lisa* on a full-time basis whilst dealing with *Absolute Beginners*. Tightly budgeted at just over £2 million, the film needed an experienced producing partner, so Woolley invited Patrick Cassavetti, a wise and very practical producer who had just completed Terry Gilliam's *Brazil*, to come on board. Cassavetti, who had been recommended to Woolley by Simon Relph, has a reputation in the industry as a personable and highly ethical operator, who suffers fools and unpaid bills badly. Attracted to the script, to the prospect of working with Jordan, and to the energy emanating from Woolley and Powell, Cassavetti accepted the job and managed to bring the film in more than £100,000 under budget. Woolley, who still never missed a single frame of the rushes, was kept informed in detail all the way through the production, but Cassavetti's precise control over the London shoot allowed Woolley to concentrate on *Absolute Beginners*.

Despite Cassavetti's bearing the brunt of the production work, Woolley found himself clashing with O'Brien, who was an executive producer on the film. Having first rowed about the casting of the lead prostitute – with O'Brien wanting Grace Jones, while Woolley and Jordan opted for Cathy Tyson – Woolley and O'Brien continued to come to blows. During the first week of dailies (evening screenings of the film shot the previous day), O'Brien argued that a minor shot of Hoskins's penis should be cut. Detesting the executive interference, and believing that with all his previous experience he could judge what the British Film Censors would allow, Woolley stood his ground. O'Brien's entire approach irritated the producer.

'Dennis can be a difficult man, and our philosophies about making films are completely different,' Woolley explained. 'He sees films like this factory. There's a place where the boffins work, where people like Neil, Michael Palin and Terry Gilliam hang out. Then there's the factory, where the producers and technicians work, and then there's the head office, where Dennis works. One day he thinks, "Oh, I'll go and see the boffins." Another time he'll decide to "check on how the factory's going, and find out why they haven't given me those reports I need".'

Woolley did not fit into any of O'Brien's categories: 'I wasn't a boffin boy or a factory boy and I didn't work in the head office. It's my job as a good producer to be all those things, and there was this man in my face, disliking me enormously. Patrick [Cassavetti] was okay in Dennis's books, but Palace had only made a couple of films, and as far as he was concerned, we could've been gone tomorrow.'

Leland vividly remembers sitting in a screening room with Woolley and O'Brien. 'It was an awful atmosphere because Dennis was sitting there with a little note pad and a special pen with a built-in torch. You knew when Dennis was making a note because you could see his pen-light going off and on at depressingly regular intervals during the screening.'

Soon full scale hostilities broke out between O'Brien and Woolley, with Jordan on Woolley's side.

'Dennis had gone into the cutting rooms when I was away, and had stated that he wanted to cut the film earlier than we had planned,' Woolley recalled. Woolley argued vociferously against such a move, explaining that Hoskins's character, George, 'needed to be given a chance to realise that he was wrong, and that you can still change as you grow older'. Jordan had shot an extraordinary sequence at the end of the film, in which the camera picks up Cathy Tyson's eyes reflected in a car's rearview mirror as Hoskins describes her as a 'bird trapped in a cage'. Jordan and Woolley insisted that this signing off emotionally was essential.

Jordan later explained that in his opinion the problems facing film-makers when it comes to endings are much greater than those facing playwrights. 'In a movie, the audience is totally dragged in and the experience is so emotional that if everybody ends up dead it's a real problem because the audience hasn't the ability to remove themselves from the experience. They can objectify the theatre experience, but it's not the same for a film. A movie needs to survive the experience, and that's what the ending of *Mona Lisa* is really about.'

Woolley's and Powell's relationship with *Mona Lisa*'s other key financiers helped save the day. Through some skilful politicking, Wooley managed to win over the film's American production executive and distributor. Jordan's ending remained.

The film went into competition at Cannes in the summer of 1986, the year Goldcrest won the Palme d'Or for *The Mission*. Hoskins was in fine form, telling Barry Norman: 'I'm having a wonderful time. It's so exciting. You know what's amazing about this place, because everyone has to dress up to go to the cinema, it's got a sort of timeless thing – it seems to go on for ever, 'cos there's people walking about first thing in the morning dressed as penguins.' Or, as Woolley later put it, 'Cannes watched Bob party.'

Hoskins flew back to London before the final awards were announced, only to find that he had won the 'Pan Dio' – 'He couldn't say Palme d'Or correctly,' Jordan explained – for best actor, which he was to share with French star Michel Blanc of *Tenue de Soirée*. It was the first time a British actor had won the Best Actor Award since Terence Stamp's performance in *The Collector* twenty-one years previously. Hoskins rushed back to Cannes in a whirlwind journey by private jet and police-escorted car, whilst those at the ceremony were kept informed of his movements by the compere: 'Monsieur Bob is on the plane . . . Monsieur Bob is at the airport . . . Monsieur Bob is now in his taxi . . . Monsieur Bob is on the Croisette . . .' until finally he arrived to steal the show. Jury member and film director Sydney Pollack ushered him out on to the steps of the Palais, where he was rapturously greeted by the 2,000-strong crowd.

The film was released in North America that June to critical acclaim, and went on to take a very notable $10 million (the equivalent of a $25 million art-house hit today). Hoskins won a flurry of further awards, culminating in a Best Actor nomination for an Oscar in February 1987. When it came to the UK release, Palace played one of its deliberate tricks on the critics. It released *Mona Lisa* at the start of September, when most of the lead critics were at the Venice Film Festival. *Mona Lisa* performed strongly, smashing the house records at the Odeon Haymarket, while taking an impressive £1.1 million in four weeks in London's West End cinemas, and going on to take just over £4 million at the UK box office. The film was just as successful on television, where it attracted a top rating of 7.8 million viewers when Channel 4 (which finally bought the television rights after *Mona Lisa* was completed) screened it in February 1989.

George Harrison loved the film, and was delighted at its success, but when HandMade sent out their Ten Year Anniversary party invitations, one arrived for Powell but none for Woolley. Powell rang HandMade and suggested that there must have been a mistake. He was told that it was no mistake. He rang back, asking if he could bring Woolley as a guest. The answer was no.

*Mona Lisa* and *Absolute Beginners* were released in America within a few months of each other. Mike Medavoy, the head of Orion and investor in *Absolute Beginners*, was by this time friendly with Woolley and supportive of Palace. He paid for an office in Los Angeles and an assistant, Kerry Boyle (who had backed *Absolute Beginners* at Orion), so that Woolley could go to America and gain an insight into the marketing of the film. Woolley jumped at the opportunity. The possibility of moving to Hollywood, the centre of the international film industry, fitted perfectly with his driving ambition and intense desire to make things happen.

When Medavoy's money for the offices came to an end following the release of *Absolute Beginners*, Woolley and Powell decided to find their own offices in Hollywood. Over the next year or so Woolley spent most of his time in Los Angeles, finding American finance for Palace projects (including US partners for Jordan's *High Spirits*) and spotting potential films for distribution in the UK. These activities alone were not enough to justify the additional expense to Powell, until his partner pointed out that the offices could be used to save money during the American Film Market and for Hollywood meetings.

The two little rooms and a reception area in an office on Beverly Boulevard were very respectable. The former owners were interior decorators and a concerted effort was made to keep the offices looking smart. In contrast to the creaking bare floorboards in Wardour Mews, the floor was covered in tasteful new carpet which they tried to keep clean. However, on one of Powell's early visits to Palace LA, some road workers happened to be spreading tarmac on the street outside the office. Powell got out of the car, jay-walked across the road right through the wet tar and entered the offices.

'There were these huge black footprints up the stairs, down the corridor, up another set of stairs, I mean they were everywhere,' Woolley explained. 'Nik sat down in the corner of the office, looked up, and yelled:

' "Who's dirtied the carpet? Look! This is terrible. Kerry come here!" ' Powell inspected Kerry Boyle, but Palace LA head of production has small feet and was wearing shoes with heels on, so it could not have been her. He then beckoned in the receptionist and everyone else.

'Finally it dawned on him when he looked down at the tracks of tar again that they ended at his own feet. Nik does this kind of thing all the time, he's like Inspector Clouseau,' Woolley laughed. 'I find it constantly embarrassing, the way you do if your wife or brother does those kinds of things.'

Back in the UK, Palace was giving birth to productions at a prodigious rate. The production drive had stepped up a number of gears following *Absolute Beginners* and *Mona Lisa*, for three main reasons. First, Powell and Woolley wanted to ensure a stream of films for Palace's distribution activities, something they felt could be best achieved by making their own films as well as buying other people's. Second, most independent production companies only make money when they are *in* production. The money for fees (if they are not deferred or ploughed back into the film) and benefits of cash flow only appear when a film is in front of the cameras. Being in production as regularly as possible, therefore, became imperative. Third, Woolley's drive and ambition were enormous.

The young producer began work on numerous films, creating a frenzy of activity within Palace productions. *Siesta*, a dreamy emotional mystery, went into development in autumn 1985 while Woolley was still completing *Absolute Beginners* and starting *Mona Lisa*. It finally went into production in 1986. *Dream Demon*, a rabid horror film to be produced by Paul Webster and directed by an American, Harley Cokliss, was set to go into production in March 1987. The low-budget Frank Deasy script, *The Courier*, was to be shot in Ireland in June 1987, while *Shag* and *High Spirits* were filmed back-to-back, also during the summer months of 1987.

Such a packed production schedule put tremendous pressure on the company's resources, and resulted in some singularly bad results at the box office. The extent of Woolley's commitment to all of these scripts is debatable. To many it appeared that he was fired not by the films but by the desire 'to be in production', to make films.

The first film that Palace produced and ultimately released during this hectic period was *Siesta*. The script, written by Patricia Louisianna Knop and based on a surreal mystery novel by Patrice Chaplin, was to be directed by Mary Lambert, a talented Arkansas-born music video director, whose pop promo background bore remarkable similarities to Julien Temple's.

Lambert had made Madonna's first pop promos and had worked with Sting, Mick Jagger and Janet Jackson among other stars. A receptive Woolley was introduced to Lambert by Gary Kurfirst, the manager of Talking Heads, whom Palace had already dealt with when the company had distributed in the UK Jonathan Demme's *Stop Making Sense*.

Woolley met Lambert for lunch in London just as he was starting to get involved in *Absolute Beginners*. Lambert was very taken by this Young Turk's gushing enthusiasm for the project. 'Steve was really into the art of film-making and the film-maker's responsibility to society – how to come up with new movies and blow apart preconceptions – and I really wanted him to produce my film,' she recalled. Woolley discussed the project with Powell, and Palace made a commitment to co-finance the film with Kurfirst, who at this stage had assumed the vague title of 'project producer'.

By the time the deal was agreed and the project underway, Woolley was up to his eyeballs in *Absolute Beginners* and *Mona Lisa*, and soon realised that with the added burden of *Siesta* he had taken on more than he could cope with. His brash 'Yes, Yes, Yes' to Lambert changed into 'Help! Not another project.' Woolley believed that he should 'spread himself thinly', nudging many projects into production, but he also felt guilty about dumping the project. He brought Chris Brown on to the film, and from that point onwards gave advice from a distance.

Despite its low budget of just under $3.2 million, *Siesta* was not easy to finance or produce. Every time the American money came together, the foreign money would drop out, or vice versa. For once, casting was not a problem. Lambert and Kurfirst rounded up some top Hollywood names who were willing to take a risk on the script in return for a little money. The cast included Ellen Barkin, Jodie Foster, Martin Sheen, Isabella Rossellini and Grace Jones, alongside some less renowned names such as Gabriel Byrne, Julian Sands and Alexei Sayle. Miles Davis was signed up to do the music, and Zalman King, Hollywood's king of raunch, joined Powell and Julio Caro, *Siesta*'s socialite record-business backer, as the third executive producer.

Powell and Palace's new head of business affairs, Katy McGuinness, were soon belting around Los Angeles trying to finalise the production's finances with Kurfirst and Caro. McGuinness recalls a trip to New York, when she and Powell arrived late at night for a meeting to be held with Caro the following day. The next morning she was woken by Wendy Broom, Powell's assistant in London, saying that she would find Nik in a Manhattan hospital. The jet-lagged Powell had decided to get up early that morning to buy a newspaper from a subway station kiosk, and had had an epileptic fit. The New York Transit cops had tried to arrest him, thinking he was a crazed junky. In an effort to escape them, Powell had run off, only to fall and crack open his head. Fortunately, the singer Chrissie Hynde of The Pretenders – who was a friend of Sandie Shaw's and hence knew Powell – was staying at a nearby hotel. Recognising the distressed Powell, she raced out on to the street to stop the Transit police taking Powell away to prison, explaining that 'He may be a loony, but he's also an epileptic.' Powell was duly whisked off to hospital for stitches and bandages.

Having badly bitten his tongue, Powell was unable to speak. McGuinness, who had only been with the company a month, had to conduct all the meetings on her own, returning to Powell's hotel in between conferences to take hand-written instructions. Powell eventually returned to London, leaving McGuinness waiting for a banker's draft crucial to *Siesta*'s production finance. On receipt of the money, she was to fly direct to Madrid. The last thing Powell wrote down for her was: 'Make sure you fly economy . . .'

In Spain, the film's main location was a little village miles outside Madrid. The August heat was intense, and dysentery started to break out. Everyone was staying in hotels in the capital, so at five o'clock each morning the cars were packed up with crews, stars and equipment to begin a hot, fraught commute to the set. Given that much of the cast and crew became eagerly caught up in Madrid's joyful nightlife (and in one another), invariably a key team member (or couple) would miss the convoy.

Chris Brown, Palace's 'man on the ground' was facing a severe cash and confidence crisis. As the producer responsible for the day-to-day logistics and paying the crew, Brown was running around in a daze, sweating buckets. He would constantly report to Lambert, 'I can't find Julian [or Jodie, or Ellen and Gabriel, who, incidentally, were later married].' Barkin had a particularly gruelling shoot, as she was in nearly every scene. Angie Errigo was handling press on the production, without access to a typewriter or phones that worked, and was constantly hassled by creepy photographers trying to snap shots of a semi-dressed Rossellini or Barkin. There were some serious breakdowns in communications between the half-Spanish, half-British crew. In Lambert's words, 'The Spanish Armada would sail up the English Channel occasionally, especially when the English crew would start making sniping jokes that riled the Spaniards' sense of machismo.'

The main problem, as usual, was money, or the lack of it. Weeks would go by with no payments finding their way to the restless crew. Brown would call meetings, at which, standing on a chair with the sun burning down on his balding head, he would explain: 'Look, I'm awfully sorry, chaps, but the cheques might be a couple of days late. I think we should all go and have a drink . . . maybe I can buy you all a beer . . . ?'

The Spanish team would sit cleaning their fingernails with big hunting knives while Brown prattled on. Powell did more than his fair share of public explanations about the cash difficulties, and was very supportive of Lambert. Meanwhile, one of the production's accountants had his passport taken away for the entire duration of the shoot by the worried crew. Kurfirst, too busy touring the world with his bands to deal with the film on a full-time basis, managed to be in Spain for only about a third of the production.

By the time Woolley flew over during the middle of the film to help steady the ship, *Siesta*'s completion guarantors were also starting to sweat about the film falling behind schedule. Woolley insisted that pages of the script needed to be cut. Lambert naturally resisted, but finally gave way under pressure. Woolley then left Spain, having promised to return and talk about what the cuts actually meant to the film's structure. He never came back to Spain. A needy Lambert would call Woolley, who would placate her by saying:

'Mary, I'll be over as soon as I can.'

Days would go by. No sign of Woolley.

'I'm flying over as soon as possible.'

He did not come. In the end he told Lambert, 'Look, Mary, I just have too many problems over here. I can't deal with this right now.'

While Woolley was dealing with the US release of *Absolute Beginners* and marketing for *Mona Lisa*, the real problems facing *Siesta* were yet to come. Although the film managed somehow to come in on budget, the financing shambles still needed to be sorted out. Powell took the negative back to London and suspended all post-production in order to force the co-producer to negotiate. Kurfirst did, but it took about two months, during which time the interest on all the debts was growing and Palace experienced severe difficulties as a result. Eventually, a deal was worked out under which Kurfirst took over the existing debt and repaid Palace the majority of its money. Palace retained the UK rights because it was the only way to get back the balance. However, just before the picture was due to be released, the financier – at the behest of the co-producer – took out an injunction and challenged the part of the contract that said Palace had UK rights. The injunction was overturned by Palace but the delay caused enormous damage to the release.

None of this amused Lambert, who watched in horror as posters across London were pulled down a few days before the aborted launch. Then Lorimar, the US distributors, were bought by Warner Brothers, and the cast became nervous about supporting the American release with publicity interviews. The film took a paltry $700,000 in the US, and little over £300,000 in the UK. Lambert later went on to direct a surprise horror hit, *Pet Sematary* (1989), but the experience of watching the *Siesta* producers fall out left some deep scars on the film-maker.

Woolley explained that the whole experience of *Siesta* was a slap around the face for him: 'I realised at that point that if I was going to produce something, and say I was the producer on the film, I'd better actually do it. The amount of attention and follow-through you give a film really does pay off, and I realised with *Siesta* that we'd tried to produce far too hands-off.' Indeed, Woolley took no public production credit for the film.

Having told Screen International prior to the 1987 American Film Market, that 'potentially, *Siesta* could be as big as *Mona Lisa*', Powell was forced radically to alter his upbeat assessment, but his perspective was more universal and less thin-skinned than Woolley's, who always took criticism very personally. In a philosophical conclusion to 'My Biggest Mistake', an article about *Siesta* in the *Independent on Sunday*, Powell suggested that 'failure is a much better teacher than success'. Palace's co-chairman then proceeded to add the immortal lines: 'Never again will we go ahead with projects before the contracts are absolutely tied down.'

By 1987, a confident Woolley had come to the conclusion that Palace should raise the money for the company's productions on its own. Encouraged by *Mona Lisa*'s success, he put the idea to a receptive Powell, and the scene was set for a significant development in the way Palace financed its movies: the dream of raising American money for Palace's productions was coming true.

Thus Palace began to move into what is known in the industry as independent packaging: bringing together financial partners while (theoretically, at least) retaining control of production. The new goal was to find co-financiers rather than interfering and demanding co-producers.

Woolley, at this time, was entering a state of 'production overdrive' from which he would not emerge for five long years. He began to believe that his main purpose in life was to produce films that would make up a body of work, a library of contemporary cinema, which in future years would be viewed with interest and admiration.

As the pressure of pulling films together grew, the time Woolley gave to others waned. A different side to the thoughtful and considerate co-chairman of Palace's early days began to emerge. Unlike Powell, who became verbose and confrontational under pressure, Woolley became increasingly uncommunicative.

'When it came down to being really tough, Stephen was usually the one who would give someone a dressing down, despite everyone thinking it was the other way round,' explained a close friend of Woolley. 'Stephen can be much nastier than Nik. He does it with his eyes, ignoring people, not saying hello.'

Woolley is naturally shy with strangers, but not intentionally obstructive. 'I find it really hard to communicate with anyone I don't know,' he explained. 'I found it hard to work out of the LA office surrounded by people I'd hardly met, and difficult to deal with Palace's ever-expanding staff as the years went by.'

Staff–employer relations were not helped by what the staff perceived to be Woolley's impressively large expense claims. While all other Palace workers, under Powell's instructions, flew economy class, Woolley would fly club or first class (mostly claimed back against movie budgets). Powell's money-sparing attitude to travel irritated Woolley. 'Nik would make a point of saying that he wasn't travelling club class, as if that was a justification for something. Why does he bother? It's part of Nik's and my "little naughty schoolboy meets the headmaster" routine. Nik always thinks I'm the headmaster and he's the schoolboy.' Powell, it seemed to Woolley, was constantly looking for approval and confirmation from his partner. From Woolley's point of view, *not* going first or at least club class was false economy, as it meant arriving exhausted and unfit for work.

Woolley was particularly keen to find American projects for Palace, and the opportunity presented itself in *Shag*. The script told a coming-of-age story set in the summer of 1963 in the Carolinas. The inflamatory title (one of Powell's favourites) comes from a fifties' jive dance indigenous to South Carolina, and the innocuous tale found its way to Woolley via its writer-director Zelda Barron, who had made her first feature, *Secret Places*, in 1984 and was keen to follow it up with *Shag*. 'I liked it,' Woolley recalled, 'so I hawked it around everywhere. Columbia took it on, and then shut the door by putting it into turnaround [the term for a studio's decision to halt production of a film, which normally leads to the film being sold to another party]. By this time I found out there was another producer involved and other writers on the project. All these skeletons started falling out of the cupboard like there was no tomorrow, and I couldn't get the four to five million dollars we needed for nearly a year. It just wasn't clicking.'

The project finally 'clicked' with John Daly, one of Britain's most notorious ex-patriates in Hollywood. The son of a cockney ex-professional boxer and dockworker, Daly had founded a company called Hemdale in 1967, initially as a talent agency but later he moved the expanded operation to the States where he began by specialising in financing low-budget studio rejects. By 1987 he had struck serious success with *The Terminator* and Oliver Stone's Vietnam Oscar triumph *Platoon*.

The word maverick is too straightforward to describe Daly. Despite his smooth charm, he developed a reputation for extreme guile when it came to business deals, and this image was fortified by his grim-tempered partner Derek Gibson. To Woolley, Daly was the classic Englishman abroad. During his first meeting, the ex-pat renamed Woolley 'Stevie' and was soon waxing lyrical: 'Oh, how *is* Zelda? I'd *love* to do something with Zelda.' He rang Woolley the next morning to say that he liked the script and that Hemdale would do it.

'Great! That's terrific John. Let's do it,' Woolley panted. A few days later he met Derek Gibson, 'who is the man at Hemdale who says let's *not* do it. So I had the usual romantic liaison with the two of them, where it was like: "I love you, fuck off; I love you, fuck off." '

The exasperated Woolley would sit in Daly's office talking about the casting for the film. Just as they were starting to agree on young starlets like Bridget Fonda and Phoebe Cates, the phone would ring. Daly would smoothly answer the call, pause to listen, and say: 'Okay, sue me for *Platoon*,' and quietly replace the handset. He would then look up sweetly at Woolley and say: 'Now, where were we, Stevie?'

Hemdale, for several days after *Shag* had entered production in Myrtle Beach, South Carolina, withheld a letter of credit that would have allowed the production's cash to flow. Stuck in the middle of fifty miles of sandy central Atlantic seaboard beaches, Myrtle Beach's 40,000 populace expands to 500,000 during the summer months, and shooting at the height of the summer season was no easy task. Woolley was sweating away in 106 degrees, handling an American crew for the first time, while Gibson and Daly were playing their delaying tactics. Finally, the money started to roll east, and Hemdale left Woolley to get on with the shoot without further delays or interference.

Palace had promised Hemdale delivery of certain music soundtracks, and Gibson was determined to hold Palace to every track. Contractually, Hemdale could reject what the industry calls the 'delivery' of the film if Palace defaulted on any one song. Palace managed to get the rights to a decent soundtrack cleared, but the songs were not precisely the ones originally promised to Hemdale, and both Powell and Woolley were aware of the potential storm brewing.

Powell likes to consider himself an expert when it comes to delivering films. In the case of *Shag*, his boast is not idle. He managed to deliver the film on schedule to Hemdale without either Daly or Gibson knowing. Somehow he succeeded in seducing an approval signature from a Hemdale executive, and all the outstanding banking details related to the $4.2 million Hemdale contribution were quickly completed in Palace's favour. A week or so later, Gibson asked to see the film in London. After the screening, he asked Powell when Palace was going to deliver the film to Hemdale? Powell was astonished. How could Gibson not know that the film had been delivered? 'Well, Derek, I'm not sure. I'll look into it,' he hedged. The following morning Gibson realised what had happened and, furious, issued a writ for fraudulent delivery, despite the fact that Powell legally had done nothing wrong. The ensuing row took up considerable amounts of Palace's money and time, and delayed the release of the film.

'Hemdale tried to avenge themselves, arguing for all sorts of different music, and it just became a horrible stew,' Woolley said. Rather too late he recalled a joke about Daly which had been circulating at the time when the two men had first begun talking about *Shag*. It was a jest of which he should, perhaps, have taken more notice.

'There's a producer who comes to Daly's office for a meeting on a Monday and the receptionist asks him if he's come to see John. The producer says yes and she explains:

' "I'm terribly sorry, but Mr Daly died at the weekend."

' "Oh, my God! Really?" asks the producer, who sits down for about an hour and then proceeds to wander out of the office. But he comes back on the Tuesday, and once again says that he's come to a meeting with John Daly.

' "You must be kidding. He died at the weekend and the funeral's tomorrow," says the surprised receptionist. The producer continues to come back until the receptionist finally cracks:

' "This is fucking ridiculous! I mean, John Daly is dead. Dead! Dead! Dead! How many times do I have to tell you? Why do you keep coming back here?"

' "Just to hear you say that." '

When *Shag* was finally released in the UK in the summer of 1988, the critics were for once relatively generous. There were no blow jobs, the cars were driven at a suitable period pace, and the music left their ears intact. In a typical, inspired PR move, Richard Branson was thrown out of the premiere screening, attracting front page newspaper coverage. For Woolley, the whole 'I love you, fuck off' experience with Hemdale was further 'marred by the fact that this concoction designed for twelve-year-old girls was inexplicably given a 15 certificate by our deaf, dumb and blind film censors. They explained they found the title and dialogue obscene, but it was clearly a backlash against our winning that *Evil Dead* court case.' Despite this, *Shag* performed relatively well at the box office.

Throughout this period, Woolley left London further and further behind. He found a small apartment off Sunset Boulevard, hired a car and hustled his way into Hollywood. As he explained: 'My feeling after the *Absolute Beginners* reviews and reception was "What's the point? It's just too bloody hard making films in Britain." So I really had it in my blood at that point to go and live in America to see what I could achieve.'

Others recall Woolley's and Jordan's attitudes altering substantially for the worse post-*Mona Lisa*. A long-time collaborator, who works closely with both men to this day and admires them greatly, described Woolley's change in personality: 'Steve went AWOL after *Mona Lisa*. He became very arrogant, and both he and Neil got caught up in the American thing. Like most British and European people, they believed it when the Americans said that they were the best thing since sliced bread. You don't realise that Hollywood is saying that to everybody until it doesn't want to know any longer, and I really think Steve was unsettled during this period.'

Woolley's and Jordan's continued collaboration resulted in 1988 in *High Spirits* which starred Peter O'Toole, Steve Guttenberg and Daryl Hannah. Jordan came up with the idea while growing bored with the lack of activity on his epic about Michael Collins, the Irish political activist who died in 1922 at the age of thirty-two, which was failing to go anywhere at Warner Brothers. The film had the support of David Puttnam, but Warner Brothers were dragging their heels, when suddenly it was announced that Michael Cimino – director of the infamous *Heaven's Gate* – was also making a bio-pic of the Michael Collins story. (Later, Kevin Costner also added to the list of Collins projects, but Jordan finally beat off the competition when in 1995 he went into production with Warner Brothers and Geffen Pictures, with Woolley as his producer.)

Jordan and Woolley were having one of their 'creative' late night sessions – which tended to result in the two men bonding or in a major row – in a pub in London, when Jordan told Woolley about a man who arranged tours around Ireland, and guaranteed his guests that they would encounter ghosts. Jordan saw the story as a potential *Whisky Galore!* comedy, and Woolley thought it was a hilarious idea. They both agreed that the concept could be developed into a decent little film.

As is so often the case when dealing with Hollywood, 'little' soon became large. Steve Sohmer, a senior Columbia Pictures executive made contact with Woolley while he was embroiled in *Absolute Beginners*, and a meeting was set up to bounce around ideas for future projects. Sohmer was attracted to the *High Spirits* idea, partly because he and his wife holidayed in Ireland every summr, and he put the project into development at Columbia as a kind of Irish 'Ghost O'Busters'.

As part of the research for the film, American co-writer Michael McDowell, who had been involved in Tim Burton's *Beetlejuice*, went to Ireland for a meeting with Woolley and Jordan. Woolley hired a limousine, and the three of them went off for four days, staying in a different rock-star-inhabited castle each night.

Within days of Jordan and McDowell delivering their script, Sohmer had moved jobs within Columbia, and his former position was filled by Puttnam. Woolley explained, 'I hadn't had a great relationship with David in the early years, because Palace had trodden on a lot of toes to get films made, and I think David's was certainly a toe we trod on – if not by me then certainly by Julien Temple, who in one American article had suggested that he be hung from the lamp-posts in Wardour Street.'

So Woolley knew the film would not get made at Columbia, and asked Puttnam quickly to put the project into turnaround. 'David was very good to us, because he read it straightaway and gave it back to us, explaining that it was the kind of film he was never going to make at the studio. We were going for a broad, very vulgar comedy, and one doesn't apply vulgarity to David. That's not his forte.'

By this stage, Woolley was into the swing of Hollywood. 'I felt cool about the whole place. I wasn't phased at all that Arnold Schwarzenegger would be sitting at the other table. Then, one day, I went to see this guy called Wafic Said at the Beverly Hills Hotel to talk about raising money for *High Spirits*. I suggested that he followed Kerry and me in his car to the restaurant, because he didn't know the way. I'm in the rental car when suddenly this huge Rolls Royce comes up behind us, flashing its lights, and suddenly I lost it.

'For the first time I thought what am I doing in the middle of Beverly Hills, completely out of my league, while there's this man behind me with all this money. I'm driving around Hollywood having a crisis, wondering who I was and completely forgetting where the restaurant was.'

Finally Woolley's rental car and the Rolls made it to the restaurant. Surrounded by three young women, Sayeed proceeded to order the most expensive wine on the list, and gave the waiter a hundred dollar bill for the drinks at the bar, except he actually parted with $200 as the notes in the new roll stuck together. He proceeded nonchalantly to explain that he could help Palace do the film for about $12 million, but Woolley held out, knowing that the wildly expensive script Jordan and McDowell had recently presented was going to need at least $5 million more than the millionaire's offer.

*High Spirits* eventually ended up at Vision PDG, a company run by Mark Damon, a sharp operator and clever salesman of films around the world. However, Vision and the film's other co-financiers insisted on various rewrites, which were tricky to engineer given Woolley's absence in South Carolina on *Shag*, and Jordan's irritation at ever having to change his script. Jordan had become suspicious of Woolley's intentions for *High Spirits*, and the producer's tendency to become distracted by his commitments to other writers and directors.

Woolley flew straight from the set of *Shag* to Ireland to contend with the production's mounting politics and a soaring special effects budget. One extravagance which infuriated Woolley was a talking horse's head, costing £150,000 which, in the final cut, appeared for only two seconds.

Although Woolley is deeply loyal to Jordan, and stressed that the film did very well for Palace at the UK box office and subsequently on video, he was personally disappointed with it. 'In the end it fell between American *Airplane* style of humour and broad comedy, and wasn't really about the little bunch of lovable Irish guys we'd envisioned at the start. Neil was in a really intense mood, and didn't want to talk to anyone on the film except me. The whole thing ended up a bad joke.'

Jordan experienced a deeply frustrating time when it came to editing the film. The main problem was that the film's American investors were in a desperate hurry to get it into the cinemas. 'The thing got mangled,' Jordan explained to the movie magazine *Empire* one year after the film's release. 'It was previewed in America before it was finished and the audience were predictably confused, so it was recut. Those previews were used as a pretext to make a different film to what I'd intended, and everybody's perspective got lost in the process.'

Steve Grant agreed with Woolley's and Jordan's assessment of *High Spirits* in *Time Out*, 'This dreadful movie carries on the love affair between Ireland and Hollywood with a vengeance, beginning as a tribute to fifties' flea-bag theatre, continuing as a banal commercial for the joys of Celtic rural life, and ending as a cross between *Beetlejuice*, *Cymbeline* and *The Quiet Man* ... It's a complete turkey.'

Jordan is now even more circumspect about *High Spirits*, stating bluntly that he is not a strong director of comedy, and that he should never have made the film. Unfortunately, after *High Spirits* he went straight on to make *We're No Angels*, a $30 million light comedy written by David Mamet and starring Robert De Niro and Sean Penn. Jordan blamed *We're No Angels*' reception and box office failure on the critics and on the studio's ineffectual marketing. He was bitterly disappointed by his first big brush with Hollywood and it was to take all of Woolley's determination and established trust with the Irish film-maker to woo him back into the Palace fold.

CHAPTER EIGHT

# Scandal

The famous picture of Christine Keeler, her legs wrapped around a chair, made a striking marketing poster and Palace's copy down one side was equally intriguing: 'In 1960 Christine Keeler met Mandy Rice-Davies at a London cabaret club. She was eighteen, Mandy sixteen. Three years later they brought down the British Government . . . This is their story.' It did not take long for Harvey Weinstein, the bull-like co-chairman of Miramax, to decide that *Scandal* was a film for his company.

Powell had got to know the Weinstein brothers in the mid-eighties, when Bob and Harvey had co-directed an inauspicious hotel rock romance, *Playing For Keeps*. The brothers were having difficulties clearing the music rights for tracks by Led Zeppelin and other artists, when Powell struck up a conversation with Harvey at the Petit Carlton bar in Cannes. Powell's considerable experience in the music business and his ability to clear music rights on Palace's films impressed the former rock promoter.

The Weinsteins' relentless passion and energy stemmed directly from their father, Max. A diamond cutter from Queens, New York, Max staunchly believed that 'No' always meant 'Yes', and instilled in his two sons a strong sense of self-belief. He would take the two boys to the cinema every Saturday, while Miriam, their mother, would go to the hairdresser.

From infancy, Harvey was considerably larger than his brother, and would take advantage of his size. Awaking in the middle of the night, thirsty for a drink, he would apparently reach over and shake his younger brother, saying: 'Bob! Bob! You awake? I'm real thirsty. I wanna drink of Coke. But you're smaller than me so you go geddit.' This apocryphal tale illustrates the brothers' relationship and respective roles within Miramax. Harvey huffs and puffs from the front, while Bob runs around chasing the details on the deals.

In the early 1970s, Harvey moved into promoting rock concerts in Buffalo, upstate New York, and even served some time as a PA to the manager of the Rolling Stones. Bob ran a local cinema that the brothers, together with a partner, had bought. The search for films to screen at their cinema introduced the two brothers to film distribution and in 1979 they launched their own distribution company, Miramax, named after their parents. The company's first film, acquired at the Cannes Film Festival, was *The Secret Policeman's Other Ball*. In true Miramax style, they created their own cut by merging the original film with parts of the sequel. Harvey's penchant for editing films after the director's cut but prior to their film's cinema release later brought him the nickname 'Harvey Scissorhands'. *The Secret Policeman's Other Ball* was a North American art-house hit, and Miramax was on its way.

It was not long before Palace and Miramax realised how much they had in common. As Powell explained, 'The bonding was immediate. Harvey was really adventurous and into making a bang. If we saw a film or a project and we liked it, neither of the companies would worry about whether anybody else thought it was any good. Harvey is a great believer that sex, drugs and rock 'n' roll shouldn't only be the province of the rock business.'

Both companies firmly held the belief that films perceived as 'arty' should not be marketed with kid gloves and that press coverage, beyond critical reaction, was an essential tool for marketing smaller films.

Unlike the big Hollywood studios, Miramax ran on gut instinct and keeping the bills down. In the early years, Bob and Harvey would write all the campaign copylines themselves, rarely delegating any creative jobs. Staff would either last minutes or many years under the belligerent brothers, depending on their ability to produce the required goods in double-quick time. Unorthodox, risk-taking, Miramax was Palace's New York equivalent: even Harvey's scruffy clothes mirrored Powell's.

Woolley also recognised the similarities between the two companies, but it took longer for him to cultivate a relationship with the brothers, and in particular with Harvey. The producer gradually developed a close bond with Weinstein, learning to appreciate the big man's 'brusque, boyish kind of charm', and admiring his 'incredible attention to detail and huge ambition'. Woolley recognised in this enormous, larger-than-life man a person who could make things happen. Others, however, were not so generous in their appraisals. Despite paying tribute to Harvey's marketing instincts in a 1994 *New York* magazine profile, Robert Redford claimed that 'You don't want to close your eyes around Harvey. You don't know what article of clothing will be missing.' Harvey loves this kind of press. He even tells stories against himself, recounting how Daniel Day-Lewis turned to him during the release of *My Left Foot* and commented in exasperation: 'There's only one part of you that works Harvey – the ability to pick scripts and pick movies. Otherwise, you're a complete disaster as a person.'

'Harvey's likely to watch a movie at two in the morning, because all his meetings have run over, and you've ended up paying the projectionist an extra two hundred quid to stay on', Woolley explained, giving an insight into how Harvey Weinstein lives and works. 'He'd arrive, say "Great Steve, let's see it", and give you notes at 4.30 in the morning and then go off and get up for an eight a.m. breakfast meeting the next morning.'

The bond between the two companies grew so strong that Miramax was directly involved in ten films Powell and Woolley produced after *Scandal*.

*Scandal* had been rejected in the UK many times during its six years of gestation. Keeler's and Rice-Davies's friendship with society osteopath Stephen Ward, and the events which eventually led to the fall of Secretary of State John Profumo, made an exciting, anti-Establishment story, which, as one commentator explained later, 'had it all – tarts, titles, tits'.

The concept had been brought to Palace by their friend Joe Boyd, the former sub-licensee of the Scala Cinema, and already a prolific independent record producer. A clean-cut and verbose enthusiast, the American-born Boyd had thoroughly researched the story with the brash, rebellious Australian screenwriter Michael Thomas. Both men were keen to rile the British Establishment by highlighting the hypocrisy surrounding the trial of Ward – who ended up committing suicide after being found guilty of living via 'immoral earnings' – and the unjust treatment of Keeler. According to Thomas, 'Christine has been taking the punishment for many years for what happened, and I really wanted this movie to redeem her.'

They had envisaged the story as a television mini-series, and Boyd had gone to considerable lengths and expense to gain Christine Keeler's and Mandy Rice-Davies's legal co-operation. Yet, despite both men's hard work, the project, like the events of two decades previously, did not win favour with the British Establishment.

Jonathan Powell, then head of series and serials at the BBC, had funded the writing of two of the three mini-series scripts, although setting *Scandal* up as three ninety-minute films for Palace was not proving easy. Thomas had prepared a detailed treatment for the scripts, and Boyd met Woolley on the roof of Palace's video shop on Soho's Berwick Street to discuss this.

Drinking beer on the sunny roof terrace, Woolley told Boyd, 'I really don't think this script works, Joe. We should consider getting another writer in.'

'Rubbish! I totally disagree,' Boyd retorted.

'Well, we should send it to Stephen Frears anyway,' Woolley bullishly continued. Boyd felt that Frears's *My Beautiful Laundrette* and *The Hit* were fine indications of the director's ability, but insisted that Thomas should be given a chance to polish the treatment before the work was sent to the director. If Frears liked it, then Thomas would remain the sole writer; if he did not, Woolley could bring in another writer to work on the project.

A few weeks later Boyd brought Thomas's revised pages to Palace, only to discover from Woolley's assistant that the producer had already sent the old treatment to Frears. Frears loved it, even without the changes, but, despite becoming involved in the project for a short while, he was heavily in demand and soon moved on to direct *Dangerous Liaisons*.

The BBC's support did not last long. When Jonathan Powell put the project to his board for production support, it turned out that internal BBC memos had been issued banning the production of any documentary or drama concerning the Profumo Affair. Politicians, learning of the project, were incensed. Roy Jenkins on BBC Radio Four's *Start The Week* said that he would be shocked and horrified if the film were made. Channel 4 turned the proposal down on the grounds of alleged bad taste, adding *Scandal* to its list of Palace productions, including *The Company of Wolves* and *Mona Lisa*, in which it had declined to invest at pre-production stage.

Following the BBC's rejection, Palace was desperate for a source of money to keep it in development. According to Powell, Palace was once again out on a limb, for by 1985 they had spent nearly £200,000 on the project. Desperate to pull some money in, Powell found himself pitching the idea to Brian Cowgill, a brusque Yorkshireman and the head of Robert Maxwell's expanding television interests. An unusually generous deal was agreed and a sum of £184,319 was advanced to Palace, allowing the company to keep pushing *Scandal* towards production.

According to Powell, 'Maxwell was wonderful to do business with.' Joe Boyd, however, has a different recollection of the Maxwell connection. According to him, getting money out of the big man was not so 'wonderfully' easy. Months passed with no agreement in place before Powell and Boyd finally found themselves sitting in Cowgill's office ready to do a deal. As the meeting came to a close, Powell uttered the fateful: 'Who's your solicitor?'

'John Stutter of Harbottle & Lewis,' Cowgill replied.

'That's funny, he's ours too. Who's going to instruct him?'

'Well, I'm not sure. What do you want to do, Nik?'

Keen to save legal costs, Powell said that, given that Stutter's contracts were always clear, precise and straightforward, Cowgill could go ahead and instruct him for Maxwell.

Boyd was horrified. 'From having this wonderfully fierce defender paid by Palace and on our side, we were suddenly locked in this room with what seemed like a rabid Doberman. In order to prove who he was being paid by, Stutter turned on us with sharpened fangs and proceeded to rip us limb from limb over the contract. We were so desperate for the money that we signed this onerous contract with all these horrible clauses.'

In the mid-1980s, Maxwell fancied himself as a future television mogul, and had organised a partnership of French, German and Italian broadcasting companies to provide programming for a European cable and satellite network. He was spotted gadding about on yachts at Cannes with his partners from France and Italy. He also let everyone in the City know that he was doing a film about the Profumo Affair. His bombastic boasting was met, however, with a very negative reaction, and his interest in the project gradually waned. Powell never spoke directly to the big man about *Scandal*, although he once caught sight of him through an open office door. 'He was smoking a cigar and bollocking someone down the phone in typical Captain Bob style,' Powell recalled, adding as an afterthought that 'he was of course very fat'.

Although Woolley was theoretically enthusiastic about *Scandal* as a television series, he was the first to suggest that Powell's and Boyd's energies would be better spent packaging the project as a movie. With the television mini-series option going nowhere, Boyd relented. However, before setting the project up as a feature film, Palace had to get out of the deal with Maxwell, a proposition that made Boyd 'sweat bullets'.

'The only way we ended up making *Scandal* as a film was because the vigilant John Stutter was on holiday when we put the project into turnaround,' Boyd explained. 'We got Cowgill to sign the documents, and I am sure Stutter would never have let that happen.' Incredibly, the turnaround contract included no clause about Maxwell being paid any share of the project's budget or eventual profits if it went into production through other means. Most private money for film development comes at a high premium; however, in this case, Maxwell had to let the project go without a fuss, because under Powell's contract there was a revision clause which ensured that the project would return to Palace if Maxwell did not come up with the finance within a specified time limit. 'It wasn't such a bad deal, as we got nearly £200,000 towards development *and* we got the film back without any further obligations,' Powell pointed out.

No longer relying on one major backer, *Scandal* needed a tangled web of supporters if it was to go into production. Palace was handling the difficulties of putting together the company's first fully packaged film with typical gutsy determination, but there were two glaring omissions. First, the film needed to be sold in North America prior to shooting. Second, if Palace were to have any chance of closing the finance for the project, *Scandal* needed to find quickly a director with whom financiers could feel comfortable.

Powell had received a call from Tim Corrie, an agent with Peters, Fraser & Dunlop, suggesting that he meet a young director, Michael Caton-Jones. The Scottish-born son of a miner from Broxburn, midway between Glasgow and Edinburgh, had set out for London at the age of seventeen. He had been a punk, living in a Stoke Newington squat and working initially in theatre before going to film school, and his reputation was rising. Frears, who had taught him at the National Film School, had suggested to Palace that Caton-Jones was a very good new bet.

The young film-maker was in a hurry to make his name. He had already completed a short award-winning comedy film, *Liebe Mutter*; a project called *The Riveter* which Channel 4 had admired; and a television drama mini-series, *Brond*. He also had invaluable first-hand experience of Palace at work, having shot the student film of the making of *Absolute Beginners* (and had no problem recalling how little Palace had paid him for his work).

Powell and Caton-Jones hit it off, although the director aired some strident criticisms of the original three-part mini-series script.

His meeting with Woolley and Boyd, however, did not go so well. As Caton-Jones walked into the Groucho Club, he thought to himself, 'Well, obviously they know I'm keen, otherwise I wouldn't be here. So they don't want me to blow smoke up their arses and tell them how wonderful the thing is. I'll tell them what I think is wrong with it.'

Caton-Jones criticised the script with gusto. Nothing escaped his attention, as, in his thick Scottish accent, he hammered into the script, scene by scene, character by character. Woolley in particular was stunned. As far as he was concerned, *Scandal* was a very strong project. Who did this young director think he was, criticising Woolley as if he were a first-timer and telling him that *Scandal* was rubbish?

Following the meeting, Palace, unsurprisingly, thought that Caton-Jones hated the project. Fortunately, a mutual friend explained to the young director that he ought to ring Woolley up and sort out the misunderstanding, which Caton-Jones decided was worth a shot. The call to Woolley went well and the mistrust dissipated after a second meeting, when a healthy compromise began to take shape.

The mini-series script needed to be brought into line with a feature film screenplay, so Caton-Jones met Thomas, who was understandably disappointed that Palace could not get the mini-series on air. Over the drink, Thomas said: 'Look, mate, I don't know how we're going to turn this thing into a film.' They ran through some ideas, and decided that if the new version were to work, it would need to focus on Christine Keeler's and Stephen Ward's stories. Caton-Jones went off to dig out the heart of the story and came up with a 180-page version for Thomas to grapple with.

The event that really bonded Woolley and Caton-Jones was a seven-hour session in a rented office in Poland Street, where the two men went through the script, scene by scene. 'We were talking about the guts of the film, not how to con people into putting money in or how to get a celebrity cast,' Caton-Jones explained. 'Steve's terribly, terribly bright. After that I had the most tremendous respect for him, because of his smartness and application, and that session really cemented it for me. It was how I always imagined it should be.'

Like Caton-Jones, Thomas became deeply impressed by the producer's ability to 'see the script from the point of view of the mob, the audience for the film. He was always suggesting ideas and raising questions, but he understands that the best way a writer works is to make him go back to the script himself and want to try harder.'

Unlike some of Palace's former projects, *Scandal* was starting to benefit from some seriously committed development work from a creative foursome – the two producers, Woolley and Boyd, Thomas, the writer, and the director Caton-Jones. Once again, however, the financial side was taking more time to come together than the creative, and Caton-Jones decided to spend six months directing a BBC project. On his return, the hot young talent quickly became attached to a Working Title film set in Kenya, entitled *Jamie*, which was being produced by Palace-rival Tim Bevan. Caton-Jones even flew out to Kenya to check locations, and was becoming increasingly keen on *Jamie* being his first feature film.

When Powell and Woolley got wind of Caton-Jones's other project they hit the roof. All the painstaking development work was about to disintegrate in front of their eyes unless they kept their director on board. Powell dashed down to Corrie's office, and planted himself in the agency's reception area, refusing to leave until Corrie saw him about signing up Caton-Jones for *Scandal*. Instead of being able to play the two films against each other over a couple of weeks of negotiations, Corrie was forced into advising Caton-Jones to take the money that Palace was offering. Nevertheless, Corrie struck a tough deal, demanding that Palace put Caton-Jones on 'pay-or-play', which meant that the director had to be paid even if the film did not make it into production. This, of course, presented Powell and Woolley with a huge gamble: on the one hand they needed the director to be secured to *Scandal* if they were to clinch the final deals on the film; on the other hand, as Powell explained, 'it also meant we had to get the thing financed and made'.

Palace had already taken on so much risk that Woolley and Powell decided they might as well take the additional leap and sign Caton-

Jones up on pay-or-play. Promoting a first-time feature film director for a £3.2 million film may have fitted neatly into Palace's give-it-a-go ethos, but Powell admits that, if he had known what was lying ahead he 'probably would never have taken that step'.

In October 1987, Woolley and Powell had written a standard letter to many US potential partners outlining Palace's production plans for the coming year. They struck lucky with Cinecom, who rang back and expressed an interest in *Scandal*. Powell pitched the project to Cinecom at Milan's MIFED film market later that month, and a script was duly sent to America. Cinecom's chief, Amir Malin, soon rang to say that he wanted to buy the North American rights. Powell asked him to put in writing all the major terms, and on 3 December he received a letter from Cinecom offering $1.75 million for the film.

A few days later, Boyd happened to be in Powell's office when John Stutter telephoned. The lawyer had been approached by Cinecom to handle the negotiations on *Scandal*, and had rung to ask if Powell minded. Boyd could not believe what he heard. The thought of the brilliantly effective Stutter working against Palace for a second time was too much for the producer. He was fed up with Powell's desperate attempts to save money, and his refusal to put the lawyer on a retainer.

'Put Stutter on a retainer *now*, Nik!'

'Argh, hang on, Joe, I'm still talking . . .'

'I'll call Steve! I'm not leaving this office – I'm going to totally disrupt your day – I want this thing settled now!'

'All right, Joe, all right.'

On 1 March 1988, when Powell, Katy McGuinness, and Cinecom's Amir Malin, Bart Walker and Leon Faulk sat down for lunch at the American Film Market, negotiations had taken place but nothing was agreed or signed. Despite plenty of discussion about the script and proposed cast, the outstanding and considerable differences – including the precise method of payment from Cinecom, and the extent of the television rights the company would control – were not mentioned at that lunch. In a dedicated effort to clarify these sticking points, McGuinness spent two weeks chasing Walker, Cinecom's head of business affairs, who turned out to be somewhat elusive, cancelling two meetings in New York, the first due to a holiday, and the second due to sunstroke.

By this time Woolley – in classic 'I start and everyone catches up' mode – was close to going into pre-production on the film. If Palace were to avoid being severely damaged by the film, Powell had to nail down a North American deal within days.

Finally, a meeting at Cinecom's New York offices was held on the morning of 16 March. The outstanding problem was Cinecom's reluctance to provide a Letter of Credit – a letter from its bankers that guaranteed the money to be paid on delivery of the film – which from Powell and his bank Guinness Mahon's point of view was a necessity.

Malin had suggested that due to other business Guinness was handling for Cinecom, the bank would discount the advance without a Letter of Credit. This was not good enough for Powell. With the deal going nowhere, the Palace co-chairman turned round in mid-meeting and said:

'Well, Amir, there's only one way to resolve this. Let's call the banks and see if they need the LC?' Powell got on the line to find out that yes, Guinness would insist on an LC from Cinecom. Powell promptly rang Harvey Weinstein at Miramax from a different room and asked if he could drop into the Miramax offices that afternoon, adding, 'I've got something that might interest you.'

Miramax's offices were in midtown Manhattan on 34th Street. They were far worse than anything Palace had ever rented: a corridor, a few tiny, stinking, smoke-filled rooms, and a filthy naugahyde couch in such a poor state of repair that it made Powell's Soho sofa look luxurious.

'Look, Harvey, I've got this deal on *Scandal*, but I've got one problem,' Powell said.

'Get to the point, Nik,' Harvey snapped.

'They can't raise an LC.'

'No problem. Let's talk.'

The meeting started at four o'clock that afternoon. By midnight a deal had been hammered out with Miramax, backed by a Letter of

Credit, offering $2.35 million for North American rights. Powell went back to his hotel and, exhausted, immediately fell asleep.

At seven o'clock the next morning, Powell was awoken by a telephone call from Cinecom. He told them he had closed a deal elsewhere. All hell was let loose, with Walker screaming down the phone at Powell, claiming that a verbal agreement had been reached, and threatening legal action. However, Malin had left New York City for Long Island, a fact which, coupled with Cinecom's inability to provide an LC, put Powell in a relatively strong position. 'They ended up throwing their arms in the air and getting really upset, so I decided that the best thing I could do was get on a plane and get back to London,' Powell recalled. 'At the end of the day, I wasn't in the best moral position.'

Quite how Weinstein was going to take to the lively Caton-Jones was anybody's guess. Woolley set up a dinner at Joe Allen's restaurant in Covent Garden, where Caton-Jones launched into how he was planning on shooting the opening scene. 'I was using films to illustrate how it would look and feel, and I was really excited – galloping along in my thick Scottish vernacular – when it gradually dawned on me that Harvey could hardly understand a word I was saying.'

When Caton-Jones finally paused for breath, he looked down at the table. Surrounding Weinstein was a large bowl of ribs, a big hamburger, a vast plate of chips and two bottles of Budweiser. In between each mouthful, he would drag ferociously on a True Blue, his favourite brand of cigarette. In typically direct fashion, Caton-Jones blurted out:

'Listen to me, Harvey. I've only met you once, but you do yourself a favour . . . you shouldn't eat this shit. This stuff's going to kill you.'

Casting *Scandal* was a considerable challenge, with the role of Profumo presenting a typically British problem as many of the senior established male actors, fearful of endangering their chances of a knighthood, were deeply wary of the part. An afternoon brainstorming session at Wardour Mews led to Powell's unique offerings on the matter:

'Er . . . what about Jeremy Irons?'

'Oh, shut up, Nik,' Woolley replied.

'Well, er . . . Dickie Attenborough?'

'Just shut up!'

By this time Caton-Jones was giggling in the corner: it was clear that Palace had promised Miramax some 'names'. In the end, theatre star Ian McKellen signed up for the part. He was keen to be involved in an overtly anti-Establishment film and, having recently come out, thought that he had waved goodbye to any titles.

By Cannes 1988, Woolley still needed to fill the part of Mandy Rice-Davies, Keeler's frisky flat mate and pronouncer of the immortal line: 'Well, he would, wouldn't he?' when told that Lord Astor, also caught up in the scandal, had denied allegations of impropriety. Palace had looked at dozens of British actresses for the part, but none of them had 'that front . . . that total brashness, innocence, lack of terror that Mandy had', Woolley explained later.

After rejecting a host of girls, including Emily Lloyd, Amanda de Cadenet, Mandy Smith, Patsy Kensit and Jane Horrocks, Woolley focused on Bridget Fonda, who had worked with Palace on *Shag* the previous summer. Fonda, the daughter of Peter, niece of Jane and granddaughter of Henry, was in Cannes that year. She had read the script, liked the idea and felt confident about the part. Palace were so desperate to clinch the casting that they flew Fonda from Nice to London during the Festival in order to meet Caton-Jones. Fortunately, the meeting went well. Despite Fonda's chronic South London accent, Caton-Jones was convinced that the actress had the technical ability to pull the part off. Fonda also kept the Weinsteins happy, and the key role was tied down at the beginning of June, just days before shooting was set to start.

Meanwhile, Powell had done a considerable amount of work on the 'chain of title' (which specifies who owns the copyright in the screenplay), and had organised extensive insurance under a production policy known as 'errors and omissions', in case the production was sued for libel at a later stage. *Scandal* was moving towards the cameras with a creative and legal fusion often conspicuously absent in certain of Palace's previous productions.

By the time the film went into pre-production, Boyd, the primary producer during *Scandal*'s development, had voluntarily taken on the more distant role of executive producer, leaving Woolley fully in charge of the production during the shoot.

Caton-Jones cut an amusing figure during the early days of the shoot. He would turn up in shorts and trainers, with half the crew wondering if he was a messenger boy rather than the director. 'Michael was so young and callow, his hair still full of shampoo, and he really wanted to shove it to the English upper class,' Thomas recalled. 'What he was looking for was that redeeming emotional climax – when Ward says in court, "This simply isn't fair" – striking the right beat at the right moment. It redeems John Hurt's character and strikes at the thing you really respect about Britain – a tradition of decency that should allow even this sinful man to have a life again.'

Redemption was last thing on the British press's mind as *Scandal* rolled into production that summer. Lord Rees-Mogg, writing in the *Independent* on 7 July 1988, condemned the production, stating pompously: 'Obviously such a film is bound to defame many people, some of them still alive. It cannot tell the story without doing so.' In Profumo's defence, he added, 'It is no man's right to renew the agony of offences, years after they have been expiated.' Meanwhile, Jim Thompson, the Bishop of Stepney and a close friend of Profumo, happened to live in Tredegar Square, where one of *Scandal*'s key scenes was being shot. According to Caton-Jones, Thompson became aware of the film when *Scandal*'s catering truck blocked his residents' parking space. Rather than turn the other cheek, the bishop wrote to the square's residents, suggesting that they make as much noise as possible in an effort to disrupt production. The clergyman also wrote to Hurt and McKellen asking them to step down from the film. Caton-Jones, however, managed to intercept the letters, leaving the stars unbothered by such divine interventions. Thompson wrote to several newspapers dismissing the uncompleted film as 'celluloid rubbish', but, of course, all the publicity only further inflamed the press and public's interest.

Refreshingly uncluttered by such moral doubts, the British tabloid papers were drooling at the cast list, which, in addition to Joanne Whalley-Kilmer, Bridget Fonda, John Hurt and Ian McKellen, included Roland Gift, Leslie Phillips (as Lord Astor), and a cameo performance from Britt Ekland as Mariella Novotny, the orgy queen. Caton-Jones was even phoned late at night by Baz Bamigboye, the *Daily Mail*'s resourceful showbusiness reporter, who threatened to write inflammatory stories about the film unless the director gave him access to one of the key stars.

Controlling the media frenzy was the job of the luckless Angie Errigo. 'Steve let *Time Out* have the press pictures from *Scandal*'s orgy scene, which they cut up and plastered all over the magazine, making it look like a porn movie,' she explained. On 27 July, the day the *Time Out Scandal* special appeared, written with great panache by Steve Grant, Errigo had to go down to the set to face the music. 'From Michael to John Hurt to Joanne, through to the camera operator and the make-up department, I had become public enemy number one. They all hated my guts.'

Woolley later explained that the magazine had been mistakenly sent the raunchy photos, so he wrote a letter to the editor distancing the five-page spread from the production. 'I had to do that to keep the investors happy, though of course it was perfect for the film.'

*Time Out* was the least of Errigo's problems. She was repeatedly woken at three a.m. by the *News of the World* demanding access to the set, and constantly hounded by assistant directors in a state of panic.

'Angie, where the fuck are you? There's a photographer down here and we don't know where he's from.'

'Well, has anyone asked him?'

'No, you've got to deal with it.'

Errigo recalls one run-in over some publicity photos of Joanne Whalley-Kilmer, which needed the actress's approval before being dispatched to Miramax in New York. 'Steve was always the good guy, the Mr Sweety Pie with Joanne. He'd been calming her down after she'd disappeared into her trailer in tears over something, and he told me she couldn't be pressured into anything just then.'

The next thing Errigo got was Miramax on the line.

'Where're the photos, Angie? We've *got* to have the photos *now*!'

The pressure was too much for Errigo. In front of Harvey Weinstein, she threw herself over the hood of Woolley's BMW, and burst into hysterical tears.

'Hey, hey, Angie,' Weinstein soothed. 'Don't let 'em upset you. It's only a movie.'

When the recovered Errigo relayed Weinstein's incredible words across the Atlantic that evening, the Miramax employee was dumbfounded. 'What?' she screeched. 'Harvey said that? Mr Harvey Weinstein said it was *only* a movie?'

Later, Errigo managed to get a piece about Weinstein on the set of *Scandal* written up by the *New York Times*'s London correspondent. Weinstein was so proud of getting a story about himself and the film into America's most prestigious paper that he sent Errigo a huge bunch of flowers. 'Given that I'd worked at Palace for eight years by now, and the most they'd ever sent me was a pot plant after an accident, and even that was from one of the office girls, I was pretty impressed,' Errigo said. 'There're no flies on Harvey. He's got more class than either of those Palace boys ever had.'

Harvey Weinstein was so eager and proud to be involved in *Scandal* that his enthusiasm amazed the British crew. He would fly into the UK at very short notice, arriving on the set in his standard black Aertex T-shirt and stretched black trousers, carrying a plastic bag full of film scripts. Weinstein had recently observed the fuss Alan Parker's X-rated *Angel Heart* had created in the US, and made sure that Palace was contractually obliged to bring *Scandal* in as an X-rated film. Consequently, he insisted that he or his nominated deputy, Susan Salonika, was present during the sex scenes to make sure that the heat was turned on. From Caton-Jones's point of view, his arrival was irksome, for the director always liked to clear everyone off the set when a nude scene was being shot, in an effort to keep the actors happy.

According to Whalley-Kilmer's contract, the actress was allowed to consult the director on all issues of nudity, and, in any event, was not legally bound to perform any scenes which involved her revealing the front portion of her body from 'above the knees and below the waist'. As an insurance against any problems, Palace had included the right to use a double in her place.

Caton-Jones knew he had a problem with Whalley-Kilmer because she had been 'pretty nervous about showing her body. She'd recently married the actor Val Kilmer [hence her name-change to Whalley-Kilmer], and had got caught up in the American way of doing things.' When it came to shooting the swimming-pool scene – a crucial act, where Profumo first sets eyes on Keeler, who is naked – Caton-Jones was determined to make the shot as accurate and as dramatic as possible. The last thing he needed was Whalley-Kilmer getting cold feet and creating a continuity problem with a body-double.

The night of the swimming-pool shoot down in Wiltshire was nerve-racking for Caton-Jones, but he was confident he could encourage Whalley-Kilmer to do the shot. Most of the crew thought otherwise. Thomas, who was on set at that time, suddenly realised that her reticence 'had nothing to do with being a star. Joanne was actually scared to do it.' Nobody was making Caton-Jones's task any easier, especially Harvey Weinstein, who would keep sidling up to the director and insisting: 'Michael, you gotta get her to take her clothes off!'

Having said it would be fine on the morning of the shoot, and having agreed to rehearsals all day, at the last minute, after a phone call to America, the actress changed her mind.

'I can't do it, Michael, I just can't do it,' she said.

'That's really fucked me up, Joanne. Listen, all I can do is ask you to get out there and let me shoot you, because we can't come back.'

After shooting Whalley-Kilmer's face and making the most of the swimsuited star, Caton-Jones cleverly managed to save the scene. A long time wary of Whalley-Kilmer's letting him down, he had spotted a featured extra, Gloria, who, with dark hair, big brown eyes and a very similar physique, closely resembled Whalley-Kilmer. As an insurance policy, he had made sure that Gloria was hired to be around the set that evening.

As soon as Caton-Jones had finished with Whalley-Kilmer and she had been whisked off the set, out came the naked Gloria. The plucky dancer did everything Caton-Jones needed to complete the nude sequence.

Whalley-Kilmer – who was putty in Caton-Jones's hands after letting him down – returned later to help with a shot filmed in the swimming pool. As she dived in, her swimming costume slipped off. 'Her tits ended up on film anyway!' Caton-Jones laughed. 'Of course, I didn't use it, but it was hilarious.'

Woolley and his young director continued to forge a strong bond throughout the shoot. Unlike Caton-Jones, the producer would always look at the daily rushes each evening, and in the morning offer encouragement and confirm that the rushes were fine. 'Steve oversees very well,' Caton-Jones professed. 'He's really good at going around and just lifting people.'

Every Friday night Woolley would take Caton-Jones out on the town, get him seeringly drunk, and let him rant about the film. Letting off steam was a crucial part of the film-making. 'I was on a mission to explain,' Caton-Jones recalled, slipping into the Friday night proselytising he and Woolley had enjoyed. 'A mission to make people fucking feel what they should have felt at the time that this poor bastard Ward was shafted. Nobody lifted a finger, and it was all because of these fucks who are still running the country today.'

Halfway through the shoot, Woolley made Caton-Jones look at a rough assemblage of everything he had shot. The bare reality of the assembled footage was too much for Caton-Jones, who was reduced to tears. Woolley gently calmed the young director down, explaining, 'Don't worry, I just think you should see where we are. Then we can see where things should go from here.' Once the shock was over, Caton-Jones simply redoubled his efforts.

John Hurt was also having a difficult shoot. Shortly before the film had started, he had split up with his wife. The emotional upset was too much for the actor to bear.

'John had gone straight out on the drink,' Caton-Jones explained sympathetically. 'He turned up to shoot late, without his hair parted. Here was my leading man, and he was as miserable as

Nik Powell (left) with
his partner Stephen Woolley.

Nik Powell with Sam Raimi at the
Cannes Film Festival, 1983, where
*The Evil Dead* was screened.

Neil Jordan and Steve Woolley during the shooting of *High Spirits*.

*From left to right*: Nik Powell, Steve Woolley, Bernie Kingham of ITC, Neil Jordan and Chris Brown during the signing of the £2 million *Company of Wolves* deal.

Steve Woolley playing in the company of a wolf on set.

*Top left to right*: Chris Brown, Steve Woolley, Julien Temple.
*Bottom left to right*: David Bowie and Eddie O'Connell during the
troubled shoot of *Absolute Beginners*.

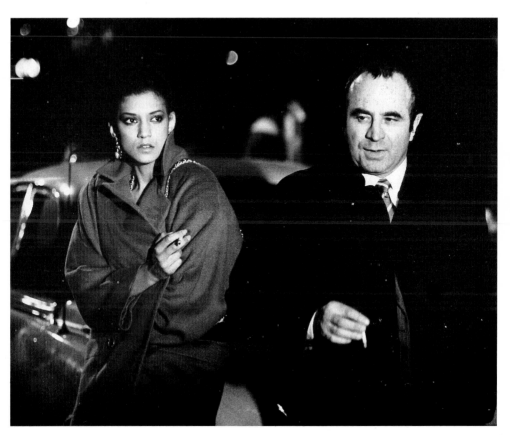

Cathy Tyson and Bob Hoskins in Neil Jordan's *Mona Lisa*, one of Palace's major hits.

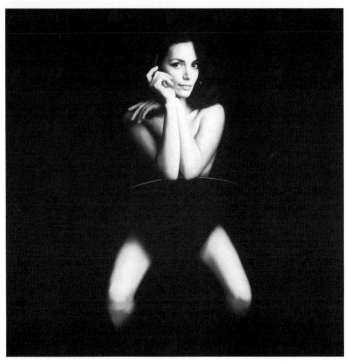

*Scandal*: Joanne Whalley-Kilmer as Christine Keeler.

*Left to right*: Michael Caton-Jones, director of *Scandal*, Eddie Collins, camera operator, and Steve Woolley just before their walk-on roles in *Scandal*.

Christine Keeler (Joanne Whalley-Kilmer) at the centre of
the infamous *Scandal* orgy scene.

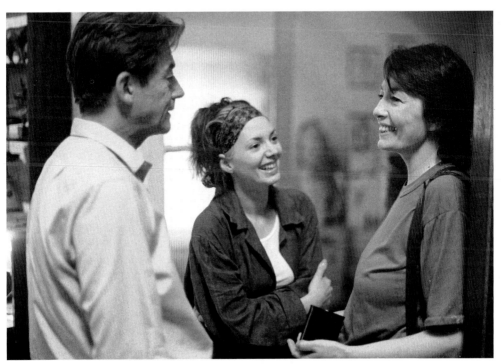

*Left to right*: John Hurt, Joanne Whalley-Kilmer and Christine Keeler
on the set of *Scandal*.

*News of the World*,
5 March 1989.

*Scandal*'s press
conference at the
Cannes Film Festival,
1989. *Left to right*:
John Hurt, Michael
Caton-Jones, Michael
Thomas and Steve
Woolley.

Harvey (left) and
Bob Weinstein,
co-chairmen of
Miramax. The
brothers collaborated
with Powell and
Woolley on eleven
movies, starting with
*Scandal* and including
the record-breaking
release of *The
Crying Game*.

Jaye Davidson refused to cut his hair for the part of Dil in *The Crying Game*; instead he wore a wig.

Jaye Davidson and Miranda Richardson in Neil Jordan's breakaway success, *The Crying Game*.

Stephen Rea (Fergus) confronts 'the soldier's wife'.

Ripping fun on the set of *Interview with the Vampire*.
*Left to right*: Redmond Morris, Tom Cruise, Steve Woolley and Neil Jordan.

Bittersweet success: Nik Powell and Steve Woolley collecting awards
for *The Crying Game* just months after Palace's collapse.

fucking sin. His pride was in tatters, and he hadn't really understood the point of his character by this stage either. When actors are insecure they start to pick on everything else.' Caton-Jones tried to build up the actor's confidence with constant praise, but found his patience sorely tested by his lead star.

Thomas recalled how 'Caton-Jones was having to put his [Hurt's] words on the dinner plates and the cutlery because he was so pissed'. Hours were being lost because of Hurt's unfortunate state.

About a fortnight into the shoot, Caton-Jones's American personal assistant, Jo Dalton, visited Hurt to give him a script. The two of them talked for a while, then went out to dinner, and within hours had fallen in love with one another. Hoping to take advantage of this budding relationship, Woolley and Caton-Jones took Dalton to one side and told her: 'Forget about looking after Michael. Here's a car. It's all yours, but you have to keep John out of the pub and get him on to the set sober every morning. Stick with him every minute of the day.'

Thomas recalls how hard the actor still found the shoot. 'I had John on his knees hugging my legs in floods of tears, saying he couldn't do a scene. Then he'd get up and do it, which is the brave thing that you've got to respect. Steve had diagnosed a very good solution to the problem and Jo worked like a bomb.' Everyone's hard work resulted in two happy outcomes: Hurt's performance was tremendous; and he and Dalton were married the following year and subsequently had two children.

Towards the end of the summer of 1988, *Scandal* was completed and Joe Boyd returned to work on the film. Boyd and Woolley had amicably agreed that due to his busy record company schedule, Boyd would be an executive producer on the film, like Powell, rather than co-produce it with Woolley. In addition to helping deal with the music clearances, Boyd took an interest in the film's editing that autumn. Harvey Weinstein also took a keen interest and demanded certain minor voice-over alterations – such as changing 'Pimm's' to 'gin and tonic' – but, ominously, he also wanted more substantial editing changes for the North American release.

Woolley, Boyd and Caton-Jones, who, due to interest charges on the film's financing, had been under great time pressure to edit and complete the film, flew out to New York to discuss Weinstein's proposed changes. Huddled together over a tiny video screen in Miramax's cramped offices, the men agonised over the film line by line. 'It was an absolute nightmare,' Boyd recalled. 'Harvey wanted a huge chunk of the second half of the movie taken out because he thought it would confuse the American audience. We had to fight, fight and fight.'

While trying to calm the quick-to-anger Boyd, Woolley had to persuade Weinstein not to re-cut and downplay the film's political climax. After Weinstein had capitulated or compromised on all but a couple of major sticking-points, he suddenly lost his temper and erupted in a classic, manufactured 'Harvey temper tantrum'.

'Fuck you, guys! If you insist on this stuff staying in, I'm releasing the film with no fucking advertising,' Weinstein bellowed, slamming the office door behind him.

None of the Weinstein–Palace arguments had dealt with the two-minute sex scene, which, as far as Miramax was concerned, had to remain graphically intact for the film's American release. In late April 1989, however, the Motion Picture Association of America awarded *Scandal* an X-rating. Such a rating signals commercial death, as seventy-five per cent of US newspapers will not accept advertisements for X-rated films, and the majority of cinemas are contractually prevented from screening them. Weinstein, however, planned to fight it and benefit from the increased publicity as a result. Although the orgy scene had got past the British film censors, the MPAA was demanding some two-seconds worth of skin and flesh tucks if the film was to drop to the desirable R-rating, which allows adults of seventeen years or more to see it.

After much legal haggling, Miramax agreed to substitute two previously unseen seconds of film for the offending original, allowing Weinstein to trumpet that the film was showing in America in the 'uncut' version. The new footage was, according to Woolley, shots of 'Christine gazing gooey-eyed at a naked black man in place of a bit of dry humping'.

Palace had obtained the rights to use the famous legs-around-a-chair shot of Keeler as one of their key marketing posters (unfortunately, it was later rejected by London Underground on the grounds that Keeler was a 'convicted criminal'). Weinstein, however, was not content to use the old photograph. He wanted Miramax to use a photo of Whalley-Kilmer in the same position. When she refused to pose, Weinstein threatened, 'Joanne, if you don't do the picture then I'm gonna do it with full breasts with a lookalike, and nobody will ever know it's not you. But if you do it, I'll make sure it's really tasteful, and we won't show any breasts or anything, and it'll look great. So whaddaya wanna do?' Whalley-Kilmer capitulated.

Palace's handling of the film's UK release was exemplary. With the exception of the *Time Out* photo fiasco, Palace had managed to limit gossip and exposure: the public had been primed but not overexposed to the film. In November 1988, special screenings were held for prominent selected critics in a deliberate attempt to gauge their reactions before the ensuing publicity bombardment could interfere with judgement. The tactic worked. In a favourable and lengthy article entitled 'Profumo: morality play for today', in the *Evening Standard* on 5 December 1988, Alexander Walker wrote that the film 'shows the aristocracy and Her Majesty's Government letting its pants down as well as its hair . . . [and] shows especially the change in the social climate which effectively abolished the distinction between celebrity and notoriety. After 1963, anybody could be famous for anything.'

In preparation for the release, Palace invested in some detailed market research. As Robert Mitchell, the company's new marketing recruit from Warner Brothers explained: 'Instead of doing the typical Palace-type research, which was to get anyone who would come for free – and then ask them to fill in our dodgy questionnaire which everyone returned with coffee stains, this time we did it properly.'

A tracking study revealed that while awareness was massive in all groups, the film still was not appealing to the crucial eighteen- to twenty-four-year-old market. Many of the subsequent posters and television advertisements were designed to appeal to that youth audience who were attracted by the Pet Shop Boys trailers which were cut from a Palace pop video directed by Caton-Jones. The guided marketing campaign worked, and eighteen- to twenty-four-year-olds piled into cinemas to watch the film.

The main body of publicity was geared towards the twelve weeks leading up to the world première at the Odeon Leicester Square. The gala screening, in aid of the Terrence Higgins Trust, created chaos in Leicester Square. The huge crowds blocked the cinema entrance, forcing stars to jump out of their cars and walk across the square. The Fleet Street snappers had a field day, and the following morning's front pages were splashed with pictures of the event. An intoxicated Woolley and Caton-Jones finally went to sleep at one o'clock the following afternoon, having read the *Scandal*-saturated newspapers at the Savoy with satisfied glee.

*Scandal* opened on the same day as the Dustin Hoffman and Tom Cruise hit, *Rain Man*, and promptly proceeded to outgross it. Hoffman was so astonished at being displaced by a small British film that he rang his LA agent to find out where the new Caton-Jones 'wonderboy' came from.

Palace employees recall standing with Woolley and Caton-Jones outside the Odeon Leicester Square during these opening days, thinking: 'This is it. This is what the movie business is all about,' as they watched the endless crowds queueing up for *Scandal* tickets.

Marshalling a prints (i.e. copies of the film for distribution) and advertising budget of around £400,000, Daniel Battsek and Robert Mitchell soon opened the film on 215 screens nationwide. Television advertisements were deliberately placed in news bulletins, targeting audiences who would probably be interested in the factually based social and political story. Ironically, advertisements within days of the film's release during ITV's *News at Ten* coincided with the Pamella Bordes affair, a scandal of a somewhat similar nature to the Profumo affair.

The six-year *Scandal* gamble had more than paid off. After ten days, the film's box-office receipts totalled £2.25 million, more than *Dangerous Liaisons* and *The Accused* had taken in their first few weeks. *Scandal* marked a zenith in Powell's and Woolley's fortunes at Palace. Here was a complex, ambitious project that the company had been able to exploit to the full. While much of the drive and inspiration behind the film's journey to the screen came from Boyd, Thomas, and Caton-Jones, Boyd later pointed out that Woolley 'very much came into his own during the making of the film', and that *Scandal* could never have happened without Powell's and Woolley's unflagging efforts.

The box-office takings from North America and the UK alone came to more than $15 million. The fact that Boyd, Thomas and Caton-Jones received their fees but no additional profits from the proceeds demonstrates how hard it can be to make money from films. According to Thomas, 'It looked like we couldn't fail to make money from *Scandal*, but somehow we did fail . . .' Caton-Jones took a fairly philosophical view on the matter, knowing that every independent distributor uses accounting techniques that tend to minimise the profits paid out.

Boyd, who has studied the accounts in detail, stressed that he was 'completely satisfied that all the monies from *Scandal* have been properly credited. The film has broken even – no small feat – and once deferments are paid, future income will be divided between the participants. Nik and Steve were always straight and fair with me, and I would trust them with any verbal or written agreement in the future.' Some investors, such as British Screen, did succeed in recouping their money. How much Palace put into the production is not clear, but the film gave both the company and its co-chairs a huge boost in the UK and around the world.

*Scandal* marked the beginning of a very fruitful relationship between the Weinstein brothers, Powell and Woolley, and brought together, in Thomas, Caton-Jones, Woolley and Powell, a team who continue to combine their creative talents. In late 1995, the film-makers came together again to make Andrew Davies's *B Monkey*.

Above all, *Scandal* was a hit. To paraphrase the famous dictum of Harold Macmillan, the Tory Prime Minister whose government fell shortly after the Profumo Affair, Palace was to 'never to have it so good' again.

# CHAPTER NINE

# Highly Geared

Some mornings Nik Powell would put on a tracksuit and trainers, and start what he called his 'three-park run' – through Hyde Park, Green Park and St James's – pacing his way doggedly up to Soho. On other days, he would walk down the road to the corner and catch the bus into town. Armed with a tattered BOAC airline bag stuffed with papers and his mobile phone, he would start making business calls the minute he found a seat on the bus. Passengers would stare, but Powell was far too immersed in his own world to notice the strange looks.

The BOAC bag rarely left his side. Woolley recalled Powell joining Paul Webster for a meeting with a sales agent. When they arrived, Powell decided to use the toilet. By the time he reached the office where the meeting was to be held, Webster had already gone in. As Powell strode confidently through the door, the bag's strong elastic shoulder strap caught in the door handle. He announced himself ' ''Allo, I'm Nik Powell' – and the elastic pulled him backwards, out of the room. Webster and their host looked on with amazement as the door slammed behind him. All Webster could stammer was, 'Oh, that's Nik, you know.'

Monday mornings and the days immediately following Powell's holidays could be difficult for those staff who worked closely with him. A compulsive workaholic, he would return to the office from his break with countless new ideas and schemes. His adrenalin level would climb as he put his mind to making things happen. As Norman Humphrey, Palace's group financial controller from early 1986 onwards, observed, 'Nik was a born deal-maker. If he was washed up on a desert island with Mr White and Mr Pink, Nik would be selling them coconuts by the end of the first day. He's the most numerate executive I've ever come across, with the ability to take in sets of numbers, analyse and retain them with great levels of concentration.'

Accounts were not the only aspect of the business which Powell liked to oversee, and his inability to trust senior staff with the full responsibility for their departments spawned increasing tension and difficulties as the Palace Group of Companies began to grow.

The one person Powell did trust, and in whose progress he showed considerable and generous interest, was Woolley. By early 1984 Woolley was still not a contractual partner with Powell. He was running the Scala Cinema, the video label and taking a major role in the first cinema releases, but his financial interest in the rapidly expanding group of companies had not been clarified. It was during the production of *The Company of Wolves* that Powell took Woolley to one side, and told him: 'I'm going to make you a partner in the whole Palace group, so we'll be fifty-fifty on everything, okay?'

One of the key reasons for Powell's pursuit of Woolley was the former Virgin partner's insecurity about the creative side of the film business. Powell's strength was in the selling and marketing of Palace's titles. As one associate explained, 'Nik would never give up on anything. He would go out and sell film tickets himself, or walk up and down with a sandwich board rather than give up on a film.' His motto would be 'never knowingly unsold'.

Powell's grasp of the creative side of film-making, however, was far less developed and assured. Tactless at the best of times, in Palace's early days he was often uncomfortable around directors and writers, and lacked experience of script analysis and development. He needed a dynamo to drive Palace Productions, and Woolley offered a less gauche, more considered approach to balance the Palace ticket. He also presented the prospect of a younger partner, seven years Powell's junior, who was likely to let Powell dominate Palace's business elements without much interference.

Perhaps Powell also missed Branson, his childhood friend, and wanted a partner for emotional as well as business reasons. In truth, in 1981 Powell could have gone into many areas of business: it was Woolley's addiction and obsession with films that took Palace into the heart of the film industry.

The twenty-five-year-old Woolley hardly paused to consider the consequences of becoming co-chairman of the growing Palace Group. Despite running the Scala Cinema, the truth was that Woolley's grasp of corporate management skills was somewhat limited at this stage. Moreover, he was more interested in dealing with films than he was in managing companies. As he later admitted: 'I was being greedy. The reality was I didn't really care about all the other businesses. All I thought about was the film side, so I got split down the middle. It was six years before it really came home to roost, when I was signing personal guarantees for things I didn't really know about.'

Although documents were issued by lawyers to confirm the joint ownership, Woolley, typically, never got round to signing them. Nevertheless, in both spirit and in title, he had become co-chairman of Palace. In the event of a dispute between the two partners, Powell would have the final say if it was of a financial nature, and Woolley if it was a creative issue. 'I was never quite sure if that was a good thing, but in the end that's what happened, because the reality was that Nik had put up the money,' Woolley said, pointing out that he had not felt able to 'tell Nik not to spend money on so-and-so, when it was his in the first place'.

Powell's personal investment of £428,900, along with the original £221,000 invested by the Norwich Union building society formed Palace's financial foundations. Norwich had already demonstrated to Powell the advantages of a long-term, hands-off partner, who did not require a director sitting on the board. Additional monies had been loaned by Norwich during July 1985, but by mid-1986 Powell realised that the overall level of capitalisation was too low to support the Palace Group of Companies' rapidly rising level of business.

The Video Palace stores were growing, the Video Editing Centre in Poland Street was fully occupied and a computer games company and music video company were being spawned. In particular, Palace Video, the theatrical and video distribution company within the group, was in need of a stronger balance sheet.

When Palace Video bought the UK rights to a film, the seller of those rights would take the contract to a bank who would lend them money on the back of it. Palace would pay for the rights only on delivery of the film. Before a bank would lend money on the back of a contract, however, it would take a careful look at Palace Video's balance sheet and it was therefore important for Palace's growth that it should look healthy. Powell decided that to achieve this he should find some venture or risk capital which would be invested in the group on a longer term basis than ordinary loan finance.

Powell's search happened to be well timed. During the early 1980s, Mrs Thatcher had criticised the big lending institutions for investing only in blue-chip companies. The Prime Minister argued that these institutions should increase venture capital investments, or Britain would never develop any successful entrepreneurs. 'And she was right,' Powell said. 'So a lot of the institutions and City people started to set up venture capital divisions, many of which I approached at that time.'

When Premila Hoon joined merchant bankers Guinness Mahon at the end of 1986, the bank's entertainment division had already held talks with Powell about providing venture capital. Based in a plush corporate building on St Mary at Hill in the heart of the City, Guinness Mahon is one of London's smaller merchant banks. Since 1980 it had developed a busy film finance division. Hoon, a prim, petite, Indian-born financier in her early thirties, had no experience in the film industry when she joined the division. Consequently, it was not surprising that she initially found it hard to 'make a case for doing business with Palace based purely on the numbers. Starting a relationship with a company of Palace's relatively small size is always difficult,' she explained. 'You have to convince yourself that the company is capable of surviving, capable of repaying debt and meeting your criteria.'

The talks between Palace and Guinness Mahon took place over a number of months and during that time Hoon became increasingly taken by the film business, and by Powell in particular. 'He struck me as a bit of a maverick – certainly very intelligent, very forceful and unconventional – although by that time I was starting to realise that the film business is full of unconventional businessmen,' Hoon recalled.

Just how unorthodox Powell could be when seeking financial support was later recounted by a rival producer in an apocryphal story. Eager to find banking sources in addition to Guinness, Powell would often eavesdrop on pub banter in The George. One night he overheard a conversation between some Working Title producers who had recently obtained financial assistance from a bank in Holland. When he questioned them about it, they deliberately fobbed him off, but somehow Powell had caught on that the bank in question started with the letter 'P' and sounded a bit like the word 'pear'. He just needed the rest of the name . . .

On his next trip to Holland to visit Boudisque, Palace's Dutch record company, Powell stopped off at a public phone booth. Leafing through the company names under 'P', he struck gold. Pierson Heldring & Pierson, a merchant bank newly involved in film financing, was bound to be the one with which Working Title had dealt. Powell's ingenuity and resourcefulness were rewarded. After a formal approach, Pierson, Heldring & Pierson joined Guinness to become supporting pillars of Palace's financial platform.

By 2 June 1987 Guinness Mahon and Pierson, Heldring & Pierson had agreed to work closely together to provide a £2 million revolving credit loan to the Palace Group of Companies. According to Hoon, the monies were to be used as a working capital facility and for project loans which were financed off the balance sheet. A project loan for a film production would normally go through a special purpose company set up by Palace specifically for that film. The new company would own the rights to the film and control its finances. So when a loan was drawn down for the production of *Shag* in the summer of 1987 – the first Palace film Guinness helped to finance – it was via

Palace (Myrtle Beach) Limited, the specific company set up for the production, and not the Palace Group as a whole.

Although, theoretically, project finance for Palace's films was fully secured against distribution contracts, the existence of sales contracts was no guarantee that the film would be finished and that contracts would be honoured once it had been delivered. It is primarily for these reasons that banks insist on a completion guarantee to protect their risk exposure. In Palace's case, there would often be a gap between the amount of finance needed to make a film and the revenues raised by pre-sales on the project. Palace would also pay a distribution advance for the UK rights, normally set at around ten to fifteen per cent of a film's budget, according to Powell. On a £2 million production, Palace Video would therefore advance more than £200,000 for the UK rights, certainly a higher price than most other companies would have paid, but the video arm was confident that with the right films and strong marketing, it would more than earn its money back. Palace would offer its own corporate guarantee to cover these gaps in the finances, something that Guinness, in particular, did not feel hugely comfortable about.

Palace's great, recurring problem was cash flow. Hoon politely described its wildly fluctuating levels as 'a moving target', while Powell's bullish euphemism for the situation was 'highly geared'. The reality was that large amounts of Powell's time were spent managing cash flow. It was a daily obsession, an ever-changing target. Powell worked his accountants overtime, night after night, demanding consolidated cash-flow projections, updated on a weekly basis. As one of his senior accountants recognised: 'Nik knew that if he could manage the cash flow, he was prepared to sacrifice profitability just to keep things going. This was on the basis that eventually there would be some luck, a hit, and then he could get everything on a stable basis again.'

The short-term juggling was not, however, without a longer term purpose. After five years of business, Powell had developed a philosophy about Palace's future. One afternoon he was visited by an entrepreneur who had established a reputation in the eighties for buying companies cheaply, running them for five years, during which time the companies would grow excessively, and then selling them and moving on to the next risk. Powell pointed out that these companies never attained the same level of profits after the sale, and proceeded to outline why he thought the short-term approach was wrong: 'You've got to spend ten years building a company, ten years consolidating it, and ten years making sure it's in a fit state to carry on without you.'

Having provided the £2 million revolving loan, Guinness and Pierson still took the view that Palace was under-capitalised if it was to survive Powell's first ten-year plan, let alone the following twenty. Guinness suggested that Palace should approach Greater London Enterprise (GLE) for further equity investment, an idea that both sides followed up. GLE was established in 1986 as a successor to the Greater London Enterprise Board (GLEB), which had been created by the Greater London Council in 1983. It outlasted its creator, whose assets it inherited. When the GLC was abolished, GLE's public funding ceased and, in a Thatcherite spirit, it started to raise investment funds from the private sector. It wanted to seek out strong entrepreneurs and help develop their businesses. The sums invested were normally too small to interest most venture capital funds. By 1989, GLE had made twenty-four investments in London companies, three of which had gone bankrupt.

According to David Walburn, GLE's managing director, Palace passed all the tests. In 1986 the company was profitable by a narrow margin, growing rapidly, and had a diverse range of income sources. Unlike many top film executives, Powell and Woolley were not lining the pockets of their own suits. The co-chairs paid themselves around £60,000 per annum in 1986/87. Their salaries were later to rise to £75,000, but never exceeded this. In contrast to some of the businesses Walburn had dealt with, Palace looked lean and mean, albeit suffering from some of the financial problems typically associated with a young independent company.

The one reservation Powell held about GLE was that, each time it made an investment, it insisted on appointing a director to the board of the company. Powell swallowed the pill, made sweeter by Walburn's accommodating, genial and supportive stance. In April

1988 GLE invested £700,000 in the Palace Group, alongside an equity investment of £350,000 by Guinness, quite separate from the £2 million loan of the previous year. The new equity investments were in the form of convertible preference shares, which would be made into ordinary shares only in the event of the company failing to meet its performance targets. Such a deal suited Powell perfectly, allowing him full rein in running the company but giving him access to badly needed capital finance.

Palace's main attraction when wooing investors was its video distribution operation, and Powell soon decided that if Palace was to grow successfully, the video distribution company would benefit from a partner. Such a move would cut down on the distribution overhead and further Powell in his aim of dominating the independent market. Talks were held with the new Virgin Vision, run by Richard Branson's brother-in-law Robert Devereux, and Palace Virgin Distribution, which dealt only with video distribution, was established in late 1982. Aware that the forthcoming release of *Merry Christmas Mr Lawrence* needed rather more than the low-level art-house service that the two companies had provided to that point, Palace Virgin approached an East End wholesaler, Golds, which had previously been operating out of the back of a sweet shop but had recently moved to large new premises. Irving Rappaport, who had researched the field, was impressed by the wholesaler, especially given the general reputation of the video business at this time. 'Barry [Gold] was trusted, honest, and people admired him because he paid his bills on time.' Newly armed with a spacious warehouse in Leyton, a computer system and the organisational rigour that Palace Virgin had lacked, Palace Virgin Gold (PVG) – later dubbed 'Pure Video Genius' for advertising purposes – was formed at the end of 1983. It was in the nick of time.

Following *Merry Christmas Mr Lawrence*, PVG released *Making Michael Jackson's 'Thriller'* (whose distribution rights PVG had bought from the American rights' holder, Vestron) and Culture Club's *A Kiss across the Ocean*, whose rights were held by Virgin. As Rappaport pointed out, 'PVG wasn't exactly a household name, but Michael Jackson definitely was. Everyone and their grandmother were after that title. Palace ended up devising the marketing campaign because Vestron only had two staff working out of the UK.'

The biggest selling music video at that time was by Duran Duran, which had sold around 25,000 units in total. Rappaport had a bet with a Vestron executive that *Thriller* would sell a massive 80,000 units in the first week of release, but the final figure was a staggering 100,000. Gold's new warehouse and computer systems were straining at the seams. After two months, the two videos had sold a combined 185,000 copies. *Thriller*'s appeal was so wide that it attracted new people into the video retail trade, with orders coming from bicycle shops, greengrocers and butcher shops.

Robert Jones was appointed managing director of PVG at the age of twenty-three. The former rock musician played a key part in building PVG's profile in an extremely conservative business. He would visit video wholesalers managed by men twice his age, determined to prove to them that Palace's titles would be financially viable. 'The only thing they'd understand was money, and that meant having to provide them with hits time and time again,' Jones recalled.

Palace was at least five years ahead of its competitors in persuading record and book shops, including WH Smith, to stock retail videos. PVG started to build an impressive and eclectic catalogue, ranging from U2 and Ultravox to the Muppets, Merchant Ivory films, *My Little Pony* and the record-breaking hit *The Snowman*. Woolley and Rappaport picked up this animated short film for a mere £5,000, and went on to shift more than half a million units.

The company's spirited sense of enterprise continued to attract bright young self-starters with no formal training who could think on their feet. As Jones put it, 'the fear of the suit was endemic in Palace, while the *corps d'esprit* was unique. Nobody suffered from having their own agenda. They just wanted to get through the day, do their best, have a laugh and go down the pub when it was over.'

While PVG was forging ahead, Palace's relationship with Virgin was sometimes strained. Suddenly it was not just Palace's films that needed care and attention but Virgin's own and third-party films handled by the distribution outlet. As Rappaport recalled, it was not long before Virgin was phoning up and asking why its films had not sold more units. Nevertheless, the business flourished overall because of the three-way shareholding of PVG, cutting down on overheads and enhancing Palace's potential profit. PVG went on to win the Best Independent Video Distributor award in 1985.

Palace started to reduce the number of titles it chose to release through PVG. During the company's early years, it had been forced to relinquish the video rights to productions such as *The Company of Wolves* and *Mona Lisa*. In order to have enough money to make films, Palace needed to pre-sell the video rights, but by 1987, as the business became stronger, the company could retain these rights and exploit them through PVG. Rather than flood the market, PVG released twelve major film titles a year, normally at a rate of one per month, and supported by other music and children's titles. Often these were smaller films with no major stars or known directors. The cinema releases and their consumer marketing campaigns would increase the subsequent sales to the video retailers.

Palace also started an interesting trend in niche video marketing when it set up Palace Classics. Specialist retail and rental video labels became much more common post-1990, but Palace once again led from the front. Films such as Federico Fellini's *La Dolce Vita*, the Coen Brothers' *Blood Simple*, Spike Lee's *She's Gotta Have It* and Werner Herzog's *Fitzcarraldo* were released through Palace Classics. Whether these films ever seriously contributed to Palace's profitability, however, is doubtful. Although they provided a fine catalogue of upmarket films, they certainly did not meet the Powell-stated need for 'hits to finance the failures'.

Gold's computing system, efficient accounting and stringent debt collection were of great benefit to Palace Video. Unfortunately, they were not matched by Palace's own methods of financial control. Before Norman Humphrey's arrival in 1986, the company's accounting 'systems' were less then reliable. In late 1985 Chris Craib, the newly appointed group managing director, had discovered that Palace was 'facing an almighty cash hole', resulting in an immediate crisis and extensive negotiations with its bank. Craib had worked out that despite there being considerable box-office takings from films such as *The Evil Dead*, *The Company of Wolves*, *A Letter to Brezhnev*, and the *Nightmare on Elm Street* series, the company had failed to invoice any of the cinemas.

Distribution box-office figures were handled by a computer system that repeatedly crashed under the overwhelming volume of information. Cinema exhibitors even rang Palace to remind them they owed the company money, but staff, who had no idea who owed what, had to consult the booker, Mike Ewin, who would patiently sort through the mess.

In the end, the old computer system had to be thrown out. Craib won Powell's grudging agreement that his wife should transfer the whole system to paper, coming up with a painstaking filing system that tracked the progress of each Palace film release. The handwritten system was sufficiently thorough to be used until the release of *Scandal* in 1989. Meanwhile, a cash-management system detailed enough to monitor the Palace Group's cash resource for the next six years was installed.

Humphrey, the group financial controller, was working such long hours during his first few months with the company in 1986 that he'd often stay at a small hotel off Trafalgar Square rather than travel back to his home near Reading. As he walked through the West End at four o'clock in the morning, he'd bump into young Palace employees coming out of the night clubs. He reflected later that his commitment stemmed from the 'spirit and dreams of the company. Palace had a team spirit and a focus that was contagious.'

When Paul Webster moved into production from running Palace's cinema distribution division, Daniel Battsek was more than ready to take his place. Leaving the detail of which cinemas to book to Mike Ewin, Battsek concentrated on conjuring up marketing ideas and schemes to make the most of Palace's films. Very often his actions led to furious exchanges with other parts of Wardour Street, but as Rank's Stan Fishman explained, 'nobody actually said what a disaster this young man was. Everybody had quite a healthy respect for him and he worked as a catalyst between Nik and Steve and other people in the industry.'

Battsek's aggressive poster policies were one of the focal points for upset. All cinema advertising posters were supposed to be vetted by a Watch Committee made up of elder statesmen who would pass the posters for the Society of Film Distributors. Their imprimatur was needed before the London Transport Authority would allow the posters to appear on the Underground and elsewhere around the capital.

The Palace poster for *Nightmare on Elm Street 3* showed Freddie harassing a coachload of young children, their faces reflecting the terror of encountering the man with the long bladed fingers. Had they been given the chance to vet it, the committee would no doubt have promptly rejected the poster. Children and Freddie in the same shot was a definite 'no-no'. One day Fishman took a call in his Odeon offices just off Leicester Square. It was the London Transport Authority. Did Fishman know that the new *Nightmare* posters did not have the official logo? Did he realise that the Authority was bitterly objecting to the poster, and that it was Odeon's responsibility to take it up with Palace?

Fishman called Battsek.

'Daniel, you've done it again . . .'

'What have I done now?' enquired Battsek innocently.

'Well, London Transport have gone up the wall about your *Nightmare* posters. Did you ever get that poster cleared?'

'Bloody London Transport, they're just being stupid, Stan.'

'You might say that, but right now they're removing all your posters from every site in London.'

Battsek would grow sheepish on the phone, apologising to Fishman while condemning London Transport in the next breath. The conversation would normally end with Battsek saying: 'Don't worry, Stan, I'll sort it out. Anyway, it's great publicity for the film.'

Fishman harboured visions of Battsek, a few months earlier, sitting in a pub meeting with Powell and Woolley and quite deliberately planning the entire fiasco. It seemed to him that Palace had probably intended never to show the committee pictures of Freddie and the children. As Fishman admitted with a wistful smile, 'Palace became the company I loved to hate.'

The year of 1986 was Palace Pictures' most successful in its then five-year history. All eight films released that year won a place in London's box-office top ten, and five of them went on to gross more than £2 million each around the country. 1987 was a far less profitable year, but in 1988 David Leland's *Wish You Were Here* was the fourteenth most popular film in the UK, taking nearly £3 million, and John Waters's *Hairspray* and *Shag* together took £2 million. In 1989, *Scandal* took sixteenth place in the charts, grossing £3.7 million, and *Nightmare on Elm Street 4* and Neil Jordan's *High Spirits* – which took a surprising £1.9 million – also boosted Palace's profile. Compared to the top grossing films in 1988 and 1989 – *Fatal Attraction* and *Indiana Jones and the Last Crusade*, which took £15 million and £16 million respectively – the above sums seem modest, but Palace was nevertheless the leading independent distributor during these years.

Palace films were also starting to benefit from an upturn in cinema attendances, which rose from 60 million in the doldrums of the early 1980s to 94 million by 1989. This boom did not massively change their fortunes, however, for the distribution of box office takings is hard on independents. On its best films, such as *Scandal* and *Nine ½ Weeks*, Palace would receive approximately forty per cent of the box-office receipts; on smaller films it could take as little as twenty-six per cent, and on average it would receive about thirty-three per cent of receipts. A film like *High Spirits* would bring in around £800,000 in film rental (from a gross of £2 million), but the release would have cost Palace £350,000 as an advance against the UK rights, and at least £300,000 in prints and advertising. Some of the advance would be earned back by selling the film to television, and through the video release, but overall the margins on theatrical distribution were tight.

The need for a hit to help the Palace Group keep its head above water was relentless. Woolley and Jones in particular would seek out projects and scripts with a view to buying the UK rights before the films were made. It was risky, but at times their taste paid off in spectacular style.

Nora Ephron's screenplay for *When Harry Met Sally* was read by

Jones at script stage. Backed by Woolley and Powell, Jones acquired the Rob Reiner-directed comedy, together with Harry Hook's *Lord of the Flies*, paying $600,000 for the titles. The two-film package did not include UK television rights, so 'it was a risky deal, but we figured that the script for *When Harry Met Sally* was funny and, with Rob Reiner directing it, it might work; but at the end of the day at least we had *Lord of the Flies* to fall back on,' Jones explained. *When Harry Met Sally*, starring Billy Crystal and Meg Ryan, went on to gross $93 million in the US, and took £7 million in the UK, coming in at number ten in the UK charts for 1990. Meanwhile, *Lord of the Flies* bombed.

Despite the film's later success, the release preparations for *When Harry Met Sally* were far from straightforward. Palace hoped to release the film in early 1990, but neither Ryan nor Crystal wanted to travel to London to support the publicity for the film. Phil Symes, still Palace's publicity agent at this stage, had an inspired idea about how to overcome this problem. With Powell's approval, he wrote to Princess Diana at Buckingham Palace, and after a number of official vetting screenings due to concern over Ryan's fake orgasm scene, Symes managed to woo the royal star to attend the première. The minute the royal première was announced, the entire cast of *When Harry Met Sally* was desperate to attend the screening and meet the princess.

The wily Symes arranged for the tabloid press to sit right in front of the royal box. When the fake orgasm scene came on screen, all the reporters turned round to see how Princess Diana was reacting to Ryan's antics, and a flash of cameras snapped her face. The resulting headlines and front page photographs ensured an opening for the film that far surpassed Palace's initial expectations.

Palace enjoyed great success taking small, niche films to the wider market, but this success was not always matched when it came to bigger fare. *Family Business*, starring Dustin Hoffman, Sean Connery and Matthew Broderick, for example, performed badly for Palace, and the film also served to highlight how poor communication was between Powell and his distribution and marketing managers.

The kind of deal a distributor does with a sales company or producer should have a major effect on the way the film is released. In the case of *Family Business*, Powell had told Battsek and Robert Mitchell that Palace needed to spend a lot of money on the prints and advertising. In good faith, Battsek and Mitchell went to town on what they thought was a poor film, hoping that their efforts would help Palace recoup its money.

'Daniel and I were busy patting ourselves on the back for getting Palace out of jail, managing to earn more than we'd spent, which on a picture like *Family Business* was quite an achievement,' Mitchell explained. 'Then we found out that it was a total disaster. Nik had intentionally or unintentionally misinformed us. Rather than Palace making money from the big release, the film was losing money. The producers were taking a percentage of the box office right from the first takings.'

Part of the problem stemmed from Powell's lack of organisational and management skills. As Mitchell explained, 'Nik never wanted anyone to know that much, which meant everyone was in the dark to some extent. It also meant that nobody could say with any authority why things were fucking up so badly, because nobody knew enough. Even the senior managers were working in the dark to a certain extent, and that's where things started to go horribly wrong.'

Whilst taking its place as the UK's largest independent cinema and video distribution operation, Palace was also running a number of 'non-core' activities. These, including the Dutch-based record company, Boudisque, and the Video Editing Centre on Poland Street, had come to Palace as part of Powell's divorce settlement from Virgin.

The video editing suite was used by Palace's pop promo company when doing post-production work on its music videos, and was remembered even by early Palace employees as being an outdated pit. JoAnne Sellar ran Palace Music, the pop promo operation, from 1986 to 1989; an operation backed by Woolley, who saw it as a natural spin-off from film. Young directors, it was hoped, would be able to make a start at Palace Music and then move on to Palace's feature films. While the scheme made sense, with five staff handling between five and ten directors (including Neil Jordan and Michael Caton-Jones), the operation cost as much as it made, and simply contributed to the rapidly expanding Palace overhead.

One of Powell's driving ambitions was to place Palace at the cutting edge of new markets and technology, creating, for example, computer games on the back of films such as *Evil Dead*. It was a policy that was fine in theory, but was never implemented. When accountant Anne Sheehan started working at Palace in 1987, she took on responsibility for the accounts for the software company, which was supposed to be launching new computer games. 'Unfortunately, the first thing they ever did was a big hit,' Sheehan explained. 'It was a game called *Barbarian* that involved chopping people's heads off. It was a sick thing that appealed to fifteen-year-old boys.' The success of *Barbarian* led to considerable amounts of money being spent on developing new video games. The difficulty with video games, however, is that, unlike films, they have to be perfect. If a video game does not work in its entirety, it cannot be released.

It was precisely this problem that sealed the fate of an *Evil Dead* video game that Palace spent many thousands of pounds developing. A launch was organised for computer boffins and journalists in the London Dungeon. Powell made a big speech about the future of the video games market, and how Palace was leading the way. Just as he was set to start the demonstration, a Palace employee came over to him and whispered in his ear. There was a problem with the computer program. The disks had a bug. Powell had to cancel the entire launch and apologise to the guests.

Many of the problems facing the young Palace companies stemmed from the fact that Powell was handling increasing numbers of businesses yet could not learn how to delegate responsibility. The executive nominally in charge of non-core activities, which included the Video Editing Centre, the Video Palace stores, Software (re-named Megawinkel), and Boudisque, in addition to overseeing Norman Humphrey's finance department, was Chris Craib. At least ten years older than most Palace employees, the well-intentioned Craib was treated badly by some of the Palace crew. Wanting to be involved in film production and distribution, Craib had found himself pushed by Powell into running the non-core businesses, many of which were losing money by 1990. Yet whether Craib was really in charge of these operations was debatable, given Powell's forceful management style.

Although Powell spent most of his time obsessed with juggling the company's finances, he also showed some concern for his employees' welfare and was responsible for instituting the annual 'Palace Day Out', a 'team steam' where the staff could behave even more wildly than usual. The 'Day Out' idea grew from Powell's idealistic notion that everyone on the staff should enjoy a strong sense of belonging to the company. Woolley, on the other hand, was convinced that the staff did not need any alcohol-induced public embarrassments to strengthen their love for Palace: he assumed that they were already devoted. Although only three 'days out' occurred in the history of Palace – mainly due to Woolley's horror at the idea of them – they still loom large in the memories of former staff.

The first 'Palace Day Out' was to Brighton. In the evening, after supper, Powell became merrily drunk. The Palace team was walking back to its hotel along the sea-front, when the co-chairman decided to play dodgems with the cars coming towards him on the main road. Finally a taxi was forced to screech to a halt. Powell leapt on to the car's bonnet, while his colleagues desperately tried to drag him back to the pavement. Powell narrowly escaped a beating as the quick-witted Michael Garland slipped the livid taxi driver a placatory £10.

By the time they reached the hotel lobby, Powell was on hands and knees, barking. In between yelps, he helpfully explained to Garland that 'Richard [Branson] and I used to do this in the early days . . .' He asked for his hotel keys, took them in his mouth, and entered the lift.

Garland recalls nearly thirty employees piling into his and a colleague's room to smoke dope and continue the boozing. The noise level attracted a knock on the door from a winceyette-nightied old woman, complaining that she was 'trying to get some sleep'. In the end, a night porter hammered on the door and sent everyone off to their rooms. 'It was a cheap, cheap hotel,' Garland recalled. 'I wanted to go to the loo, which was outside the room, so I didn't bother putting any clothes on. But the door locked behind me.' His room-mate was so stoned he did not hear Garland banging to get back in. By this time it was five a.m., and with just a tiny towel around his waist, Garland was frozen.

'I decided to keep warm by running a bath, which I fell asleep in and woke up like a frozen prune. But I was still facing the same problem about getting into my room. I was like this drunk, naked Irishman who had no option but to go down to the night porter, who went ape-shit.'

The following August the Palace crew went to Edinburgh for a weekend during the festival. About forty members of staff travelled up on the night train, which according to one employee 'was awash with alcohol and every South American substance known to man'. By the time the 'Day Out' started, most of the staff were drunk. The employees were to do as they pleased during the day, and meet up in a Chinese restaurant for a big supper in the evening.

Rather than hire the whole Chinese restaurant, Powell had decided to save money by booking only half the room – which was unlucky for one middle-aged couple who had decided to celebrate their wedding anniversary in the other half of the restaurant.

Dressed in white trousers and shirt, Powell, the worse for drink, stood up on the table to make a speech:

'Anybody from Palace shut the FUCK up! Anybody who isn't can leave if they like!'

Powell fell off the table, pouring red wine all over his white clothes. Palace employees were either roaring with laughter or sitting sheepishly in their chairs, thinking, 'Oh, God, I'm not here.'

Behind his embarrassment at his partner's antics, Woolley – who deliberately avoided the Edinburgh débâcle – was often genuinely worried by the amount his partner drank and by the way he drove himself. He was particularly concerned that these frenzied excesses might trigger an epileptic attack, but Powell remained oblivious of such thoughts, and was quite capable of happily rising the next morning to don the same wine-stained white shirt.

In 1989, the Palace Group had a sales turnover of £20.5 million, compared to £14.8 million in 1988 and £11 million in 1987. Its full-time staff had risen from sixty-eight to ninety-two over the same period, and after a net loss before tax of around £100,000 in 1987, the company had managed a net profit before tax of nearly £500,000 in 1989. Palace had also managed to keep producing films at a time when the UK production industry had sunk to a new low. Just twenty-seven UK-produced films had gone before the cameras in 1989, nearly half the previous year's total. As a consequence, Powell and Woolley were fêted by budding directors and producers as the bright new hope, which further enhanced the film company's maverick image both at home and abroad. According to one European producer, 'Palace was a legend that you just couldn't help hearing about, even though you weren't quite sure what it was all for.'

Despite the growth and glamour, Guinness Mahon, Pierson, Heldring & Pierson, GLE and Norwich Union considered the company was still significantly under-capitalised. More money was needed. Powell managed to nearly double the share capital of the Group in early 1990 to £3.45 million through the creation of £1.55 million new shares. Norwich came in for just under £1 million, GLE for £400,000, and Guinness's Development Capital division and Pierson invested £200,000.

The investors firmly advised Powell that a strategy review was essential if the Group were to survive the approaching onslaught of recession. Powell took the advice to heart, instructing accountants Stoy Hayward to carry out a thorough strategy review of the Palace Group, which was presented to the board in March 1990. With the new capitalisation and action following the review's recommendations, Powell thought he had done enough to steady the ship before the tidal wave of recession crashed on to Wardour Mews. But neither he nor the prostitutes next door knew what was coming.

# CHAPTER TEN

# Cinema Fodder

It took nineteen-year-old Richard Stanley just one week in early 1988 to write the script for *Hardware*. It was a grisly, comic-strip-style horror story, and, like his countless previous scripts, inspired little enthusiasm in potential developers and producers. The South African-born long-haired hippy had already directed music videos but he was in a rut, having split up with his girlfriend and made little progress in feature production.

During a particularly badly organised animated picture shoot, Stanley met a militia-obsessed youth who was trying to save enough money to return to Afghanistan to fight the Russians. Eager to find a new project, Stanley suggested that they could raise some money by filming a documentary from behind the Jihad guerrilla ranks, and it was not long before they found themselves doing just that. Stanley explained that he 'had a lot of theories about Afghanistan', and now he had his 'chance to put them to the test'.

Back in London, the script for *Hardware* remained with a young music video producer, Paul Trijbits, who was supporting Stanley's efforts in Afghanistan. The small but pushy Trijbits had come over to London from his native Holland in the early 1980s, and set up Wicked Films to handle pop promos. His real ambition, however, was to forge a way into feature films. Engagingly chatty, Trijbits loved to spread his distinctive independent gospel, telling people with whom he worked that they were all 'Thatcher's children, doing everything for themselves'. Some of his crews were less than amused by the analogy, and neatly adapted the producer's patter, describing him as one of 'Thatcher's illegitimate kids'.

The ambitious young producer finally got round to reading the first draft of *Hardware* and, impressed, passed it on to his Caribbean-born partner, talented writer Trix Worrell, for a second opinion. Reading, in the first few pages of the script, the passage describing the discovery of the droid, the partners were taken with Stanley's vivid images.

> Slowly a face emerges from the earth. A steel face with eyes like red jewels, features scorched and marked by shrapnel wounds.
> The nomad begins to dig more swiftly now.
> He glances furtively around himself, and then looks down, smiling at his discovery.
> The steel skull returns his smile . . .

The Wicked partners thought *Hardware* was a tremendous, futuristic script, and were eager to produce it, but as Trijbits bluntly admitted: 'We knew jack-shit about horror films, and had no real idea how to raise the money.'

One evening, Trijbits and Worrell were drinking upstairs at Freds, a small trendy media club next to *Private Eye* magazine, just off Soho Square. Michael Caton-Jones introduced them to Steve Woolley, who thought the duo were film school friends of the director. After sharing a few rounds of beer, the duo set about convincing the producer that *Hardware* was the best new thing to hit the horror genre, and that Stanley was nothing less than a genius crying out to be discovered. Woolley was interested, and read the script a few days later.

A couple of weeks after that, Woolley rang Wicked, wanting to option the rights to the screenplay. A long-time fan of the horror genre, Woolley believed that *Hardware* could be a great project for Palace, and his experience in releasing horror films made him confident that in *Hardware* he had found a strong, horror sci-fi film which could be made on a low budget. He also gave a copy of the script to his former girlfriend, JoAnne Sellar, a horror film addict whom he knew was keen to start producing films instead of pop promos.

For Wicked to do a deal with Palace, however, Trijbits needed to present Stanley to Palace and set the project in motion. This was somewhat difficult, given that the young writer-director was thousands of miles away in the Afghan mountains, trying to cope with a badly wounded cameraman, hundreds of minutes of war footage and credit cards way over their limits. Trijbits finally contacted Stanley but failed to convince the young hippy to return immediately to London. Undaunted, he tracked down Stanley's ex-girlfriend, and badgered her to ring him. The ploy worked. When Kate told Stanley she loved him and that he should come back, the young hippy did not hesitate to return.

The shock of returning to Britain, 'back in my flat, no bullets, well-stocked shops and where the people were nice', did not stop Stanley from being wary about Trijbit's promises. Unconvinced by Wicked's talk of a £250,000 shoot, he went to Wardour Mews to confront Woolley.

'You don't need Paul on this film,' Stanley explained.

'Why not? They brought it to us,' Woolley retorted.

'It's nothing to do with him. I've never worked with him in my life. I mean, I hardly know the guy.'

But Woolley, who at this point was releasing *Scandal*, preparing *The Big Man* and dealing with a myriad of other projects in development, felt that the best way forward was for Trijbits to co-produce the film while Palace oversaw the project from the executive sidelines. Stanley was sent back to his digs in Finsbury Park, from where he was promptly evicted by his girlfriend. Wicked and Stanley signed over the rights for a minimal sum, and, as the film started to be prepared for production, in mid-1990, *Hardware*'s writer-director was living on the street.

Putting together the budget for *Hardware*, which Wicked now estimated would cost £500,000, was, of course a complex job. Trijbits later modestly confessed that he had not realised that even though Palace had said 'Yes' to doing the film, the budget still had to be raised from a range of sources. According to Sellar, who had joined the team as Palace's producer representative during pre-production, 'It soon became apparent when I went through the budgeting side that there was no way it could be done for under a million.'

Palace put its money where its mouth was, investing £125,000, guaranteed by its new banking deal with Guinness Mahon, in return for UK rights. Other backers were also needed, and, given Stanley's age, experience and the nature of his cyborg-infested fantasy, it was unlikely that they would be fighting their way to the table. Fortunately, Simon Relph, the chief executive at British Screen, already knew of Stanley from a short film the teenager had previously made. 'I thought he was a very talented boy, so I was very positive about *Hardware* and delighted when Nik and Steve took it up,' Relph explained genially. He also thought the budget of just over £1 million was 'sensible, because a lot of the films we made at British Screen were far too expensive, and we were never going to make money on them'. As it turned out, investing in *Hardware* was one of Relph's more shrewd decisions during his time at British Screen. Relph's involvement also highlighted how shrewd Trijbits had been in getting Palace to oversee Wicked's first film. 'British Screen would never have come on board with just Wicked, Stanley and that weird script,' Trijbits laughed. 'But with Palace's help, we were in there.'

Miramax, elated by their first Palace collaboration over *Scandal*, were licking their lips at Stanley's screenplay. Harvey Weinstein, in particular, was excited by the prospect of a cheap (for he managed to knock down the advance Palace were hoping to obtain from Miramax), bloody, gutsy, deviant and futuristic movie. At least, that was how Harvey envisaged the film, and as co-executive producers, the brothers were entitled to give their opinions on the casting, script, editing and other creative decisions with a heavy-handed freedom that would leave the naïve Stanley stunned.

In the interests of budget-control, Woolley had insisted that the film should be shot in desperately cheap London locations. Dom Shaw, the young location manager employed for little more than

£100 a week, approached the person responsible for relaunching the derelict North London arts venue, the Roundhouse. Shaw, fed up searching for a location, was determined that Palace should commit to the Roundhouse. Woolley insisted that he send a report regarding the sound problems the vast, echo-filled space might present for the production. The new arts centre manager found a detailed report in the files, which had been commissioned by the defunct Roundhouse Arts Centre Trust, with a complete breakdown of noise levels, including diagrams and detailed decibel measurements.

Shaw promptly faxed the relevant pages to an impressed Woolley at Palace. The fact that there were clanking trains grinding past the building every twenty minutes was somehow overlooked. 'It was a post-apocalyptic film, so I didn't give a shit really,' Shaw laughed.

The first round of fights with Miramax was over the lead actors. Auditions were held in the States, where Stanley and Sellar agreed that a lithe young blonde actress, Stacey Travis, was perfect for the young woman's role. In return, Miramax insisted that a 'name' played the lead male role. All Stanley's choices were rejected in favour of Dylan McDermott, an up-and-coming Hollywood actor whom the Weinsteins, according to Sellar, 'were convinced was set to be a big, big star'. While Travis gamely made every professional effort to share Stanley's vision of the film, including listening to the director's imaginative post-apocalyptic ramblings, McDermott showed little desire to understand either Stanley or the film.

The real star of *Hardware* was MARK 13, named after the apocalyptic verses of the Bible, a brilliantly designed deviant robot that pieces its 'life' back together with murderous consequences. The robot's importance irritated McDermott, and he would constantly turn to Sellar during the shoot and exclaim, 'We're not making a horror film are we?' to which Sellar would reply, 'Dylan, you *have* read the script, haven't you?' Their repartee became a running joke amongst the crew and producers.

McDermott, having just split up with his girlfriend Julia Roberts, spent hours on the phone to America. 'He was very busy talking to mates in LA, trying to find out which guys Julia was seeing,' one crew member explained. McDermott was so obsessed by his failed fling with Roberts, that Travis had 'virtually to do it' to get him even vaguely interested in the film's key sex scenes.

Throughout the shoot, Miramax would send executives to the set, armed with alternative scenes, script amendments and new characters. 'It got really silly and it wasted a lot of time,' Stanley explained. 'Halfway through they suggested that a next-door neighbour be changed into a twelve-year-old child. A week later they came back, having changed their minds again, saying it should be a dog.' One Miramax-inspired street scene incensed Stanley so much that he walked off the set, explaining 'that it was best just to let them get on with it. I just wasn't interested.' Woolley later argued that 'most of Harvey's suggestions were completely sensible', and that Palace had even hired an additional screenwriter in an attempt to give the script a sharper narrative drive.

Sellar was smack in the middle of Miramax's line of fire. The tough début producer did a sterling job of protecting Stanley while placating Miramax's foot soldiers.

Harvey Weinstein made a few visits to the set, picking his way through the rubble, scrap metal and skirting around a half-open sewer which the crew was trying to shift. His answer to the chaos initially was to keep cool, but towards the end of the shoot he started spotting minor members of the cast whom he thought could be sacrificed to the bloodthirsty robotic anti-hero. One key crew member recalls him saying: 'Hey, who are these guys anyway? Can't we just get the killer-droid to take them out with the rest of them?'

Unlike Stanley, Sellar kept in mind the fact that Miramax would have to believe in the film if they were to give it their full commitment when releasing it in America, a market where the film would desperately need support if it was going to make any mark on the public. 'I had huge rows with Harvey, but if you stand up and stick to what you believe in, he'll basically see sense,' Sellar explained. 'Some of Miramax's ideas were good, some were bad, and my job was to divert the bad stuff.'

Despite the expanded budget, *Hardware* was still being produced extremely cheaply. 'Everybody was working for peanuts,' admitted Sellar when asked about the crew's salaries. 'It was everybody's first film, and they were all doing it for love, really.' Despite the enthusiasm, the lack of expertise showed. Elizabeth Karlsen, Woolley's new assistant and soon-to-be wife, recalled how the film was hampered by the small budget and first-time crew. Hardly a novice to low-budget film-making after working on numerous movies in New York, Karlsen was nevertheless concerned as to how they could make the film with *no* experience whatsoever.

'They were just boys playing with the little models and story-boards as if they were dinky cars, but when it came to the horrible practical housekeeping side of the production they had no idea,' she explained. They had huge enthusiasm, but 'I don't think they really knew what they were in for.'

According to one crew member, the production manager had done a deal with AppleMac, so he spent much of his time playing with the expensive computer hardware, producing beautiful computer-generated schedule sheets. One of Trijbits's contributions to the production was to sign a sponsorship deal with Schlitz Beer, in which large cases of beer were donated to the team for the wrap party, in return for a neon sign saying 'Schlitz' and a bottle of beer appearing on screen. The neon beer sign was meant to appear in a futuristic landscape, shot in the Royal Victoria Docks. Assistant directors kept trying to edge the sign out of the camera frame, while Trijbits would hover around asking,

'Is it going to be in? Are you sure it's in?'

'Yeah, yeah, Paul, it's in,' a weary voice would answer.

Trijbits would sneak up to the video monitor and squeal: 'It's not in, guys. The sign's got to be in!' The crew found the affair so ridiculous that, in the final version, they doctored the sign to read 'Schit'.

One of the few people who really knew what was happening on set was Ray Corbett, an experienced first assistant director. Sellar was aware that if Stanley failed to communicate properly with Corbett, the production would come unhinged. Corbett was from the old school of production, working very hard but still managing a daily half-hour snooze in the pub during pre-production. He would watch the strangely orange-tinged daily footage with an amused grin, laughing at the audacious stylistics Stanley was throwing at the film in abundance. Seeing young film groupies with trendy haircuts creeping round the Roundhouse, trying to fix lights and props, Corbett would suddenly boom across the set, 'Can anyone tell me a reason why we're not *doing* it?' The footsteps would stop. A long silence would ensue. 'Right. Well, let's fucking do it!'

Stanley's personal life throughout the film was not very stable. He had adopted a late-80s grunge-style hygiene and clothing and, having no home of his own, was sleeping in the Portakabins at the Roundhouse every night. This hardly impressed the owners of the premises, who were concurrently using the cabins as offices. They would turn up in the morning to find a bundle of stinking rags in a corner, only to discover it was a person. Karlsen let the director sleep on her sofa for a few nights and remembered the high stench in the living room the next morning.

Stanley's vision of a particularly controversial shower scene in the film managed to inspire a walk-out by the female staff in the art department. In the sequence, Travis is attacked by a long, twisting iron drill belonging to the robot. The robot's rape-hungry antics were too much for some of the crew, who refused to contribute to the sequence, but the scene went ahead anyway.

While most of the shoot's production troubles were quickly resolved, one particular problem proved more difficult to overcome. Halfway through production it became known to Sellar and Karlsen that there was a query over the source of the material for the script. A friend of Stanley and an artist were claiming that the *Hardware* story was taken from a *2000 AD* comic strip which they had written and had been published by Robert Maxwell's D. C. Thompson at an earlier date. Rather than worry Stanley in mid-shoot, Sellar and Karlsen decided to keep quiet about the dispute and deal with it once the film was in the can.

Stanley had signed a legal letter before production began confirming that the idea behind *Hardware* was entirely his own original work. This letter formed a critical part of the 'chain of title', a legal term for the documents needed to confirm all relevant rights to the film are owned by the production company.

When confronted by the 2000 *AD* claim, Stanley was adamant that he had not based his script on the material. Trijbits, who said he knew nothing about the issue, suddenly found himself 'in meetings, surrounded by seven lawyers, and only one of them was mine'. Although he and Worrell were surprised by the resemblance between *Hardware* and the disputed 2000 *AD* cartoons, they were convinced of Stanley's innocence because of a £500 original film Stanley had previously shot in his bedroom which starred a MARK 13 robot.

Others at Palace were less certain, and Sellar pointed out that although the strip 'was incredibly similar, it was hardly a terrible thing to admit, yet Richard was acting like he was being accused of committing some crime'. Stanley now explains that the concept for the android came from an assembly of different sources, including films such as *Terminator* and *Alien*, as well as recycled 1970s' slasher movie routines, and that '2000 *AD* were following lots of the same influences'.

Such disputes normally fizzle quietly away with a hushed-up agreement between lawyers, but not in the case of *Hardware*. Before any settlement was agreed, the story found its way to *Time Out* magazine, which bluntly suggested that Stanley had plagiarised the story. Palace settled the dispute by paying an undisclosed sum – estimated to be around £20,000 – and agreeing to the inclusion of a small title credit at the end of the film, acknowledging the two comic-strip artists.

Despite the inexperience of the crew and director, and the rows over the final cut between Stanley and a united Palace and Miramax, *Hardware* came together by early-1990 with surprising vision and vigour. The film had provided a first break for the majority of the young crew and marked the coming of the next generation of film-makers. Most notably, the art director, production and special effects designers are all working in feature production today. Thanks to Miramax's investment and gutsy marketing support, the film reached number six in the North American box office charts, and its performance on video was also impressive. Relph's faith in the project was vindicated, as British Screen for once more than made its money back.

The relationship between Wicked Films and Palace, fractious throughout the project, took a nosedive on its completion. Trijbits had always teased the thirty-three-year-old Woolley about Palace already being 'past it' and 'too old', jokes that had not gone down too well with the Palace co-chairs. To rub salt into the wound, after the film was released, Trijbits and Worrell had taken a full page in *Screen International* cheekily thanking all the senior companies for their assistance in the making of *Hardware*, which amused Powell and Woolley.

While Wicked and other young film companies were the new generation in Trijbits's eyes, he was aware of the many tricks he had learnt from the 'Palace School of Film-making'. Powell, in particular, he thought, had been brilliant at balancing the demands of *Hardware*'s financial and creative teams. His admiration was dulled somewhat, however, when more than £40,000 of Wicked's production fee for *Hardware* remained unpaid after the film was finished. His claim mystifies Powell to this day: 'The film was fully-funded and audited, and the books show that everyone was paid.' Trijbits, on the other hand, believes that the lost monies contributed significantly to Wicked's music video company going bankrupt in March 1992. All was not lost, however, for Trijbits and Worrell had sensibly signed up Stanley's next screenplay, *Dust Devil*. Trijbits confirmed that Palace later paid the young producers 'around £9,000 per page, for an eight-page story "treatment" for a film, which worked out pretty well for us in the end.'

*Hardware* played at the Cannes Film Festival in May 1990, an event Stanley remembers vividly. The first midnight screening went relatively well, and by the second night news of the film's merits had spread. Trijbits and Worrell had packed the audience with French school children to give the sense of a full house. 'I thought I'd done everything I had to by then, so I did a load of psycho-chemical drugs, and was off my face when I saw the second night screening,' Stanley recalled. 'Of course, I really enjoyed the screening, but when I got out there were heaps of distributors grasping at me and Harvey kept talking to me. I was tripping out of my mind so I panicked, and ran out on to the street. I ended up in a coffee shop where Nik was sitting drinking. He didn't seem to notice anything wrong with me, and started chatting about chess. In the end I was hunted down by a group of girls who kept throwing their arms around my neck. I eventually had to make a run for it and ended up in a hotel swimming pool where someone accidentally rescued me.'

By the start of 1990, Woolley's Palace Productions was as highly geared as the rest of the group. The company's shooting schedule that year – and thereafter – was extremely hectic. *Hardware* and *The Big Man* were shot simultaneously in London and Glasgow respectively and, as the two films entered post-production in spring 1990, Woolley was planning four further films, three to go into production that year (Jordan's *The Miracle*; US director Bill Duke's *A Rage in Harlem*, and Peter Richardson's *The Pope Must Die*, which was to be shot in Zagreb and Dubrovnik) and Stanley's *Dust Devil*.

*The Pope Must Die* became known as *The Pope Must Diet* in North America after a row between Miramax and the Catholic Church led to Harvey Weinstein making a subtle title change. The film was initially going to star Steve Martin, but in the end Robbie Coltrane played the oversized pope.

Powell's emerging Palace TV operation was also preparing to go into production that year with *Woman At War*, an ambitious television mini-series to be shot in Poland, and a project with comedian Lenny Henry, *Lenny – Live and Unleashed*.

This frenetic activity was financially underpinned by a key three-picture deal with Miramax, which was concluded in the summer prior to *The Big Man* shoot. Powell and McGuinness, eager to seize the opportunity to secure considerable amounts of money towards Palace's productions, albeit at Miramax's knockdown rates, flew to Miramax's New York offices for the difficult negotiations.

'Nik and I spent three days in a room with Harvey with nowhere to go to confer, so we'd go out on the fire escape for half an hour and try to figure out what we were doing,' McGuinness recalled.

Weinstein would bring a huge crate of Diet Cokes and a box of 200 cigarettes into the stuffy room. The thirsty, stressed-out Powell would eye Weinstein's nourishment longingly, until he realised that it was 'all for Harvey'! Of course, the Cokes were eventually passed around.

When the North American deal for *The Big Man*, *The Pope Must Die* and *Dust Devil* was finally completed late in the evening on the third day, McGuinness was ready to collapse into bed. 'But Nik wanted to celebrate,' McGuinness recalled. 'So he took me to a really cheesy restaurant, where they did $9.99 specials. The waitress asked if we wanted wine, and Nik said, "Narh, can we have a bottle of your cheapest house champagne? We're celebrating." '

In terms of effort, expense and expectations, *The Big Man* was the film into which Powell and Woolley put their hearts and wallets. It was to have major ramifications on the future stability of Palace.

The idea for *The Big Man* was brought to Woolley by Don MacPherson, one of the screenwriters of *Absolute Beginners*, who suggested that William McIlvanney's gritty novel could be adapted into a screenplay for cinema. The story of the unemployed Dan Scoular – a gentle giant, living in a tightknit Scottish community – which climaxes in a violent bare-knuckle fight, was eagerly optioned by Woolley and adapted by MacPherson. Determined to bring out the iniquities and social injustices of the Thatcher era, they introduced a backdrop of the 1984 85 miners' strike, making the renamed 'Danny' an unemployed miner. Woolley in particular saw the film as 'quite epic and heroic, but at the same time a moral story'.

A draft of the script was sent to David Leland, Jordan's co-writer on *Mona Lisa* and director of *Wish You Were Here*, who quickly accepted the project and began working with MacPherson on the screenplay. Leland was particularly concerned that the film should not become another television 'play of the week'. Like Woolley, he wanted a strong, cinematic, large-scale film, shot in widescreen and with a cast big enough to fill the cinema screen. Liam Neeson, the Northern Irish rising star, was soon signed up to play Danny, and Joanne Whalley-Kilmer joined the cast as his wife, Beth. A host of

British names were also lined up, including Billy Connolly and Ian Bannen.

Palace raised the initial £3.1 million budget through its deal with Miramax, an equity investment by British Screen, pre-sales by The Sales Company to German and Spanish distributors, and sales to Scottish TV and BSB for UK free and pay-TV rights respectively. Palace Video advanced a considerable sum for the UK theatrical and video rights, but the confident Powell and Woolley were convinced that *The Big Man* was worth every pound.

The upfront commitment from Miramax resulted predictably in their contributing reams of notes and amendments to the screenplay. Senior crew members recall Weinstein and his faithful assistant, Susan Salonika, flying into Glasgow on several occasions in a sweat about the Scottish accents. 'They drove me mad,' Leland explained. 'Harvey would bombard his minions, who would come up with all these pages of amendments, mostly about elements they didn't think would work for an American audience.' Woolley would patiently sift through the paperwork, reducing Miramax's angst-ridden outpourings to five or six points, which he would then discuss in detail with Leland. 'It was diplomacy *par excellence*, because Steve was both protecting me and letting me get on with the job in hand.'

The nine-week shoot before Christmas 1989 went well, despite freezing weather interfering with the cameras. The atmosphere grew increasingly tense as the film moved into the third week and the story's brutal climax. The staged fist fight between Danny and ex-boxer Cutty Dawson (played by Rab Afflick) is the centrepiece of the film, and Leland's actors did not let him down. Both men, surrounded by a heaving male mass of punters, back-stabbers and miners, threw real body punches. After the intensity of the five days of shooting the fight, the cast and crew felt a huge anti-climax as they soldiered on to complete the film. In a moment of typically acerbic insight, Leland told one journalist on the set, 'This is a shit or bust movie.'

Finding a suitable ending to the screenplay had presented great difficulties for MacPherson and Leland. Neeson's character either needed to be redeemed, and given the chance to reassess his life following the fight, or he could be killed. 'Most producers come up with very daft suggestions, but Steve kept talking to us, and often coming up with the hardest options,' Leland explained. One message all agreed upon was that *The Big Man*'s violent sequences were to call into question macho behaviour rather than reaffirm it. It was a central message that was to become bitterly lost on the critics ten months later.

When *The Big Man* had wrapped, Woolley and Leland began to seek a suitable soundtrack for the film, and particularly for the fight scene, which, as Woolley recognised, needed to be scored in 'a dramatic and vivid way, creating a lift into another arena and away from just being a kitchen-sink movie or turning on the telly'. Tapes were sent out to the Oscar-winning Italian composer, Ennio Morricone, who agreed to compose the score. Leland recalls travelling to the Italian's studios in Milan, only to find himself seduced by the pedantic, precise craftsman, who insisted on calling him '*Maestro*'. He went back to Morricone's apartment, which looks on to the sunny balcony from where Mussolini made all his big speeches, and listened to the composer's comments.

'I've decided that there will be a *Big Man* theme, and a fight theme for your film, *Maestro*,' Morricone intoned bossily. He then sat at a piano, and played a selection of tunes, asking Leland, 'Which ones do you like?' Leland and Woolley came back a few weeks later and listened to a recorded tape next to a video of the film. When Leland started to demand a transition at the climax, and made some religious allusions, Morricone became deliberately confused. The great composer rammed a tape upside-down into one of the machines, which rendered it useless. 'So, *Maestro*, you will have to sing it for me.' These antics amused Leland greatly, but he bravely started to sing what he wanted.

'When we got back to the recording, Ennio had understood everything. Unlike most composers I'd worked with, he'd composed and written every quaver. He had extraordinary flexibility at the point when most people became increasingly restricted. It was a revelation to watch him conduct a sixty-piece orchestra, making changes and alterations to the score on the spot,' Leland recalled.

Dealing with the talented Morricone was clearly an experience that Woolley and Leland remember with affection, but the charming Italian did not come cheap. Palace ended up settling a bill for more than £200,000 on top of their original investment. The decision was taken by Woolley, who later explained that he was so confident of the film's success that he took another gamble.

*The Big Man* premiered at the Edinburgh Film Festival in August 1990, where it was met with a shockingly negative reaction. 'They were passing the knife, standing up and chatting, and as soon as the film was twenty minutes in, everybody was going for a piss,' Leland recalled despondently. Despite positive reviews in the women's magazines, normally the earliest to review a film, critics who saw *The Big Man* at Edinburgh spread the bad word of mouth with a vengeance. Many of them disliked the downbeat, depressingly monotonous mood of the film. It was not hard to argue that Neeson's performance was distinctly one-toned and lacked the inspiration and zest that the role demanded. Whalley-Kilmer's unmastered accent left her a sitting duck, and the film's overall message did not fit the times. The 1980s audiences desired to be entertained, not pummelled into sympathising with the downtrodden Danny.

'I think the film is very good,' Woolley said five years later. 'I am very pleased with it, very proud of it. There was a solidarity around the making of *The Big Man* that was very important to me and to Palace. I'm not just another producer just doing it for the buck. There is a long-term plan here – I don't even know what precisely that long-term plan is – but this film was part of a brick that went towards it.' However, he also recognised that a film that centred on how a 'community came together under the worst strain of the Thatcher years [had] a theme which wasn't a very popular notion at the time'.

Woolley also suggested that whereas female reviewers understood the anti-violence message of the film, most of the men said, ' "This is just sick. This isn't boxing, it's completely over the top".'

And yet our research into this kind of boxing had shown that people just keep on going and going. As long as the guys were standing, they'd bash each other down.'

Against a backdrop of that summer's poll tax riots and the film's critical assassination, Palace prepared a big publicity campaign. More than £350,000 was spent on prints and advertising, and yet the film died within its first two weeks, amassing a paltry £268,000 at the box office. As Mike Ewin, Palace's cinema booker, admits, '*The Big Man* never really started.'

Although Woolley recalls most of the Palace staff getting behind the film, there were certain crucial exceptions. Having never begrudged the amount of time and effort the company demanded he put into its productions, Daniel Battsek had started to have second thoughts. 'Until *The Big Man* I had allowed myself to ride along and, despite my doubts about every other movie, had found ways to be persuaded that we could reach the man on the street. It was only when Palace reached *The Big Man* – when suddenly I couldn't be persuaded that anyone would want to see that movie – that I began to reject the Steve-like "You must make this film work" and we began to fight properly.' It was a change in attitude that was to weaken one of Palace's strongest assets.

When Harvey and Bob Weinstein first screened the completed film, they loved it. 'They were incredibly excited,' Woolley said. 'Harvey thought that it was a work of genius, and so did Bob.' After the film had bombed in the UK and had met a lukewarm response at the Toronto Film Festival, however, Harvey cornered the shell-shocked Leland, and insisted that a new title and a major re-cut and re-voicing were required before the film could be launched in America.

Leland was dragged into a lengthy and exhausting re-edit of a film Harvey retitled *Crossing The Line*. Everything was going wrong; Woolley recalls a hasty preview screening in Cincinnati, where Miramax and Woolley were overseeing the shoot of *A Rage in Harlem*. Leland flew down specially for the screening, only to find in the cinema a pitiful audience of around twenty, including a mother with three children below the age of seven. Whatever *The Big Man* might have been, it certainly was not a film for infants. Woolley and Leland were furious with Harvey, who promptly screamed at his poorly organised underlings. When the radically altered film was finally released in North America, it lasted just a few weeks in the cinemas.

Woolley, though deeply disappointed at the film's failure, moved quickly on to other projects. The Palace co-chairman's production schedule for much of 1990 took him thousands of miles from Wardour Mews and the financial problems Powell was contending with on a twenty-four-hour basis.

The first film of the year was a $9 million all-American project, *A Rage in Harlem*, to be produced by Woolley and Kerry Boyle. It was precisely the kind of film the ever-ambitious Woolley had hoped Palace's Los Angeles office would inspire, raising the company's profile in America and providing a potential boost to the UK distribution operation.

Backed by Miramax and Powell's independently-raised finance, and set to be made with an entirely black crew, *A Rage in Harlem*'s cast included Forest Whitaker, Danny Glover, Gregory Hines and Robin Givens, the former wife of Mike Tyson. The eight-week shoot in Cincinnati was scheduled to take place almost entirely at night, a strain on any film but made acute by the American union crew's disdainful treatment of the entire production. The costume designer resigned one day before principal photography, costing the production hundreds of thousands of dollars.

Typically, Palace rolled into production before the Canadian Imperial Bank of Commerce and Pierson had come through with the money, once again exposing the company to considerable financial risk. Woolley's patience with touchy directors was tested by Bill Duke, a former actor, who was empowered under the Directors' Guild of America's rules to disappear for ten weeks to edit the film before showing a frame to the frustrated producer. Their relationship had gone from bad to worse during the shoot, which, in stark contrast to most of Woolley's productions, certainly was not a strong, collaborative effort.

Jordan's *The Miracle* went into production in Bray, a small town just south of Dublin, at the same time as *Rage*. Woolley, aware that *Rage* would demand his presence in America, asked Redmond Morris, a line producer, to take a leading role in the production. Having fought hard to help raise £2.7 million for this, Jordan's first film after his semi-successful sojourn in Hollywood, whenever Woolley turned up on set he encountered a nervous director. After all, this was Jordan's chance to re-establish his reputation. He did: the critics adored the film, which went on to win both an exhibitors' award and the public prize at the Berlin Film Festival alongside a Best Original Screenplay award from the London *Evening Standard*.

According to Simon Perry (who in 1991 would take over from Relph as chief executive at British Screen), by late 1990 it was obvious to him that British Screen's relationship with Palace had to change. The relationship was crucial to Palace, which was always hopeful that the government-backed organisation would help fund every project it presented to them. For the man in charge of British Screen's investments, dealing with Powell and Woolley was not always an easy prospect.

As Milan's MIFED film market got underway in late October 1990, Perry (who knew he would be in the job in three months' time) took a fresh look at Palace. 'Nik was in a high old state in Milan, claiming they were going into production on *The Pope Must Die* any day, but also still trying desperately to get the money together. I thought that something was happening here. Instead of Nik raising the money and Steve spending it, things were happening in the other order. Steve was spending the money, and then Nik was having to raise it. That was a very dangerous situation, because it meant that the rug was being pulled from under Nik's feet by the fact that in Yugoslavia there was a production rushing towards a start date. It meant that Palace's position in negotiations was growing weaker and weaker.' Perry decided that it was time to review British Screen's investment.

Since 1987, British Screen had invested in five Palace films, and earned their money back on two. Perry's concern was such that he decided 'to drive a train' – as Powell later described it – through

British Screen's relationship with Palace. He set about altering the pattern established by Relph, telling Powell: 'I'm not going to ask Palace to protect my downside and guarantee some of British Screen's investment back. Instead, I'm going to fight hard to get a bigger share of the upside of the films which work.' Powell accepted the change with an air of relief, all too aware of the need to keep British Screen content. He was right to do so. On this basis, Perry would become involved with three further films after *The Pope Must Die*.

Despite Woolley's already hectic schedule, far from calming down by the middle of 1991, Palace Productions was shifting into sixth gear, preparing to roll out two more films, *Waterland* and *Dust Devil*, and later put into pre-production Neil Jordan's then-titled *A Soldier's Wife*. It was to be Palace's last film.

CHAPTER ELEVEN

# Woman
# at War

Thinking back to 1990, Powell described himself, somewhat disingenuously, as a 'reasonably busy person'. He took around twenty-five decisions an hour – constantly barking a stream of instructions at Katy McGuinness and the recently appointed Angela Morrison – and a phone call every minute (to the intense irritation of people already in meetings with him). His attention was demanded by more than a dozen major companies, as well as the well-being of the Group as a whole, and in 1990 he was overseeing the financing of three feature films and a TV mini-series, together worth more than £12 million.

From 1988 Powell took an increasing interest in Palace Television. One of this division's and Powell's major achievements had been the winning of British Satellite Broadcasting's Power Station programming contract in 1989. To Palace, the new rock rival to MTV was worth more than £1 million in cash flow a year, and a healthy profit of around £350,000 per annum.

Powell had wooed former *Time Out* editor Don Atyeo to help run the outfit. The Power Station was perfect Palace territory. Young, funky and entertaining, the cheap-and-cheerful satellite television provided Powell with an ideal flagship for his television ambitions. It was a franchise he guarded with great pride and care. Having beaten off four competitors for the rock-cum-pop channel licence with 'the lowest cost per hour in UK television', the last thing Powell needed was any trouble with the government authorities. So, despite his 'reasonably busy' existence, when Powell received a phone call from Bob Hunter, a British Satellite Broadcasting executive who oversaw the channel's programming output, he dropped everything.

'Hello Nik. You'd better come over right now and take a look at these tapes. We've got a problem with the Independent Broadcasting Authority,' Hunter said.

Powell leapt into a cab and turned up at Hunter's office minutes later.

'The IBA are really hopping up and down, Nik,' Hunter warned, shoving a video tape into a machine. 'Take a look at this.'

The video tape showed the Power Station's ginger-haired twenty-four-year-old presenter, Chris Evans, sitting behind his desk. He got up from his chair to reveal a very short pair of running trousers and jumped to the other side of the desk. Hunter stopped the tape.

Powell was puzzled. He still could not see anything strange or offensive, so Hunter showed the scene frame by frame on BSB's state-of-the-art equipment. As Evans's scissor-kick jump straddled the table, one of his testicles happened to drop from his shorts.

'But nobody could spot that in a million years,' Powell stammered, incredulous that he had been dragged away from Wardour Mews for this.

Hunter agreed, but insisted that Powell had to placate the IBA. Powell rang the Authority and sent a letter in which he undertook that nothing like the Evans 'slip' would happen again, adding that from now on Evans would be instructed to wear 'tight bicycling shorts'.

Evans later moved to Channel's 4's *Big Breakfast* show and, despite being voted the ugliest man on television in 1993, gained national celebrity status. The Power Station's fate was less blessed. In November 1990, the expensive satellite war of 1989 90 came to an abrupt halt. BSB merged with Rupert Murdoch's Sky in the last week of October 1990. Despite Powell being one of the few BSB executives who had stuck strictly to budget, Sam Chisolm, Murdoch's executive henchman in charge of the new BSkyB, promptly dumped the Power Station.

In addition to wiping out the healthy cash flow so coveted by Powell, the BSkyB merger had a further important effect on Palace. Palace's independent distribution wing had done extremely well selling the pay-TV rights to its films to both BSB and Sky. Competition for the films had been intense, and prices had been buoyant. As soon as the merger was signed, BSkyB, which was losing a staggering £10 million a week, stopped buying all new product.

Powell faced his staff at the Power Station's leased studios in Parson's Green with a brave face, as he explained to them that the operation had to come to an end but would, he hoped, be revived with the help of new investors. The studio, cheap, cheeky but also experimental and energetic, had been a testimony to the most creditable elements of the Palace philosophy. Once again, Palace had provided a starting block for many talented young people, who have since gone on to work in the British television and film industries.

The Power Station's closure was a stroke of badly timed misfortune which marked the rise of an ill-wind swirling around Wardour Mews. Despite the blow, Powell tried to raise additional capital to relaunch the satellite music station, and approached numerous potential investors, including Richard Branson, about the venture. Unfortunately, the pan-European strength of MTV and the relatively low profile of the Power Station counted against him. So, instead, Powell turned his attention towards making a bid for a forthcoming ITV licence franchise.

PolyGram, the $3 billion Dutch-owned music giant, epitomised the new corporate face of Europe at the start of the 1990s. Like German-owned Bertelsmann, France's Hachette and Branson's Virgin Group, among others, PolyGram was keen to use the security of its sales to expand into the audio-visual business, an area it saw as enjoying growth potential. It was also starting to take a renewed interest in the British media scene, having invested in it for a short period during the late 1970s, although its film investments had not met with much success. Powell, sticking to the entertainment business's definition of capital – i.e. using someone else's money, not your own – had had an eye on PolyGram as a potential partner for some time.

PolyGram's film, video and television interests were run by smooth, dapper Michael Kuhn, a lawyer by training, who had come into contact with Powell during his days at Virgin. According to Kuhn, it was at the 1990 Cannes Film Festival that Powell approached him about the idea of a joint bid for an ITV franchise. To both men it made sense. Palace had a foothold in television via the Power Station, while PolyGram was a strong corporate partner able to help underwrite the expense of a television franchise bid, and already owned a majority stake in independent film producer Working Title, which was just starting to move into television drama. For Powell's fledgling Palace Television, a stake in an ITV licence would not only propel his new division forward in leaps and bounds, but help underwrite the entire Palace Group. He was also keen to put a genuinely independent bid together, rather than a corporate conglomeration that would merely replace the old ITV bosses with more of the same.

When it came to costs, Kuhn was clearly on Powell's wavelength: 'Given that it was likely to be the usual British kind of fix, we wanted to do something that was as inexpensive as we could manage, but still a serious bid.'

Knowledgeable in film and video but lacking experience in television production, just before Christmas 1990 Powell and Kuhn approached Tom Gutteridge, whose Mentorn Films each year produced more than 250 hours of programming for the BBC, ITV and Channel 4. Gutteridge specialised in arts, drama and entertainment programming, and had produced *01 For London* and *Challenge Anneka*, the primetime BBC1 show. By the New Year, Gutteridge had told Powell that he would join the consortium.

After a lengthy debate regarding which ITV franchise to bid for, the group decided to go up against London Weekend Television.

They named their consortium 'London Independent Broadcasting', and few groups came in for more criticism both from rival bidders and the press. One observer said, in the television trade magazine *Broadcast*, that 'All [of LIB's directors] are driven men with monstrous egos,' adding that the chances of them not falling out with each other were very small indeed. The consortium was quickly dubbed 'The Groucho Club Bid'.

Part of the television establishment and the City's scepticism was due to their deep-rooted suspicion of independently run film and record companies. This distrust was augmented by PolyGram committing itself to only a twenty-five per cent stake in the company. Their caution was probably dictated by the then poor financial state of Philips, the Dutch electronics company, which held eighty per cent of PolyGram's shares. Palace, Working Title and Mentorn each took fifteen per cent – the maximum allowed for independent production companies – while the final thirty per cent was to be taken by City stockbroker Hoare Govett. The chief executive set to run the station if the bid was successful was Stewart Till, then running Rupert Murdoch's Sky Movie Channel, who joined PolyGram's film operation a few months later anyway.

Andrew Davidson's book about the ITV franchise battle, *Under The Hammer*, contends that the LIB bid came together in an increasingly haphazard manner. On the evening in May 1991 before the completed bids had to be delivered to the newly appointed Independent Television Commission, Gutteridge was finalising the eight-page summary on a portable computer in his Wardour Street offices. Surrounded by lawyers, advisers and consultants, Gutteridge worked until midnight, when he finally finished the summary. Unfortunately, at that point, one of the lawyers got up to make some coffee. As he walked across the room, his foot caught the computer's power cable, dragging the plug from the wall socket. The screen went blank. Gutteridge had not saved the summary document.

Kuhn, who had just entered the room to check that the bid had been completed, was horrified at the news, and quickly dictated a new, generously spaced, summary of why the LIB was the right choice for the London weekend franchise to a rapidly summoned secretary.

Five months later, on 16 October 1991, the ITC rejected LIB's £35.41 million bid on the grounds that it failed the quality threshold. The incumbent LWT was reinstated for a mere £7.58 million.

On reflection, Kuhn felt that while the consortium may not have had the resources of an ITV company, it was nevertheless an 'extremely powerful bid'. 'We had the money guaranteed, a company in Palace that had set up a broadcasting operation from scratch on a zero-based budget basis, programme providers who before and since have proved themselves the best in the world, and one of Europe's biggest management companies in the entertainment business. The fact that it was finished off late at night with computers going down and last-minute scurrying around was true of every single bid,' Kuhn explained.

Despite the LIB bid's failure, Powell argued that the consortium could have run London's weekend broadcaster as well as anyone else. He felt that the bid failed partly because the government added the quality hurdle half-way through the process, but ultimately because LIB's image was wrong. 'You know, a bunch of youngish entrepreneurs like Palace backed by a foreign record company like PolyGram isn't really English Establishment.'

The bid did have one positive effect in that it cemented the relationship between Palace and PolyGram, a relationship that was to have enormous ramifications for the future of Powell's company.

A key player in a consortium competing with LIB in the ITV franchise bids was Allan McKeown. After a period in American television, McKeown had developed populist comedy series such as *Lovejoy* and *Birds of a Feather*, building his Witzend Productions into SelecTV, which by the end of the 1980s was a thriving independent production company. Although McKeown believed that LWT was always going to win back its franchise, he talked to Powell about joining the LIB bid, and in the end decided to join the Meridian (Clive Hollick's) MAI group/Central TV bid. In October

1991 the Meridian bid won the South/South-East franchise, beating TVS and two other rival bidders.

Tough, funny and seasoned, McKeown – who is married to actress and comedian Tracey Ullman – knows the television business inside out. Having learned the hard way from Lew Grade (who helped him produce many of his early television programmes while controlling and exploiting the international rights for himself), McKeown wanted to set up a company that would distribute his own product and gradually build a library of programmes to exploit.

Powell approached McKeown at the Cannes MIPCOM Television market in October 1989 about the possibility of a joint venture between Palace and SelecTV. Powell's idea was to set up a company to handle the product of SelecTV and Palace. Palace Television was completing a Channel 4 series, *Beyond The Groove*, hosted by David Rappaport and co-produced by his brother, former Palace executive Irving Rappaport, and Martyn Auty. The musical drama series' star cast included Little Richard, Barry White, Bob Geldof, Harry Dean Stanton and the Eurythmics. Powell planned that *Beyond The Groove* would be Palace's first project to be sold by the new TV Sales Company.

McKeown liked Powell a lot, and was very impressed by the Palace Group's success at producing and distributing films. His one concern was Powell's approach to the television business. 'I think Nik had gone about financing *Beyond The Groove* in the same way as he'd done the movies,' McKeown said. 'He'd had the idea, gone out to find a few broadcasters who'd take it, had a pretty chunky deficit and thought, "Well, I'll pick that up in overseas sales". That's not quite the way you need to attack television.'

Having worked in the US and the UK markets, McKeown has strong views on the television business. His contention is that the BBC, by being able to afford to dump its shows around the world at unrealistically low prices, has effectively spoilt the entire UK marketplace. Powell's notion that Palace was likely to find big sums of international money for its television projects was anathema to

McKeown, who found it hard even to sell his primetime hits, let alone a late-night musical roadshow.

'Nik had a kind of 1960s business acumen,' McKeown explained. 'During that decade, we all ran these businesses on the principle that you didn't want to make a profit because the Labour government would take ninety-eight per cent of it away in tax. So you lived out of your business and you never paid your bills until the writ or the bailiff arrived. It was a bit macho to operate like that, but as time went on we changed our attitude, especially in television.

'So going round to Nik was like going back in time. Here he was in a sweat shop, making jokes about how there were always people outside trying to get their bills paid, and there often were. I could hear him on the phone telling people to fuck off whom he owed money to, but it was a game, just like we used to do in the sixties.'

So when it came down to jointly running The TV Sales Company, despite their mutual admiration, Powell and McKeown soon found themselves at loggerheads. First, there was the problem of the programmes – or Palace's lack of them. Apart from *Beyond The Groove*, the only key programme Palace Television was producing was *Woman At War*. The mini-series was supposed to be handled by The TV Sales Company, but it never made it to the joint venture because Powell had been forced to sell the show in key territories in order to finance production. McKeown remembers his jaw dropping open at the meeting when Powell explained the deal over *Woman At War*. He was staggered at the amount of money the company had lined up for a product with little to no upside left even at that early stage.

McKeown did not mind that Palace operated differently from SelecTV but he did object to the difficulties he had in getting money out of Palace for the joint running costs of the new company. Following the MIPCOM television market at Cannes in October 1990 a SelecTV accountant billed Palace for around £50,000. The sum was to cover the costs of the market, the overhead of the company and bridging revenues from anticipated sales receipts.

Weeks passed, but no cheque arrived from Palace. SelecTV accountants raised the issue with McKeown, who called Powell.

'What, didn't it get there? I put it on a bike this morning. That's ridiculous,' Powell shouted, turning round to scream 'Tony, you did put that cheque for Allan on a bike?'

'Yes, Nik, it's on a bike. We'll find out where the bike is.'

Days were spent looking for the bike. Eventually it was established that the cheque was not on a bike, but in the post.

'Allan, it'll be with you in a few days,' Powell said.

A week later McKeown called back, explaining that the cheque never arrived.

'Unbelievable! Let's stop the cheque and issue a new one,' Powell said.

'Well, okay, Nik, but we really do need the money. We'll send someone round to pick it up,' McKeown patiently suggested. An employee was sent round to Wardour Mews, but the cheque needed a second signature, and nobody was senior enough to sign it.

In the end, this particular payment was made at a hotel in Cannes at MIP TV in the spring of 1991. McKeown and Powell had a meeting where one of The TV Sales Company's employees (unaware that Powell had pre-arranged to pay a reduced sum) recalls asking for the infamous money. 'Nik was sitting there in his terrible knee-length shorts, fumbling in his pockets for something. In the end he pulled out a screwed-up cheque, and threw it on the floor in front of me. The amount had been crossed out, and changed to half the original sum. It was post-dated.'

By late-1991, SelecTV was producing nearly 100 hours of television programming a year, and building a library of nearly 300 hours for The TV Sales Company to get its teeth into. Palace had delivered six half-hours of *Beyond The Groove*. The joint venture was about to go into profit, with half the healthy commission about to slip away from SelecTV to Palace.

'But Nik was a bloody good partner,' McKeown stressed. 'He wasn't out to score points, and he was embarrassed that Palace wasn't making enough shows. Sure, Palace never paid its bills on time, but they did eventually get paid.' In early 1992 Powell, anxious to keep McKeown clear of certain other problems looming before the Palace Group, sold Palace's shares in The TV Sales

Company to McKeown for £1. Palace left a few outstanding bills, but the deal quietly put the debts to rest once and for all.

Initially, Palace Television was going to be run by Irving Rappaport. However, by 1988 Rappaport had moved away from both distribution and television and was developing Bob Geldof's feature film, *Cowboys*, one of the few Palace projects that never made it into production. In spring 1988 Powell phoned Martyn Auty, hoping that he would be interested in setting up the new division. Powell knew Auty from his days as *Time Out*'s television editor in the early eighties, and when Auty went on to produce drama for the BBC Powell kept in touch. The chance to run an independent television operation within the bustling Palace Group seemed an exciting prospect to the intense and brooding Auty, and he soon accepted Powell's offer.

'Characteristically, Nik felt he could learn about television on the hoof,' Auty recalled. 'We'd walk down the streets in Soho, New York, Cannes or wherever, and Nik would bump into people and tell them we'd started a TV company and we should have a meeting. Most of the contacts came from broadcasters to whom Palace had sold its film rights, but no matter who it was, Nik used every single contact.'

Auty was hired for more than £55,000 a year, a salary which caused considerable consternation within the Palace ranks. Woolley in particular detested the idea of Palace moving into television. Rather than try to stop the new company at birth, however, he decided it was something Powell was so keen on that it would be churlish to stand in his way. So Palace Television was born to a single parent rather than embraced by a united family.

The television project soon dearest to Powell's heart was a 189-page book that the Palace co-chair had bought at an airport, read on a plane, and proudly presented to Auty the first day he joined Palace. *Inside The Gestapo – A Young Woman's Secret War*, was written by Hélène Moszkiewiez, who lived in Vancouver but had grown up in Belgium during the Second World War. The true war thriller tells the story of a woman who worked under the Nazis during their occupation of Brussels between 1942 and 1945. According to the book's jacket copy:

> By day she typed deathlists of prominent Belgian Jews – by night she risked her life in a frantic race to warn them to leave town. She harboured stranded British soldiers in her lodgings and, under orders from the Resistance, stabbed to death a high ranking Gestapo officer . . . [*Inside The Gestapo*] is the unforgettable story of one woman's will to survive against all odds.

As far as Powell was concerned, the book had everything – war, guns, sex and Nazis – and the chance of a documentary with the real woman which could be scheduled to air prior to the mini-series screening, a device the Americans were particularly keen on in the late eighties. Powell told Auty that Palace Television should make the mini-series a top priority. Palace Television's development executive, Valery Ryan, flew to Vancouver with Reg Gadney, the proposed writer, to meet Moszkiewiez. Meanwhile, Auty was carrying out extensive research on Belgian war records in an attempt to find out more about Moszkiewiez's story. Powell remained obsessed with what he saw as the project's commercial potential and ordered him to soldier on. In addition to overseeing the development of the script, Auty was talking to numerous potential investors and considering various locations, including France, Germany, Luxembourg, and made a week-long trip to Eastern Europe to check out possible studios for the shoot.

Powell had succeeded in wooing the BBC's Head of Drama Jonathan Powell to the table, but instead of bankrolling the project himself, Powell suggested that the money for the project should come from Alan Howden's BBC buying department. Howden offered $750,000 towards the mini-series, which, at the time, was budgeted at £1.2 million. After months of cultivating Canal Plus, Palace managed to win $1.2 million from the French pay-TV giant. Edward Bennett, a British television director who had made a host of popular British television dramas, including some of the *Poirot* series, was signed up to direct and was willing to try to improve the script. All Palace now needed was a place to shoot the production.

Eastern Europe had become the leading contender for such a privilege. In the end, Auty felt it was a toss-up between Hungary and Poland. His and Bennett's preference was Hungary, which had become a vibrant production centre in the early 1990s, and was an increasingly popular choice for Hollywood producers. Poland had a less stable infrastructure, lacking experienced crews, cameramen, studios and daily screening and processing facilities, but was correspondingly cheaper.

Powell received a phone call in spring 1990 from Boy George's manager, an old contact from his Virgin days. Powell remembers him saying: 'I've got this Polish producer who's right up your street, really entrepreneurial, so you should talk to him about your TV project.' Within days, a Polish man called Wictor Grodecki [pronounced Victor Grodetski] turned up at Wardour Mews. He claimed an extensive track record in production in both Poland and California. Powell was impressed, and looked forward to working with a man who, he believed, could make things happen, rather than with one of the old bureaucratic Polish or Hungarian studios.

At Powell's prompting, Auty later met the Pole, though he was not quite certain what the meeting was to be about. Grodecki instantly whipped out his business card from a breast pocket, explaining: 'It's about *Woman At War*. I can help you. I am Polish producer. Whatever they quote you in Hungary, I can do cheaper. It's no problem. We can do it for million dollars.'

Auty asked if he had read the script, which he had not.

'Well, how do you know it's going to cost a million dollars?' Auty asked.

'I give you crew, cameras, everything for one million. It's no problem,' Grodecki replied.

What the Pole was offering was the below-the-line costs of the Polish shoot – which meant the inclusion of physical costs such as extras, equipment, studios and locations – all based on a figure that was plucked out of the air as far as Auty could see. A few days later Auty had a meeting with Powell.

'How'd you get on with Wictor then?' Powell asked.

'Bit iffy really,' Auty replied.

'Argh, you know these Poles, Martyn. He's okay and anyway, it's a cheaper deal,' Powell said.

Auty proceeded to point out that Poland was five hours' flight away, that the country had no real production infrastructure, and that Palace had no idea who Grodecki was, and whether they could trust him. Powell, mindful that Palace had already invested more than £100,000 in development costs, ignored the arguments in favour of the cheaper deal.

*Woman At War* raced into pre-production, with Hollywood actors Eric Stoltz and Martha Plimpton cast in the lead roles. In a practical sense, neither actor was a wise choice, as Plimpton was a vegan and Stoltz a lactose vegan. As Poles tend to favour products considerably higher up the food chain, a cook had to be flown out to look after the actors' diets.

Bennett, who had initially been unhappy about the switch from Hungary to Poland, changed his mind when he reached the Polish town of Wroclaw. During the 1930s, the Nazi Albert Speer had designed a huge film studio just outside the town. Bennett thought the place looked extraordinary, and was confident the town could double for Brussels in the early 1940s.

By the time Auty, Bennett and the British side of the crew reached Poland in early October, Palace had already realised that certain key costumes and props would have to be flown in. Palace employees flew in with hand-held props, and on one occasion Katy McGuinness came over from London with some thirty-foot sheets of metal that the designer needed to complete the set.

During pre-production in September and October, Auty knew a lot of things were going badly wrong. During the first few days, he did not spot one camera, costumes for the extras, or 'any of those things you need to make a movie'. When questioned, Grodecki replied: 'It's no problem. They'll be here tomorrow.'

Following an inspection of the local film processing laboratories, a decision was taken to ship all the footage back to England rather than risk ruining it in the local facilities. Getting a phone line out of Wroclaw, it transpired, entailed paying two women to sit all day trying to get a connection to London. Although fax machines were provided, none of them worked. Walkie-talkies were everywhere, but also did not function.

Grodecki's office at the studios had a large photostat blow-up of a US hundred-dollar bill, underneath the sign of his company, AMPOL FILM. The name served as a neat demonstration of Grodecki's desire to unite the eastern and western worlds. The 'AM' stood for America and the 'POL' for Poland.

The crews had originally been working to a production start date of 5 November. It was put back a day when Auty found Grodecki in a local bar, when he was supposed to have been at a production meeting. He sobered the Pole up, explaining: 'Look, tomorrow morning I've got to see a camera.'

'Come to studio at eleven o'clock. There will be camera.'

By this stage some members of the Polish crew had started to ally themselves with Palace rather than with their employer, Grodecki. Auty was warned by his first assistant director that there would be a camera the next day, but it would have been borrowed from another unit. Sure enough, Auty could see the labels of the other unit plastered on the sides of the boxes when, the next morning, Grodecki proudly unpacked a twelve-year-old Arriflex camera.

'Look, Wictor, I don't care where this came from, but tomorrow morning we're turning over on this camera. Right?'

'It's no problem,' came the stock reply.

On the first morning of production, Auty gathered together the crew, who wore cheap faded blue denim and whose long faces bore heavy moustaches, and gave them a talk. 'It was a very rousing kind of speech. I'd like to think that was something that really set the tone of the whole thing,' Auty recalled. Standing next to Bennett, he told them what Palace was going to do, and how the project was all about 'building bridges, rather than coming all this way to tell people how to make movies'. One of the things Auty mentioned was that the production would aim to shoot five minutes of footage a day. However, when the interpreter reached that line, most of the crew broke out laughing. Auty and Bennett looked quizzically at each other, while the interpreter leaned over and explained: 'We only shoot two minutes a day. That's all we do.'

Within three days of entering production, it became clear that Palace was not getting what it was paying for. Auty would compare Grodecki's budget with what was actually being shot each day, and challenge the Pole with the discrepancies. Initially the answer would be that the price was right, then Grodecki would claim that the goods Palace was being charged for had gone astray 'on the way from Kiev'. Finally, a reluctant apology would be forthcoming, and a promise that everything would be all right the next day. At the end of the first week Auty sent a telex to London explaining the severity of the situation. The only way to send it was via an office where the message would be open to scrutiny by Grodecki's people.

At this point, just as the temperatures were starting to drop below zero, Palace's production accountant Michael Garland flew to Poland, armed with a calculator and a thin denim jacket. Powell had instructed him, somewhat optimistically, to get the project's finances under control, and to find out what was happening to the money Palace was paying Grodecki. Most production accounts are set up in a way that allows the producer to draw down money on a weekly basis. The cash flow levels are set next to anticipated budget requirements, which are normally steep in the first few weeks, reach a peak, and then drop away towards the end of a shoot. Palace was paying for the English and American actors and other above-the-line costs, while Grodecki was responsible for the production's below-the-line costs, for which he was being paid $1 million. (Above-the-line costs cover the creative elements, including story rights and screenplay, executive producer, producer, director and principal cast; while below-the-line covers the physical cost of the production.)

Grodecki had arranged with Palace that tranches of his co-producing fee and costs would be paid at regular intervals into his London account by Palace. The money came to Palace from Canal Plus, which delivered its payments on time. Palace would then pass the money on to Grodecki. The Pole's money would be converted by his London bank into US dollars, which would be brought quite legally into Poland in suitcases by Grodecki's courier.

By the time members of the Polish crew started to approach Auty and Garland about their lack of pay, Grodecki had received more than $400,000 of Palace's money into his account. Garland would patiently sit down with the Pole and go through the figures on each day's shoot, but however hard the accountant tried, they did not add up. Scenes where 2,000 extras had been promised were shot with 800 Polish locals, with the pay for the other 1,200 disappearing into thin air. Grodecki would resort to blaming the production's Polish-born designer, an easy target, but one that Auty and Garland both found difficult to accept.

Auty's petty cash was running out, drained by countless costs for which, he argued, under the contract, Grodecki was responsible. Bennett would ask the producer to slip the odd few notes to loyal members of the crew to keep them happy. Auty even had to pay people to turn on a gas ring to heat soup for the crew. Isolated and under great pressure, Auty found himself having to explain to the Polish crew that he could not pay them because that was Grodecki's responsibility. The paranoia and mistrust was intense. Garland would sit down to breakfast with Polish crew members who would then move to a different table.

At the end of the second week, Auty requested some legal support from Palace in his war with Grodecki. Katy McGuinness flew out, and two lawyers representing Grodecki also boarded planes from London to Poland for a show-down. Garland and Auty joined McGuinness in the heated meetings, which were held in a damp, smoke-filled caravan. Also present was a representative from Film Finances, the project's completion guarantors, who were understandably alarmed by the break in production. The lawyers failed to come to any agreements and no progress was made. As the weeks dragged on and Christmas approached, the production froze to a standstill.

When McGuinness finally returned to London, the word flew round Wardour Mews that 'things are getting really bad in Poland'. Nobody really knew why, but the obvious scapegoat, as producer, was Auty. Woolley, who at this stage was dealing with *The Pope Must Die* on location in Yugoslavia, declined to help sort things out. He had his own problems to deal with, not least making a film in a country on the brink of civil war, and being arrested and shoved into jail for a night for throwing snowballs with Adrian Edmondson. However, he did suggest to Powell that the best person to help Palace complete *Woman At War* was Patrick Cassavetti, the outstandingly efficient producing partner on *Mona Lisa*.

In the middle of December Auty flew back to London to tell Powell that Palace had to get out of the deal with Grodecki before any more money was lost. He and McGuinness started to look for an alternative Polish producer to help bring the project in. A few days later, Powell flew to Poland and summoned the crew to a meeting at a crumbling pre-war hotel (where one of the cast had just watched a rat jump out of a toilet).

'Right, we're going to get this show on the road,' Powell stated boldly. 'We're going to change over from Wictor to a different company, we've rescheduled from the original twelve-week shoot to fourteen, and Ed is still directing. Michael is here from Palace's production department, Katy is here from our legal department, and Palace is right behind you. Good luck.'

That evening, Grodecki arranged to have a meeting with Powell in his hotel room. Garland and other members of the crew had, without Powell's knowledge, been hiding in Powell's room film stock they had removed from Grodecki's house. Garland raced over and warned the bemused Powell, who was in his pyjamas, that he had to shift the boxes before Grodecki spotted the stock.

When Auty saw Powell that same evening, he asked the Palace chief if he was staying on the production, given that his name had not been mentioned in Powell's rallying speech that afternoon. 'If not, you should tell me to my face,' Auty insisted. Powell was evasive, saying that he would confirm everything in a few days. Several days went by, with no news from Powell, before Auty was invited by Bennett to go for a drink. Bennett explained what Powell had failed to say, namely that Auty's position had been sacrificed to keep Film Finances happy, and that Cassavetti and Ray Corbett, the first assistant director from *Hardware*, would be joining the production shortly.

'I think what happened was that in Nik's enthusiasm to prove that Palace Television could function, he basically said to his head of television, "Fuck off",' Cassavetti explained later. 'It wasn't fair on Martyn, who wanted someone out there on site all the time so that he could get on with his own job.'

Cassavetti had privately advised Powell to pull out before Christmas and write the disaster off, but Powell managed to persuade the guarantors to back the new team and schedule, and told Cassavetti, 'Narh, we've got to go on and finish it.' By the time the producer arrived in Wroclaw, 'the crews were exhausted and despondent, and the director was beside himself'. He recalled that 'Grodecki was still around, but he was in an office being guarded. It was deeply unpleasant, something similar to the Wild West.'

On the first night of re-shooting there was a show-down between the new Polish crew and Grodecki's team. Grodecki and his crew and minders marched with petrol cans towards the set, which was in the middle of a city wasteland. The British crew also rushed to the set, together with all Poles loyal to Palace. 'It was like a Mexican stand-off,' Garland recalled. 'The bad guys blinked first and it all fell to nothing.' It was the last the production saw of Grodecki and his crew.

As February came to a close, *Woman At War* limped towards a wrap. Both Palace and Film Finances lost thousands on the project. According to one source close to the project, the final cost, when post-production and a further re-shoot in March were included, was more than double the original budget of $2 million. The budget was not the only casualty. Auty left Palace towards the end of 1991, depressed and disappointed at the lack of loyalty Powell and Palace had demonstrated. If he had been too inexperienced to handle the production, he felt, Powell should never have put him out there. Once committed, Palace failed to stand by its man.

Garland's reward was a virus he picked up during his four-month stint in Poland. He was very upset by the lack of support from London and shocked by the Polish nightmare. Deciding that he'd prefer to take a step back, he asked Powell if he could leave Palace. A deal was cut where he was given first option on Palace's films as a freelance production accountant, which suited Garland perfectly.

Grodecki attempted to launch a court case against Palace during post-production. Powell explained that there 'was quite a bit of litigation, but it was obviously going nowhere'. The mini-series was shown on Canal Plus (where it was a surprise ratings hit) in 1992, but the BBC has yet to screen *Woman At War*.

'I was never keen on that book,' Woolley said later about *Woman At War*. 'I couldn't care less about TV. That's the whole point about my profile. I am Mr Film. I am Mr Cinema. I love cinema. Nik loves TV as well as films, and was desperate for this TV company.

'I think he launched into it in a very bad manner, going for it in the way we have always done films. I should have put my foot down and said No.'

# CHAPTER TWELVE

# The Show
# Must Go On

The cost of doing business was starting to hurt the Palace Group by the time Stoy Hayward's strategy review landed on Powell's desk in March 1990.* Marked 'Private & Confidential', the thirty-three-page 'presentation of recommendations' confirmed to Powell what he already suspected. His company was suffering from 'an excessive spread of activities, an inadequate level of financial resources, and weak organisational structure and management expertise'.

From the banks' point of view, the review provided a sense of relief, finally putting in print what they had been saying to Powell over the past year. Fearful of the growing recession and the increasingly low profit margins in Palace's video distribution operation, Guinness, Pierson and Barclays Bank's Soho Square branch – which handled the Palace Group's trading account – all took a keen interest in the review's findings.

The Stoy Hayward report had taken more than six months to prepare, and cost more than £20,000. Far from being 'superficial', as one Palace senior manager later complained, the report contained a relatively accurate assessment of the Group's position. Powell had no quarrel with Stoy Hayward's overall findings, and neither did the Palace board when they met to discuss it. 'It wasn't a long

---

* The report was leaked by a private source, not by Stoy Hayward.

discussion, as we accepted their recommendations pretty much wholesale,' Powell explained philosophically. Rather than get upset or take things personally, the Palace chief decided that the best approach was to digest the material and act on it as fast as possible.

As well as praising Palace's strengths, including marketing skills, entrepreneurial flair and 'cash flow awareness' (a quality not to be underestimated), the document detailed losses and problems for which both Powell and Woolley had to take direct responsibility. Although Palace Productions was supposed to be financed off the balance sheet (with production monies flowing through individual companies rather than the whole Group), the finance for development, pre-production costs, constantly deferred production fees and what Powell called 'enhancement monies' took their toll. He estimated that enhancement monies, spent to 'enable us to finish off the final film in the way we wanted – and it was incredibly important to realise the vision of say Steve, Neil or Julien – obviously were to be written off'; they came to a total of between £100,000 and £300,000 per Palace production. In 1987, due mainly to a 'significant loss by productions' such as *Siesta*, the pressure of these costs brought pre-tax profits down by nearly eighty-five per cent. While the growth in both theatrical and video distribution since the company's inception had been impressive, 1989 witnessed Palace Video's annual turnover dropping from nearly £8 million to £4 million as a result of the changing market and underperforming films. The video operation had been slow to adapt to the new buoyant video retail market. Rental figures were dropping, while sales in shops were rising rapidly, but Palace was not benefiting much from the change. As Woolley later conceded, 'We knew the way the market was going, but we didn't assess the importance of the sell-through market as quickly as we should have done. In a sense we were victims of our own early successes.'

The review's three principal findings struck at the heart of the Group's difficulties. First, Palace's limited resources were spread too thinly over too many of its activities, resulting in the Group becoming both small and weak in most of its markets. Palace's historical development had been shaped by 'having a finger in a number of pies', while individual directors had 'pursued activities which interested them'.

Second, the board of directors, including Powell, Woolley and Craib, were too involved in the day-to-day operational problems to have a proper overview of the whole Group and consequently were 'stretched'. In particular, Craib was so involved in non-core businesses by the time the recession started to bite that the group managing director had little idea of the state of the Group's other major activities. Craib later explained that 'Nik was starting to make productions his little empire, and no one else had a look-in. Given the impact that productions were having on the rest of the group, I considered that dangerous.' Indeed, the review argued that too much reliance was being placed on Powell to 'make things happen', suggesting that the Palace co-chairman was either not delegating sufficiently or was suffering from a lack of effective middle-management. In reality, both scenarios were true.

Stoy Hayward demonstrated Palace's business portfolio by placing its main companies in boxes marked 'Stars', 'Cash Cows', 'Question Marks' and 'Dogs', alongside a commentary. Palace Pictures' cinema distribution operation fared well, landing in 'Cash Cows', while Palace Productions and Palace Video were boxed in 'Question Marks'. Significantly, four of Palace's 'non-core' companies – the Video Editing Centre, the Video Palace shops, Palace's software company and the record company, Boudisque – were all branded 'Dogs'.

The review did not pull its punches. By page twelve it was recommending selling three of Palace's 'Dogs', and fifty per cent of the Video Editing Centre. The maximum amount Stoy Hayward estimated Palace could raise by such action was £5 million, the minimum £2.5 million.

The report pointed to a history of poor forward planning and unrealistic projections which had left the Group 'consistently underfunded', a problem that was to take on increasing importance as Powell attempted to put the recommendations into action.

The report's criticisms also raised questions about Powell's role in the company. During the previous three years, Powell had found himself increasingly caught up in the search for finance for Palace's films. Following the report, some of Palace's bankers wanted to ensure that Powell focused on the Palace Group, rather than the ever-greedy Palace Productions.

Ironically, just as Stoy Hayward had been preparing its final presentation during the last days of March, Palace had hit a typical cash flow crisis. Palace Productions and Palace Television had clawed down around £500,000 of the Group's resources due to post-production costs on *The Big Man*'s music score, late costs on *Scandal*, and the unanticipated cash-flowing of the television series *Beyond The Groove* for Channel 4. In addition, due mainly to the mismanaged release of *Family Business*, further funding was required for Palace Video, which served to underline once again how severely under-capitalised Palace was. Without more capital, it could hardly cope with its high level of production and releases, let along keep the rabid 'Dogs' ' heads above water. Yet the Group had been re-capitalised only two months previously. It also had £1 million and £500,000 paid in advance by Parkfield and Guild Entertainment respectively for video distribution rights. In their report, Stoy Hayward estimated that by May Palace would have a shortfall of capital of more than £1 million.

In addition to the strategic sell-off and financial restructuring, Stoy suggested three new appointments. These included a new chief executive officer to take over day-to-day control of the Group and help raise new money; a productions director who, unlike the frequently absent Woolley, would remain in London and 'hold the fort'; and a distribution director who would sit on the Palace board.

During 1991 Woolley spent just one month in London, dividing the rest of his time between *The Miracle* in Ireland, *Rage in Harlem* in the US, and (after squeezing in a wedding to Elizabeth Karlsen) he flew out to Yugoslavia to produce *The Pope Must Die*. No wonder it was suggested that Woolley needed a supporting production manager in Wardour Mews.

Powell and Woolley were encouraged to delegate their daily responsibilities, while Craib, as the adviser to the new chief executive, was to focus his efforts 'on ensuring that financial affairs are under control'. In the end, no production manager was appointed, although

Daniel Battsek was promoted from head of UK theatrical operations to take charge of all of Palace's distribution operations, including video, and was appointed to the board as the non-executive distribution director recommended by the Stoy report, while Robert Jones was appointed to the board as non-executive acquisitions director. The moves reflected the extent to which Battsek and Jones had become a link between the co-chairmen and a staff from whom, in their efforts to keep Palace breathing, they had become increasingly alienated. Yet Powell recognised that Palace still needed a new senior executive to come on board.

Stoy Hayward had gone into considerable detail on the profile of the new chief executive. The person needed to be between thirty-five and forty-five years of age, experienced in either broadcasting or video record distribution, and offer strong entrepreneurial management skills. Aggressive, eager for a challenge, but also profit-conscious, Palace's new whiz-man should ideally come to Wardour Mews with an established 'high profile in the industry'. It even referred to specific Channel 4 and Zenith TV senior executives, suggesting 'a Colin Leventhal/Charles Denton type'.

The person that Palace finally appointed was the twenty-eight-year-old Tony Kelly, the former head of programme finance at British Satellite Broadcasting. Kelly joined the Group in early August 1990 on a salary of £75,000, full of enthusiasm for the task in hand. It was the most senior appointment in his high-flying career, and a long way from his childhood days in Manchester on the biggest council estate in Europe. Kelly's background attracted Powell, who did not want a corporate executive with little experience in raising money or operating financial controls. Kelly had worked at International Computers Limited, Mars Confectionery (which Powell had always admired for its 1930s open-plan offices, its cost-saving efficiencies such as sharing secretaries and its lack of company cars) and at the Goldcrest group before joining BSB, where Powell had worked closely with him during the Power Station negotiations. Kelly's bright and breezy manner was appealing to Powell, who saw the young executive as a 'no thrills, no bullshit' appointment. In his enthusiasm the Palace co-chair omitted to explain to Kelly Palace's true financial situation.

The Palace family was collectively appalled at Powell's choice. Craib felt threatened and constantly put the new chief executive down in his first weeks at the office. Beyond a deep love of football, Woolley found he had absolutely nothing in common with Kelly – and whereas Woolley supported Spurs, Kelly was an avid Manchester United fan. The greatest animosity, however, emanated from Palace's young employees who, addicted to hip movies, club music and black clothing, found Kelly's financial patter, Prince of Wales suits and polka-dot ties too much to bear.

Over the next twenty months, Kelly doggedly worked his heart out. He would reach the Palace offices at seven every morning, and insisted on an eight o'clock management meeting every Monday. As Woolley was hardly ever in the country, he was rarely able to attend.

Kelly's approach to management differed from both Woolley's and Powell's. 'The former management would say, "Here's a problem, Nik, solve it." My view was to address the issues and also come up with some suggestions of how to solve them. I'd keep putting deals forward that weren't all that great, but actually made us money rather than cost us money at the end of the day.' Unfortunately, just as Powell had dominated his other managers and accountants over the years, so he rather overwhelmed Kelly. 'I should've been a bit stronger with Nik, because he's quite a domineering character,' Kelly admitted. Along with Powell's bark, he was also intimidated by the size of the co-chair's shareholding, often keeping his advice to himself when he thought Powell was doing the wrong thing.

Just days before the ill-fated Kelly joined Palace, Parkfield Group PLC collapsed into administration. Palace Video had, by this time, stopped using Palace Virgin Gold (PVG) to distribute its product and Parkfield was now responsible for sell-through (retail) and Guild Entertainment for rental.

Parkfield's chairman, Roger Felber, was a business entrepreneur and former airline pilot, who had acquired an engineering combine in the early eighties and then diversified into information and entertainment services, notably video. During the late eighties the Parkfield conglomerate became one of the best performing companies on the stock market. However, the group started to shake following the resignation of Paul Feldman, who left his position as head of Parkfield's entertainment division in January 1990. Under his management, thousands of video units, worth around £50 million, had been bought in the build-up to Christmas 1989. The move was disastrous, resulting in a huge stockpile of unsold cassettes. A combination of the recession and the cancellation of Parkfield's exclusive Hollywood distribution contracts triggered a downwards spiral in the share price, which fell from 518 pence in January to 48 pence by 19 July, the day before the conglomerate went into administration.

The Department of Trade and Industry investigated Parkfield's collapse in the spring of 1991 after allegations that the company had 'window-dressed books to avoid bankruptcy' appeared in the British press, (although, in the event, no formal charges were pressed). In April 1991 the *Guardian* alleged that Parkfield had 'attempted to stave off bankruptcy by inflating earnings to the tune of £27 million'. One deal injected a paper income of £14 million into the group, but the accounts failed to show the other side of the bargain – a total of nearly £30 million going from Parkfield to the other party. Shortly before Parkfield finally crashed, owing more than £280 million, Roger Felber had privately assured management executives that the company was sound. By early 1991, Felber was understood to have left the country to take up residence in Peru.

Parkfield's collapse was terribly timed for Palace and put under further pressure the company's cash flow. The advance, in total worth £1 million, which Palace had been drawing down from Parkfield on a monthly basis in return for the Palace catalogue, was suddenly turned off, and Palace Video's retail operation was out of the market for three months whilst a replacement distributor was sought.

Palace's relationship with Guild, its other video distributor, was more stable but considerably less effective than Palace's former arrangement with PVG. However, by 1989 PVG had been disbanded, following Branson's sale of Virgin Vision. Guild had begun to dominate the market for mainstream independent movies, buying distribution rights to such big-budget films as *Total Recall, Terminator 2: Judgment Day* and *Dances With Wolves*. Guild's success at picking up independently made US films normally associated with the Hollywood majors left Palace Video's staff irritated by the distribution arrangement. They felt that Palace's films were getting short shrift when it came to marketing and distribution opportunities. As Powell explained, 'Guild was going through a purple patch, enjoying massive and easy sales, while our product looked less interesting and was harder to sell. There was a feeling that Guild's day-to-day managers were only paying lip-service to our requirements, and that we were seen as relatively small beer.' Palace, with its high-quality but less mainstream rental titles, was also struggling to compete with Hollywood's major distributors who had started to exploit fully the blockbuster-led rental market.

Already charged with finding a way to plug Palace's existing finance gap, Kelly was sent reeling in shock by the Parkfield collapse. 'Unbelievable! You've just got to just picture it. There's me thinking that the world's collapsing around me within days of arriving. What am I doing here? Why is this happening to me?' Kelly quickly set about patching up the cash hole and clinched a new video retail deal by early November. Contrary to one board member's snide observation about Palace's new chief executive – 'I thought we were going to get the ventriloquist, not the dummy' – Kelly was proving that he could fight with a vigour that Powell began greatly to value.

In addition to the appointment of Kelly, Powell accepted Stoy Hayward's recommendation that he should sell Palace's peripheral activities. This was not an easy move, practically nor emotionally, for the Palace co-chairman. The sell-off exercise was later aptly dubbed by Humphrey the equivalent to *Sophie's Choice*, a case of 'which babies should he choose to sell or keep'. However, by the time the software company, the Dutch record company and the video stores were packaged properly, with sales brochures and housekeeping in order, it was too late. Just as, by late-1990, home owners were finding it impossible to sell their houses for anything approaching what they had paid a few years previously, so the Palace companies failed dismally to attract the level of offers Stoy Hayward had forecast at the start of the year.

Boudisque, the Dutch record company, was successfully disposed of for around £225,000 with the buyer also taking on its outstanding debts. After considerable efforts by Craib, a French company agreed to buy the software company. The £200,000 price-tag was not far from Stoy's top estimate, but the buyer backed out at the last minute, and the deal did not go through. Meanwhile, finding a fifty per cent partner for the Video Editing Centre on Poland Street proved impossible. Each week, across Soho, film, video and television editing companies, whose equipment was often more up-to-date than the VEC's, were closing down. Palace was not helped by an enforced delay due to VEC forming an essential part of its Power Station deal with BSB. By the time the Power Station had collapsed, the market was dead.

It was the retail stores, however, that caused Palace's managers their biggest headache. According to Powell, a deal was done to rent out the Berwick Street premises, which brought in some extra income. 'We should have closed Palace Video at that point, but instead we moved into Oxford Street and took on a lease which caused considerable problems later. I should have just said "No".'

The company found itself paying an annual £250,000 lease on a large store in Oxford Street, taken on at the height of the property boom. The shop was half-heartedly filled with racks of videos in an effort to keep some cash rolling in. Far from a Branson-style Megastore, the Oxford Street space was fitted with a knocked-up counter, and the floor was covered with old cuts of carpet from previous tenants. 'It was a nightmare,' Kelly explained. 'We couldn't get rid of it because the lease agreement was cross-guaranteed by the Palace Group which, like a lot of Palace companies, made it difficult to just chop off. I started flogging some of the other shops off at next to nothing just to get them off our hands.' In the end Palace sub-let the Oxford Street site to some

businessmen selling anoraks, who were subsequently replaced by
The Bankrupt Jeans Co.

The BSB merger with Sky was another misfortune for Palace.
Following the collapse of the Power Station deal with BSB in
October 1990, Kelly and Powell managed to negotiate a brief
termination period, which gave them time to find a back-to-back
deal to lease the Parson's Green studios to a new company, Middle
East Broadcasting. The deal was worth £1.1 million to Palace and
got the company off the hook on the extensive leasing commitment.
The deal, however, as Kelly stressed, was not closed until June
1991, by which time Palace's relationship with one of its banks had
changed beyond recognition.

Following the Stoy Hayward review, Powell increasingly spent
his precious time handling Palace's banks, which he knew were so
crucial to keeping the Group in business. Contrary to the external
griping about Palace's 'useless administration', Powell's senior staff
were proving themselves outstandingly brilliant at making the most
of the Group's resources. Many companies heaving under Palace's
pressures would have collapsed long before this point. What Powell,
Craib, Kelly and Humphrey managed to avoid was too many bills
and debts falling due at the same time. They all knew that that
delicate balance was desperately vulnerable. One false move and the
whole company could collapse.

The relationship between Powell and Barclays Bank's Soho
Square business centre did not date back very far. Coutts had been
Palace's trading bank, handling its central clearing operation,
including staff salaries, payment systems and production accounts,
but not equity investments or loans. Powell's relationship with
Coutts dated back to his Virgin days in the 1970s, but the co-chair
became irritated by the constant turnover in managers at Coutts. In
1988 Barclays began to pursue Powell, trying to persuade him to
move the Group's business to them. Given that Powell wanted to
increase the account's overdraft limit, which under Coutts was set at
£350,000, it seemed like a good time to play two banks off against
each other. When Barclays offered a significantly higher limit,
Powell decided to change banks.

'It was one of the few times in my life when I overvalued the usefulness of the additional facility and undervalued the incredibly long relationship I had had with Coutts,' Powell recalled. Money was not hard to come by in the late-1980s. Barclays initially offered Palace an unsecured working capital overdraft of £400,000 and later raised this to £750,000, secured by a second charge on the company. According to Guinness's Premila Hoon, when Barclays first approached her and asked if there was any way in which Guinness could share some security with them by allowing Palace to provide a second charge, she had refused, although later the bank allowed Palace to offer the lower form of security against the loan. It was this facility that was soon to become the subject of a major falling-out between Barclays, Palace, Guinness and Pierson.

By summer 1989, Peter Hitchen, a tall, solidly built silver-haired man, had taken over the Palace account for Barclays. Hitchen, with his friendly style, has a reputation for providing the smooth, publicly acceptable face of Soho Square. Despite his good humour, he had his work cut out. Soho Square, like other clearing banks, was taking a long hard look at its most risky exposures, although in the case of Palace, Hitchen was still happy with Palace's account and credit. Hitchen genuinely liked Powell, but he soon became fed up with the manic meetings with Palace's managers. 'Firstly, I didn't understand why every meeting needed at least three of them. That, together with Nik's mobile, drove me demented,' Hitchen recalled. When Powell's phone (long since banned at the Groucho Club) did ring, Hitchen would bellow: 'Can we have one meeting at a time please!'

What Hitchen was looking for was regular, accurate management and financial information; something he contends was in short supply from Palace. 'It [financial information] was out of date before they even got it,' Hitchen said, adding that the great deference shown to Powell struck him as particularly unhealthy. 'Even from the out-of-date financial information that we received and in the absence of any success in the numerous survival and rescue plans which had been presented to us all through 1990, it was obvious that the Group's financial position had deteriorated markedly from when the overdraft had first been agreed. It was also apparent that we were not being provided with information that was available to other lenders and this above anything else severely undermined the trust between bank and customer which is the corner-stone of any banking relationship. The need for security to bolster the existing facility therefore became paramount.'

Hitchen was right to be suspicious about the level of detailed information Palace was providing. Powell had by now developed a close relationship with Guinness's Premila Hoon, who had a detailed knowledge of Palace's financing and cash flow situation. 'I kept nothing from Guinness, but I wasn't so open with Barclays because they weren't for me our prime bankers. They weren't the ones with anything like as much money at risk as Guinness, and that's where the problem arose,' Powell explained.

By the time Barclays had begun to get cold feet about the £750,000 facility, Wardour Street was rife with rumours about Palace's financial situation. Powell's occasional pub jest – 'Why run a big company well when you can run a small one badly?' – was coming back to haunt him. Talent agents, entertainment lawyers and rival companies started to spread gossip about the company, while larger creditors did not hide the fact that they were being asked by Palace managers to extend payment terms on a weekly basis. Most of this backbiting did not alarm Palace employees. After all, Wardour Street had been predicting Palace's collapse for eight years, so why should they take the rumours seriously now?

Barclays Bank's Soho Square branch is less than two minutes' walk from Wardour Street and its rumour mill, while many of the bank's other customers were entertainment businesses which dealt with Palace. Barclays soon decided that it needed a first charge against Palace Group's assets, in place of the existing second charge, to safeguard its £750,000 exposure. A senior account manager at Barclays met Hoon in Jamuary 1991. This time Barclays asked if it could share a first charge on a *pari passu* basis. Powell was under the misapprehension that Guinness and Barclays would find a workable solution to this new problem, but the two banks were so worried about the deteriorating state of Palace that they were both determined to have a first charge against the company.

Hoon told Barclays bluntly, 'If you want to share the security on a *pro rata* basis, then you should also share the overall risk on a *pro rata* basis.' At the time, Guinness and Pierson were proposing to refinance Palace to the tune of £1.5 million, and it seemed to Hoon that this provided the perfect opportunity for Barclays to come in with them on an equal basis. However, the suggestion of refinancing Palace made Barclays exceedingly nervous.

Palace was owed a considerable sum of money by Guild as part of its video deal, due on or before 15 January 1991. A transfer of £400,000 was expected any day. Hoon was aware of the payment, and wisely asked Palace's management to set up a special (and entirely proper) account for Guinness and Pierson into which the money could be paid. She wanted to ensure that Guinness and Pierson, the principal lenders to Palace, could, if necessary, obtain priority over other creditors, including Barclays. She also wanted to keep Barclays' clearing facility of £750,000 available to Palace; whereas Barclays might possibly attempt to reduce this facility if a sizeable sum came into the account, thus reducing their exposure. Letters were sent by Maarten Melchior, one of Pierson's entertainment executives, to Guild to confirm that the monies would be paid into a Dutch account, whose details he provided. Guild duly signed a fax in agreement on 8 January. Pierson agreed to lend the cash-strapped Palace £400,000 in lieu of Guild's payment.

During the second week of January, a key refinancing meeting was attended by Powell, Craib, Kelly, Hoon, GLE's David Walburn and a representative from Norwich Union, all of whom were prepared to sign off on a new financial package for the company. The plan relied on Barclays' existing £750,000 facility continuing, as well as on other deals Palace had made.

Half-way through the big meeting, the phone rang. It was a Barclays manager from the bank's Regional Office. Could he speak to Hoon? The bank informed her that it was not prepared to lend more money and indeed the continuation of Palace's existing overdraft facility now required 'a thorough review' by the bank's 'intensive care' team from their Regional Office.

What had happened was that the cheque for £400,000 from

Guild had been mistakenly paid into Palace's Barclays account, which reduced the bank's exposure considerably. According to Pierson's Melchior, someone from Palace's accounting staff had received the cheque from Guild, and, unaware that it was destined for the Dutch account, had promptly deposited it in the Barclays' Soho Square account. So the monies failed to reach Pierson, leaving the Dutch bank and its partner, Guinness, a further £400,000 out of pocket on Palace. Hoon was apoplectic with rage.

Barclays set about withdrawing Palace's overdraft facility and warned bank clerks to refer Palace employees to senior management, while cheques were not to be cashed on any account. Powell was devastated. 'My whole restructuring was based on keeping the £750,000 [facility], and now I had to get that refinanced. What [Barclays] collapsed was a much better refinancing package, but had I been a bit harder, more of a Branson and less of a Powell, that would never have happened. I have to take full responsibility for it.' Palace was not using the whole Barclays facility at the time, but the company's cash flow forecast showed that the whole £750,000 would be used within the month. As Powell admits: 'We had enough bills to pay to use it up.'

A meeting was held between Powell, Kelly and Barclays' regional 'intensive care' team. According to one source, the self-styled 'Rottweiler' – namely, the Barclays Regional Office manager who handled the meeting – 'told Nik his fortune in words of one syllable' and in such a ferocious manner that Powell and Kelly just sat, stunned.

'Well, you could have given us some warning. I mean, a bit of notice would have been nice,' Powell grumbled. At the end of the meeting, Powell provided an otherwise deeply unpleasant discussion with some light relief when he asked, 'Are you sure you don't know who your parents are?' Kelly laughed out loud, and the two men, wondering how they were going to survive this battle, left the meeting and went to the pub. Powell's stubborn optimism kept shining through as, over their pints, they searched for new ways to refinance the Group.

Optimism, however, does not interest banks. Numerous small

businesses were experiencing difficulties in 1991, and many were foreclosed on due to the clearing banks' damage-limitation policies. Hitchen explained a clearing bank's point of view: 'We needed then, as we do now, to protect our shareholders and especially our depositors. We are secured lenders, not venture capitalists or equity providers. Barclays was very supportive of the relationship with Palace, and indeed we had spent many of the previous weeks and months working with Norman Humphrey – who was working heroically and seemed to be the only one at Palace able to give us accurate information – doing whatever we could to help manage the rapidly deteriorating cash position.' Powell's and Palace's senior management team's pain would have been less acute had Barclays not withdrawn their facility. But as one financier stated: 'The outcome would have been exactly the same. Palace was waiting to fall apart.'

There were indications that it was not just Palace's finances that were coming apart: the Palace family, too, was disintegrating. Videos started to disappear from the offices. By the summer of 1990, it seemed to staff that the Wardour Mews offices were being frequently plundered. One person close to Palace saw its staff steal some of the company's equipment.

Palace had grown so quickly, with more than 100 full-time employees by 1991, that the original family atmosphere had been diluted. Despite Powell's notion that the company was still small and intimate, the truth was that employees no longer felt so intensely part of Palace. A brand of corporatism had emerged, breeding a mild sense of disloyalty among more recent recruits. Resentments about rivals' pay had escalated, while freelancers would appear with increasing regularity in the accountants' room on the top floor. They were there to demand their cheques. Battsek in particular confronted Powell about his pay, making it unequivocally clear that the day Palace stopped paying him he would leave the company.

As the pressure on Palace mounted, Powell's business and personal life grew more hectic and uncertain. On 16 October 1991, the night that the London Independent Broadcasting bid for an ITV franchise was rejected, Sandie Shaw drove a tired and inebriated Powell back to their flat in Harley Street. As she parked by the house, a police car drew up beside the couple. Shaw, a confirmed teetotaller, was incensed by the policeman's enquiry about whether she had been drinking, and marched up the stairs to her home only to be followed by the constable. When she screamed, 'Get your hand off my tit', Powell leapt across one of the officers in an attempt to protect the dignity of his wife. He was promptly arrested for resisting arrest.

At six-thirty the next morning Kelly arrived at London Heathrow, ready to join Powell for a meeting with a French company.

'Nik, you look terrible. You can't go to Paris looking like this!' Kelly exclaimed.

'I've just got out of the police station,' Powell replied.

Kelly nipped off to buy Powell a new shirt and a razor so his boss could have a shave in the men's room. When they arrived at the meeting in Paris, he carefully placed Powell well back from the table at which the meeting took place, keeping his breath out of the way.

Only six months earlier, on 6 May 1991, *Variety*, the American entertainment business magazine, had printed a glowing tribute to Palace. Headlined 'Nik Powell's star is one to watch in Britain', the article by film expert Terry Ilott explained that 'No other company in the UK can boast such a broad range of activities and, other than broadcasters, few can claim to be more expert than Palace in any of them. It is an integrated company, a studio in miniature.' Ilott stressed, however, that Palace would need considerably more capital to play with if it was to scale greater heights.

In the article, Powell suggested that it would take the company eight or nine years to achieve both financial and artistic success. 'What we need is a major hit that will generate cash flow and eliminate our debt. We won't make any decisions about the future of the company until that happens. My gut feeling is that we will have a major worldwide hit at some point, but I have to run the business on the basis that we won't.'

What nobody knew at that point was that Woolley and Jordan were about to embark on making *The Crying Game*. Neither did anybody know that Powell was deadly serious about eliminating Palace's debt. He had already started to consider selling the entire company.

# CHAPTER THIRTEEN

---

# The Emperor's New Clothes

---

'Hello, I'm Mr Woolley.' With these 'restrained, almost corny' words, the young, pony-tailed producer introduced himself to property millionaire Roger Wingate in 1984. Wingate, a tough-minded businessman and the owner of Mayfair-based Chesterfield Properties PLC, had come to know Powell and Woolley through his ownership of the Curzon chain of West End cinemas. Alongside Merchant Ivory films and a smattering of specialist and foreign language pickings, numerous Palace films played at Wingate's cinemas during the 1980s. But it was not until the 1990 Cannes Film Festival that the relationship between Wingate and Palace became close.

Palace had scored a coup by acquiring rights to David Lynch's *Wild at Heart,* starring Nicolas Cage and Laura Dern, before it won the 1990 Palme d'Or at Cannes. Wingate congratulated Powell, saying he would like to run the film at his cinemas, at which point 'Nik sort of made it clear that whilst it was a good acquisition, he wasn't quite sure how he was going to pay for it.' Wingate was asked several times during the 1990 Festival if Palace was in financial trouble. He responded that as far as his dealings with Palace were concerned, everything was quite satisfactory.

Wingate had long admired Palace's flair for selecting interesting films and marketing them to both commercial and art-house audiences. At the end of June 1990, he advanced a revolving sum of

£400,000 to Palace to allow the company to buy the UK rights to films for which the Curzon cinemas would have first option. Mayfair Entertainment, Wingate's newly named distribution company, would charge interest on the loan and take its advance out of the film's box-office sales.

A year later, Kelly and Powell approached Wingate about the possibility of his making an equity investment in the Palace Group. Wingate, an experienced businessman, was surprised by their presentation in the summer of 1991. 'They provided me with a whole lot of confidential information which was amazing. The numbers as they went into the future just got bigger and bigger. I told them, "Gosh, it's impressive but I don't know about it." '

Rather than being rushed into a snap decision, Wingate asked for some time to consider the proposal. He came back with a different proposal from the equity investment Powell and Kelly had been angling for. Wingate suggested that Mayfair Entertainment should take over the entire physical distribution of Palace's films. In return, Palace should go out and buy new films, armed with a provision of £2 million from his parent company, Chesterfield Properties. The marketing and promotion would remain under Palace's control, while all films would be jointly released under a new Mayfair/Palace banner.

'There was a certain logic to it,' Wingate explained. 'We had the halls, the money and the organisation, whereas Palace had the buying and selling strength, and Robert Jones was brilliant at spotting films.' From Powell's point of view, given that the initial equity deal was clearly not on the table, the £2 million facility was an opportunity to keep some kind of Palace distribution operation alive before his other plans had reached fruition. He was buying time.

A press release trumpeting the Mayfair/Palace deal was prepared on 11 November 1991 by Phil Symes (whose PSA public relations company was by now incorporated into the much larger Rogers & Cowan International Public Relations). After outlining the surprising arrangement, Symes added: 'Formalities connected with this intended long-term collaboration are expected to be concluded by the end of November at the latest.' As far as Wingate was concerned, the Heads of Agreement was 'in reality a fairly detailed document reciting steps to be taken by both parties to bring the partnership into effect, and was legally binding.'

The Mayfair collaboration, far from being the 'formality' publicly heralded, was plastered with problems on both sides. Mayfair Entertainment was run by John Hogarth, an experienced but stubborn old-style industry veteran and a sworn enemy of Powell's operation. In his view, Palace had long flouted a number of rules 'for the good of the industry'. Members of the Society of Film Distributors – the established trade body Palace had always refused to join – did not fly-post in the West End. 'It's illegal, and we didn't do it. Palace did, and that summed it up pretty well for me. I was not only pissed off [with the deal], but I was worried, because you can't split film distribution and marketing; it's one function.'

The key Palace staff affected by the Mayfair deal were Daniel Battsek, Robert Mitchell and Robert Jones. Aware of Palace's desperate need for money to keep the distribution operation alive, they were nevertheless collectively dismayed at the deal. 'Nik couldn't have picked a company that was more opposite in every way, shape and form. It was quite hilarious,' Mitchell recalled. More ominously, from Battsek's point of view, Palace's prized marketeer was no longer really running his own distribution operation. It had always been a hard slog making the most of Palace's releases, given the company's financial constraints, but now Battsek had to put up with Mayfair interfering in his strategy every day of the week.

Hogarth, who was just months away from retirement when the deal was announced, prided himself on dealing with the minutiae of releasing films into cinemas. 'Palace was hopelessly useless at it,' he contended. 'A cinema owner once said to me, "When I am waiting for a Palace film to be delivered I am always very happy when an aircraft flies over my theatre, because I think it might well come down by parachute that day." ' He was also deeply concerned about Palace's ability to meet its end of the bargain financially. After all, advertising space and marketing costs still had to be paid for. 'Wardour Street is a tiny, tiny place,' Hogarth explained. 'Once the word goes round that people are not paying their bills, people get to know about it.'

At a tense meeting between Powell, Woolley, Hogarth and Wingate, Hogarth bluntly demanded to know how Palace was going to solve its creditors' problems. 'Argh, well, John . . . I'd rather answer that particular question to Roger in private,' Powell hedged, asking a reluctant Hogarth to leave the room. At that point, Powell finally told Wingate about the PolyGram deal.

When Powell's refinancing plans had collapsed on the back of Barclays' withdrawal in spring 1991, the Palace co-chairman had started to consider a far larger deal than the one with Mayfair. As the weeks went by, and creditors and operational bills mounted, a reluctant Powell came to the painful conclusion that nothing short of selling the company would save the Palace Group.

A formal presentation of all the companies was prepared, unbeknown to Palace's employees, putting a bullish gloss on the Group's situation. A number of French companies expressed interest in the Group. However, according to one party, something did not quite add up in the package that was being floated. 'Nik and Steve were quite arrogant about the prospective deal,' the source explained. 'They both suggested that it was best for us not to go into too much detail on the company, and that we should leave the financial details to them to sort out.' 'Don't worry, that's not your problem. This is the deal we want to do,' Powell had said boldly. On hearing those words, this particular company walked away from the table.

By late summer 1991, there was just one bidder left in the running. PolyGram, one of Europe's largest entertainment companies, was the obvious potential buyer. The corporate situation seemed right, given that the Dutch-owned record giant had just launched a $200 million new film operation, PolyGram Filmed Entertainment, and was looking to expand into production and distribution on a major scale. It was taking a record label approach to picking up new production companies – buying into different production and distribution opportunities in different countries – and by June 1990 had already taken a forty-nine per cent stake in

Working Title Films. Also encouraging was the personal relationship between Powell and Michael Kuhn, the dapper, smart-suited lawyer who was masterminding the corporation's expansion into film. The relationship had been forged in the early eighties and cemented during the two companies' increasingly close alliance during their preparation for the LWT franchise bid in 1991.

When Powell put his formal presentation of the Palace Group on the table, Kuhn was certainly interested. Palace Productions was just the kind of company PolyGram was acquiring for its film operation, while the corporation's video outfit was interested in the catalogue of film rights which Palace Video had built up over the previous nine years. Also, 'Nik was a mate, and I wanted to help him in any way I could,' Kuhn stated.

Two major assets and a friendship was where Kuhn decided to draw the line. He was not interested in Palace Pictures, the theatrical distribution company, because PolyGram had its own plans in that area, so the Mayfair deal was seen as an irritant by Kuhn and his colleagues. He certainly did not want to deal with the Group's non-core driftwood. PolyGram's film chief put these companies' existence down to Powell's eternal search for cash-generating vehicles desperately needed to pay for production and distribution in the severely under-capitalised Palace Group. Kuhn did not mince his words, explaining that 'It was ludicrous to have that small company with so many different things. I understand why Nik did it, but the tail was wagging the dog.'

When Wingate was finally told of the prospective PolyGram deal he was not amused. It was difficult to see how the new Palace/Mayfair distribution operation was going to fit in with PolyGram's ambitions. His first step was to put a stop on the £2 million advance and start negotiating.

One of the key films to which Palace had picked up the rights was Merchant Ivory's *Howards End*, starring Anthony Hopkins and Emma Thompson. Powell had bumped into Ismail Merchant on the corner of Poland Street and Broadwick Street and had asked if *Howards End* was available. Merchant explained that Wingate had already offered a very acceptable £300,000, to which Powell promptly added an extra £25,000, coming away with a deal. Or so he thought, but a few months later Palace did not have the money to pay for it. He then approached Wingate about sharing the acquisition of *Howards End* on a fifty–fifty basis, quite separate from the overall Palace/Mayfair joint deal.

Subsequently, most of the monies for the initial Palace down-payment of £32,500 had come from Wingate's original float. When a nervous Merchant Ivory demanded the outstanding £292,500 for the film, Palace could not deliver, and Wingate took over responsibility for all payments.

To Wingate, a deal is a deal. Powell, however, having agreed and announced the Mayfair/Palace distribution pact, was having second thoughts about signing it. 'I misjudged it, because I thought that PolyGram would like to buy a company with a £2 million cash facility in place to buy films, but of course PolyGram regarded themselves as a cash-flush company anyway,' Powell explained. 'Roger wanted me to sign the deal, mainly so he had securities for monies that he had already advanced for *Howards End* . . . I didn't want to sign it because I didn't want the [Mayfair] deal to jeopardise the PolyGram deal.'

Wingate was seething. Having paid out considerable sums for *Howards End*, he wanted the film back and the new deal signed. He issued a writ against Palace, forcing Powell to sign the full Mayfair/Palace deal. During negotiations with PolyGram UK's newly appointed managing director Stewart Till, it became increasingly clear to Wingate that PolyGram considered the Mayfair deal 'was a bit of nuisance, and would have to be changed'. While Wingate could quite understand Till's point of view, he stuck to his guns. A compromise was finally reaached whereby PolyGram would handle the marketing and Mayfair the physical distribution of films. It was far from perfect, but Wingate felt that at least he had not let PolyGram bully him out of the picture.

As 1992 approached, relations between Palace and Mayfair were deteriorating fast, and matters did not improve when, during the third week in January, Mayfair hit a problem with Rank, who claimed that Palace owed it more than £20,000. Rank argued that Mayfair should pay the outstanding sum, and threatened not to release Mayfair's existing films prints from Rank's central despatch department. The powerful corporation had Mayfair in a corner. Wingate and Hogarth had no option but to pay up if they wanted to continue to do business.

By November 1991, having examined the Group, PolyGram had decided that it wanted to buy the Palace Video library for £4.86 million, including hits such as the *Nightmare on Elm Street* series, *Nine ½ Weeks* and *When Harry Met Sally* and around 150 other films that had formed the backbone of the company. According to the proposed deal, Powell and Woolley would act as consultants. PolyGram also offered £2 million for Palace Productions' interests in the rights to the company's sixteen completed films totalling a production investment of £65 million. The rights to Palace Television's rather less impressive output were also to be included in the deal.

Although respectful of the Palace Production's creative clout, track record and energetic level of output, Kuhn was highly circumspect about the way Palace Productions had been run financially. During one of their early talks, Kuhn made this clear to Powell and Woolley: 'Look, if we're starting again we'd better capitalise, because it shouldn't be done the wrong way round a second time. So how much do you need for development, how much for your overhead, and how much for that period of pre-production before all the financing is closed? Let's do it properly this time.'

The production deal that was finally agreed looked good for both sides. PolyGram would provide a £500,000 development fund, a £525,000 overhead facility, and a stand by provision of £250,000 for the period just prior to going into production which had created the most severe stress on cash flow and had so often resulted in a call on the parent Group's funds.

PolyGram's accountants pored diligently over the figures provided by Palace, 'the sort of stuff *behind* the figures we were presented with before we actually dive in,' Kuhn explained. Powell thought the deal was as good as done. Two identical press releases were sent out by Palace and PolyGram International on 27 November 1991, stating that PolyGram *'had reached agreement in principle'* to spend approximately £7 million in acquiring Palace Video, Palace Pictures and to enter into a long-term agreement with Palace Productions. Effectively, the contract had been signed, but the deal was still to be completed. No mention was made of the deal being subject to any further due diligence or an independent audit. At that point, Powell stopped lining up any other potential purchasers and put his considerable reserves into closing the PolyGram deal. Announcing the PolyGram deal to his staff had not been easy. On the day he told Wardour Mews about the imminent sale, he burst into tears.

Wardour Street breathed a collective sigh of relief as the story hit the front pages of the trade press that week. 'Thank God for that,' thought the creditors. 'Now we're going to be okay.'

Powell employed the legal services of John Stutter of Harbottle & Lewis to front the negotiations for Palace. He needed a reliable spearhead, given that as a shareholder he could not lead the sale of his own company. The original terms of the deal involved PolyGram putting the initialled contracts into escrow (in trust) with lawyers. The deal would be completed following further confirma- tin of Palace's 1991 financial position. A mechanism was included whereby the £7 million price tag would be reduced on a sliding scale if the value of Palace's balance sheet fell below a set level. Unless Palace's and PolyGram's assessments turned out massively differ- ent, the deal looked set to go through.

The internal politics at PolyGram were growing heated, how- ever, regarding the pending Palace deal. According to Powell, Kuhn warned him that there were certain senior figures at PolyGram who were putting up staunch resistance to the deal. Powell set up meetings with PolyGram executives, but, despite his charm and lucid sales pitch, came away from the meetings deeply concerned.

These executives were playing multi-million-pound corporate politics, a game that Powell was well aware was not his best strength.

Jan Cook, the company's chief financial officer and his legal and financial team, decided that a full-scale independent audit should be implemented by chartered accountants Ernst & Young. Powell later contended that he was not aware that 'highly conservative Dutch accounting practices were going to be applied to Palace's books'. Other senior Palace employees were less polite, suggesting that because of PolyGram's internal battle over Palace, a deliberately negative audit had been commissioned from Ernst & Young. Kuhn adamantly denies that this was the case.

Whatever the reasons for the moving goalposts, Powell still remained buoyantly optimistic that the PolyGram deal would be closed. In the meantime, the pressure of debt was growing ever more acute, and at Christmas Powell and Woolley agreed to sign personal guarantees worth £1.25 million to Guinness and Pierson. Powell claimed later, 'When the directors of a company enter into those major personal guarantees, it means they are very confident. While the books might not have been in accordance with multi-national standards, they were still good basic books, and showed a realistic picture of the company on a forward-going trading basis.'

Kelly, who had been working sixteen-hour days, seven days a week, thought Powell and Woolley were 'stupid' to sign personal guarantees. He would have prefered the co-chairmen to hold a board meeting and put the company into administration rather than see them hang nooses around their necks. By this time Powell, Woolley, and Kelly had all taken pay-cuts of more than a third to lessen the Group's £200,000-a-month permanent staff salary burden. In February they took a further cut, and staff salaries were not paid. Everyone and everything at Wardour Mews – including its renegotiated and now excessively high lease – was on hold pending the PolyGram deal going through.

Part of Powell's and Kelly's role by the New Year was to handle angry creditors demanding payment. One night, Kelly was the last person left at Wardour Mews, when four heavily built men broke into the offices and cornered him. 'These were seriously angry people ready to beat the crap out of me because they hadn't been paid,' Kelly recalled. 'The Irish blarney really poured out of me that night to keep them cool.'

Couriers hovering outside the Mews block waiting for creditors' payments became more frequent and more tense and, on some days, getting in and out of the office was like crossing a union picket line. Agents, trade journalists, post-production houses and other film service companies fed the rumour mill, gossiping about whether Palace would survive until the PolyGram deal was closed.

The pressure on Palace also told on Powell's and Woolley's relationship. The partners had often had healthy yelling bouts over differences of opinion, but communication seemed to be quieter rather than louder between the two men during these fraught weeks. Powell's innate tendency to keep certain pieces of information to himself – telling much but not everything about a deal or turn of events – was increasingly frustrating Woolley, and Powell's manic save-the-company schedule and frenzied manner hardly made it easy for Woolley to access his partner's thoughts.

On the other hand, by this stage Powell clearly needed emotional and moral support as much as tactical advice. One evening at the height of the troubles, Powell and Woolley were set to go to a key industry event together. Powell, stuck in a meeting, told his assistant to make absolutely sure that Woolley did not leave without him. Twenty minutes later, Powell could not find his partner anywhere. Woolley had inadvertently disappeared, leaving Powell looking utterly crestfallen.

The majority of Kelly's time was spent mortgaging the future of Palace to keep the company alive while the PolyGram deal was being closed. Desperate measures were taken to find cash. The Palace Video catalogue was plundered, with rights sold off wherever possible. One film that Mayfair thought it owned outright turned out to have been sold for television to the BBC. When Hogarth contacted the BBC about the matter he was told, 'Yes, that's right, but we've already paid Palace. Someone came to see us and offered a discount for cash.'

Until late 1990, distributors and producers had trusted Palace.

They had not been too concerned about the money for distribution contracts being late, because they had known it would eventually arrive. By late 1991, however, people were starting to lose their nerve. Frantic calls, faxes and visitors were flooding into the offices, not only demanding payments but in many cases the return of rights to films.

Despite the pressure on Wardour Mews in January 1992 – and notwithstanding the odd incidental theft – the staff remained loyal. Pushed into the back of a blazing bunker, the majority rallied round the besieged company. The bouts of drinking at The George continued apace, tinged with a manic edge. Life after Palace was unimaginable for the young employees, mainly because they had become so used to denigrating everyone else that there was nowhere else they wanted to work. Palace had given many of them their first job and first taste of the film industry. Dozens of Palace workers continued to turn up at the offices without pay for many weeks, and in some cases months.

Palace's long-standing do-or-die mentality reached intoxicating heights as the company lurched from day to day, desperate to crawl into the protective comfort of a corporate cradle. As Robert Mitchell explained, 'We were all hoping that the PolyGram deal was going to come through and I really wanted Palace to survive. I didn't want all those people who'd knocked it for doing things differently being able to rub their hands in glee when it went down.'

The pressure from and on Palace's three film productions, *Dust Devil, Waterland* and *The Crying Game* throughout this period was intense. All three financing packages had been tortuously late in completion, costing Palace nearly £1 million, causing inevitable casualties. While spirited commitment to *The Crying Game* helped pull the film through production just before Christmas, the other two films were beleaguered by problems.

The Richard Stanley-directed *Dust Devil* shoot proved a nightmare experience in the Namibian desert, creating great difficulties for JoAnne Sellar, the film's producer. With little support from Palace's London office, she performed a remarkable job bringing it in. When a 120-minute director's version of the film reached Palace

in December, major disagreements flared up and the film was cut to
ninety-five minutes. It was screen-tested at Wimbledon in the New
Year.

*Dust Devil* became the focus of a lengthy and bitter row, when
Stanley wrote a vitriolic thirty-five page diary about the making and
release of the film, 'I Wake Up Screaming'. The diary infuriated
Woolley, who felt it was a blatant betrayal by the young director of
his producer. Woolley blames himself for going forward with
Stanley's script, which he felt was never as strong as *Hardware*. He
is fiercely supportive of his old girlfriend and Scala colleague Sellar,
who had 'worked incredibly hard', and succeeded in achieving
'terrific production values'. Woolley publicly slammed Stanley, and
the two film-makers have not spoken since.

*Waterland* was also highly problematic, stretching Powell's
reserves of energy so far that employees could not fail to notice the
strain beginning to show. Powell's attire slipped to a new level of
shambolic disorder. He turned up at the office often unshaven,
while his mind was so overloaded with information that he found
normal daily chat difficult.

As one senior employee recalled, 'You couldn't talk to him about
anything, and he kept losing his temper, screaming and bawling and
becoming completely irrational.' Some staff even told their boss to
'fuck off', past caring if he sacked them, especially since they were
not being paid. Outside the office, Powell's mobile phone remained
glued to his ear, as he frantically tried to scrape together more cash
to keep the company alive.

Powell's search for money did not always take him far from home.
Patrick Cassavetti and Katy McGuinness were doing their best to
bring *Waterland* in under its £3.4 million budget. The shoot that
autumn 1991 was difficult, especially as Miranda Richardson had
opted to join *The Crying Game* at the last minute. Their efforts were
not helped when Powell, without Cassavetti's knowledge, rang
Michael Garland, the production accountant on the film, and fully
aware that Palace was owed some money from the production,
asked, 'How much money have we got in the account?' Garland told

him, at which point Powell, said, 'Argh, we'll take £150,000 out, but don't tell Katy or Patrick. I'll put it back later if you need it.'

Garland was in an unenviable position. Torn between loyalty to his boss and loyalty to the production, he decided to tell McGuinness, who was closer to the project than anyone, having developed and produced the film. Scared that Cassavetti would blow the whistle on the whole production, the pair opted not to tell the producer about the transferred funds. Some of the money removed by Powell came back in small increments – a process Garland described as 'jiggery-pokery' – but as post-production came to an end, a gap of around £80,000 remained in the production's final budget, taking it dangerously close to its contingency limit.

Garland finally told Cassavetti about the missing monies, and that Palace did not have any more cash available to plug the gap. The producer was livid. Cassavetti, still owed considerable monies from the film, went to see Powell and Woolley 'to clear the air', and was met by a shifty, deeply embarrassed pair of co-chairmen. Although incensed, Cassavetti could see the severe pressure Palace was under: 'It's not as if they were embezzling money or buying Rolls Royces. It was going to pay their staff salaries for God's sake.'

Despite the obvious severity of Palace's problems, many Palace staff had enormous confidence that Powell would pull them out of the hole. As one of his accountants explained, 'Nik is a brilliant businessman because he never wastes time over regrets. Whatever the circumstances that are thrown at him, he absorbs them, thinks about them and always moves on, and that's why everybody thought we would just survive.' Powell's *modus operandi* may have worked on a short-term basis, but he was now facing a crisis that stemmed from a long-term pile-up of problems. His overriding goal – to get the PolyGram deal closed and keep as many of his staff paid as possible – was proving to be far more difficult than he had anticipated. While Stutter was fronting the PolyGram talks, Powell was racing around 'supervising, guiding and managing this incredibly complex set of negotiations.'

Powell had to deal not only with PolyGram but with the banks, the shareholders, Mayfair, the release of new films, keeping his staff going, and the ongoing company business. He was also contending with the fact that neither GLE nor Norwich Union initially wanted to go with the PolyGram deal.

Woolley put great faith in Powell's experience and his partner's demands for extraordinary temporary measures. However, as the sands kept shifting beneath the elusive PolyGram deal, Woolley grew increasingly pessimistic. 'I'd come into meetings fresh from a plane from somewhere or other and say: "Well what the fuck's going on? This was promised, that was promised . . . I thought we had this?" '

Meanwhile, PolyGram's accountants were poring over Palace's administrative files in an effort to assess what they were to take as the company's 'true' financial position. Ernst & Young were instructed to carry out an audit on the Group's 1991 finances in strict adherence with PolyGram's corporate accounting policies. As Kuhn saw it, 'PolyGram was waiting for our due diligence and audit, which were conditions for the purchases, when Palace started to experience terrible cash flow difficulties.' Kuhn was not exaggerating.

On 24 January, the High Court ordered that Palace Video should make a payment of £31,130.76 to HandMade Films, to pay for the rights to the released *Nuns on the Run*. Woolley's old foe Dennis O'Brien, executive producer of *Mona Lisa*, was sticking the knife in. Cork Gully, administrators for the collapsed Parkfield Group, was chasing Powell for the return of part of the advance that the former video distributor had paid Palace. That the £350,000 should be returned was debatable, Powell and his accountants argued, given that Parkfield had failed to keep its end of the bargain. Every time creditors phoned or appeared, Battsek, Jones, Craib and Kelly would ask them to try to hold on, telling them in good faith, 'It's going to be okay. We think PolyGram will come through any day now.'

The time taken by PolyGram to conduct its aggressive audit – from the end of November 1991 to late March 1992 – was choking Palace to death. In late January, PolyGram, realising that the assets it was supposed to be buying were in danger of disappearing, offered to put in a facility of £2 million until 2 April 1992, to enable the Group to keep trading. 'This loan was made in the belief that the Ernst & Young report would show positive net assets as presented to us by the management of Palace,' Kuhn explained. In return, PolyGram demanded a first charge on the company, something to which Guinness and Pierson were deeply opposed. Kuhn's answer was blunt: 'If we hadn't [lent £2 million], then Palace would have gone bust and they would have all been sunk.' Powell fought for the bridging deal to be accepted, partly out of desire to pay off colossal debts, but also suspecting by now that PolyGram might otherwise walk away. PolyGram's first charge gave it first rights to 'all and any sources' of income, including the rights to Palace's film catalogue, and was finally signed on 17 February.

The £2 million loan, however, proved to be too little too late. Having already lost *Howards End* to Wingate due to its failure to pay Merchant Ivory in full, Palace proceeded to lose the rights to a series of important films. Robert Jones had already arranged to buy the rights to Quentin Tarantino's début feature *Reservoir Dogs*, but Palace could not lay its hands on the money to close the deal. Consequently, Jones persuaded Kuhn and Till to conclude the deal on behalf of PolyGram. *Reservoir Dogs* went on to take more than £4 million in the UK over an extraordinary two-year extended run, and laid the foundation for *Pulp Fiction's* huge success in 1995.

Jones had also spotted a strong package of films being sold prior to the February 1992 American Film Market. US sales company Spelling Films International, part of the Hollywood Entertainment giant responsible for *Dynasty* and other long-running series, had virtually closed a UK distribution deal with Palace for three of its films, including Robert Altman's *The Player* and David Lynch's film adaptation of the cult television series, *Twin Peaks: Fire Walk With Me*. Once again, there was no money for the deposit, allowing rival Guild Entertainment to step in and snap up the pictures.

Notable films that Palace normally would have pounced on, including the French art-house hit *Delicatessen*, and Cannes discoveries *Strictly Ballroom* and *Man Bites Dog*, went to other distributors. Despite the lack of money, Palace was still supporting

British film-makers during these final months, backing films by Mike Leigh, Derek Jarman, Ken Loach, Peter Greenaway and Terence Davies. The UK film market was changing shape, with both small and large distributors copying the marketing tactics Palace had pioneered a decade previously.

Back in the offices of Ernst & Young, accountants were edging closer to a final report on Palace's 1991 year. Applying PolyGram's multinational accounting policies to a fledgling independent group of film-related businesses, however, was the equivalent of comparing Marks & Spencer to the local corner shop. Corporations normally write off investments and losses within the same financial year; others will sometimes try to spread losses over a much longer period of time. Large companies take a conservative view of the value of their stock and assets; small companies tend to put forward the best figures possible. Neither way is necessarily right nor wrong, as long as the accounts don't transgress the law.

According to one financial insider, Stoy Hayward, the Group's auditors, had long tried to make Palace's company directors aware of the Group's accounting policies followed in the preparation of end-of-year accounts. Palace's estimates of the value of its library of film rights were probably no more optimistic than those of most independent production companies. Nevertheless, Powell severely underestimated the cultural and financial distance between the ramshackle Palace family and the corporate face of PolyGram.

Kuhn, however, argues that there is no such thing as 'different rules for different companies. All company accounts, whether they are big ones or little ones, have to be prepared in accordance with Generally Accepted Accounting Practices (GAAP). In the case of movie accounting, if you open a movie theatrically and it's a failure, you should recognise that loss at the time; if it's a failure at video, you should recognise that loss at the time of the video release and so forth. What you should not do is delay recognising that loss until the last possible revenue-producing opportunity has failed you – for example, living in the hope and expectation that a television or catalogue sale down the road will be sufficiently large to cover the failure of a movie theatrically, or at video. That is the classic way to go bust. [But] to suggest that there are different rules for big and little companies is not correct.'

By March, Kuhn was standing back from the Palace sale, setting up new deals with other UK, French and American companies. Powell and his management staff were in the hands of PolyGram's money men, who were screening the financial minutiae. Films that Palace had sold on to television companies such as Channel 4 and the BBC were the subject of major disagreement. Palace's auditors would treat approximately twenty per cent of each agreed but not-yet-paid deal as a sale, and acknowledge eighty per cent as a debit rather than as an outstanding liability. PolyGram insisted on treating the whole sum as an unpaid debt – hence a liability – and, moreover, were interested only in receipts, rather than receivables.

The movies PolyGram singled out were an ironic choice: their own subsidiary, Working Title, had produced *Chicago Joe And The Showgirl*, which was a flop for Palace at the cinemas in 1989 and which PolyGram picked on as a significant loss. Powell explained that these losses were being written off over a number of years, but PolyGram's clean sheet tactics meant the film was written off immediately. PolyGram's unrelenting attitude led some Palace employees to speculate that the record giant was looking for a way out of the deal.

Throughout March, Powell and Woolley, growing ever more anxious, awaited Ernst & Young's report. On one of the last days of the month, a bike drew up outside Wardour Mews and delivered the document to Powell's desk. Woolley, Powell, Craib and Kelly gathered round to discover its findings. 'I knew it was bad news because I could see it on Nik's face,' Morrison recalled. 'All their faces were black as anything. I didn't know quite how bad the news was, nor how much perseverance Nik had left in him.' The report's findings were more appalling than any of them had wished to believe.

At PolyGram, Michael Kuhn was outraged. Not only was the 1991 net asset value below the agreed minimum level, it was so far from anything Palace had presented to PolyGram's management that the company's senior executives were furious. From a corporate point of view, PolyGram was absolutely within its rights to withdraw from the deal. 'I am not green about these things,' Kuhn explained later. 'I know a lot of the numbers that independent companies think of are wishful. I had allowed for a tremendous margin of error and made the loan on that basis. When it turned out to be much, much worse than even I, who was not an unsophisticated banker, could have suspected, we said, "That's outrageous. Give us our money back!" '

Palace, withering under a flood of winding-up petitions from creditors, did not have anywhere near that level of money to hand. Powell, normally so canny in setting up rival bidders, had for once not cultivated a second bidder. Perhaps that was due to his belief that the deal had been as good as done back in November, but by then there were no other interested takers in any case. Meanwhile, PolyGram set about engineering a damage-limitation exercise in the trade press and succeeded in planting comments in *Variety* that placed much of the blame for the failed deal on Palace's history of mismanagement and firmly on Powell's and Woolley's shoulders. The article was fair but brutally tough. Ironically, it was written by Terry Ilott, the same journalist who had praised Powell and his Palace Group so highly just ten months earlier. The article demonstrated how keenly the trade press is read in such an unsteady and insecure business. Image and perception is all. As a senior consultant at a *Screen International* lunch commented just days after the 1992 *Variety* article, 'That *Variety* piece was the most damaging thing I've read about a company for years.'

Yet even at this late stage, Powell's belief in his company led him to hope that somehow a new agreement could be hammered out. In one particular aspect he was right. PolyGram was still hungry to close a deal with Palace Productions, and stuck to part of the original deal by going ahead with a separate production arrangement with a company later to be named Scala Productions. The development and 'first look' deal – giving PolyGram a first option to produce Scala's upcoming films – was slightly reduced in terms of financial investment, and it allowed PolyGram an earlier option to withdraw support. Nevertheless, the new company, Scala Productions, with

Powell and Woolley at its helm, rose from the ashes of Palace, and enabled Palace's numerous film projects, including *Backbeat*, *Jonathan Wild*, *The Neon Bible*, *The Hollow Reed*, *Galatea* and *B Monkey* to keep heading towards production.

After two years fighting for its life, Palace was having to face the inevitable. A combination of bad luck, lack of capital funds, a bitter economic downturn and a desperately ambitious production slate had all contributed to the firm's demise. Cash flow, that quicksilver lifeline, had been greedily devoured by the number of films the company had put into production over the previous three years. Meanwhile, distribution hits had been elusive, while the former advantages of diversification had backfired when it had become too difficult to offload the loss-making non-core business into a decaying marketplace.

When it became clear during the first days of April 1992 that the PolyGram deal had been terminated, Palace's board met. David Walburn of GLE, alongside lawyers and other advisers, suggested that Palace should file for administration. Powell turned to John Stutter, who in turn started to talk to representatives of Smith & Williamson about handling an application to the court. It was clear that the Palace Group of Companies was as good as insolvent and in desperate need of protection from the onslaught of creditors hammering at Wardour Mews's doors.

Bailiffs were appearing in the offices. Never the best-kept corporate building even at the height of Palace's business, the bustling office was now a fast-emptying shell. On one occasion, two large bruisers in suits turned up at Wardour Mews. An employee shouted across the floors, 'Quick, they're coming!' The heavies passed grimly from room to room, checking the office furniture and electrical equipment still left in the building. As they strode around the rabbit warren, employees quickly formed a human chain and passed some computers through a window, into a van waiting below, to be returned when the coast was clear. Powell, desperately making a call on his mobile phone, found himself cut off in mid-sentence. The phone company had closed the account. Resourceful to the last, Powell dug in his bag for another set, dialled a number and carried on his conversation.

By February 1992, Daniel Battsek had left to head up Buena Vista UK, the first part of a new Walt Disney distribution operation for the whole of Europe. The new job made him one of the most powerful distribution executives in Europe. The offer was well-timed, making it hard for either side to see a realistic alternative to Battsek leaving the collapsing Palace for such a wonderful position. Powell was tremendously pleased for him, seeing the appointment as proof of the elevated status of Palace's former distribution operation. Indeed, both Woolley and Powell are very proud of the senior positions Battsek and many of their former staff now hold in the industry. They have great respect for Battsek's flair and imagination, which is now applied to films with the advantage of a major's money and clout.

Tony Kelly finally left the company, exhausted and disappointed. He clung to his view that the banks should have converted their debt into equity at least a year prior to Palace's collapse. The banks had told him firmly that it was too much too late even then. No matter what the staff had thought of Kelly, together with Craib, Humphrey and Powell, he had given everything he had to save the company from going down. He left owed many weeks of pay. To mark the end of his eighteen-month nightmare, Kelly went on holiday with his family to Lanzarote, only to experience a different kind of cash flow problem. He was mugged at knife-point and had his wallet and credit cards stolen.

'The staff had been phenomenally loyal, buoyed by Nik's infectious optimism,' Woolley later reflected. 'There had always existed a feeling that Palace lived on borrowed time. Yet, incredibly, when it finally crashed, that staff spirit never burned out. We were the Eric Cantona of distributors: all too capable of running into the terraces at any moment, but what else could we do? We were part of a film industry, not part of a business.'

The depleted staff still coming into Wardour Mews had increasingly less to do. Films were not being released, and business had disintegrated. Gallows humour ruled the day, followed, at night, by depressed drinking sessions in The George. The Palace family was splitting up for good. Staying together for the sake of it was unhealthy and unrealistic. Morever, so many of its key workers were such good friends that they knew their ties would survive the collapse of the company that had brought them together. The family, doubting it would experience again the buzz and intensity it had found in Palace, was dispersed throughout the film industry.

On 16 April 1992, Powell and Woolley issued a statement explaining that although the PolyGram deal was dead, an offer had been received for Palace Video. Gartmore, a publicly-listed investment fund, was interested in the library of remaining rights, and a provisional offer was on the table. The press release also confirmed that Palace had applied to go into administration. Under the 1986 Insolvency Act, an administration order offers companies a half-way house between total liquidation on the one hand, and voluntary settlements between a company and its creditors on the other, with the object of allowing the company, or some part of it, to continue trading. Powell had to gather extensive information proving that parts of the company could be sold as ongoing concerns in order to apply to the courts for an order. Having never applied for adminstration before, however, Powell did not realise how long it was going to take or how much it would cost to file the paperwork required.

Palace's remaining assets were on a knife edge. Had Palace Video been forced into liquidation, the value of Palace's film licence rights would have plummeted because they would automatically revert to the producers. Most companies deal in product; fleets of cars, buildings and other tangible physical assets; but Palace Video's value was its expert staff and the library of rights. Holding on to the rights, however, was proving impossible. As soon as Palace filed for protection, producers started reclaiming the rights of their films, despite the fact that they technically belonged to the administrators. The library of films was besieged by claims made by film-makers all over the world. Palace Video's book value of nearly £9 million suddenly dropped to next to nothing.

Despite Powell's prompt attempt to set up the administration, it was not until 27 April that the full information required by the High Court was finally delivered. It was just in time to freeze a host of creditors' winding-up petitions due to be heard two days later. The majority of Palace's companies were formally put into administration on Thursday, 7 May 1992; the last time Powell and Woolley saw the Palace staff under one roof. It was the worst day in Powell's life. 'To admit failure and to admit that I had let them down . . . to admit that I had not succeeded when for a year I had been telling the staff that we would survive, was terrible.'

Despite the continuing talks with Gartmore, the administration had already been dealt a body-blow by PolyGram. Smith & Williamson had hoped that the costs of running the administration would be covered by a £200,000 offer by PolyGram for the UK distribution rights to *The Crying Game, Dust Devil* and *Waterland*. By the time the High Court had approved Palace's application, that offer had dropped to £70,000 – hardly enough to keep Palace's management afloat, let alone protect and repackage what was left of the Group.

Why, after six months of informal discussions, and seventeen weeks of intense negotiations, did the PolyGram deal not come to fruition, Powell asked himself. He took upon himself the blame for failure to conclude the PolyGram deal. 'When things have gone right in one's life for twenty-five years, as they had in mine, you're always suspicious that several things would come at you at once. I am not as brilliant a businessman as Richard [Branson], and if it had been him in charge . . . him and me, we probably would have found a way to survive. At the end of the day, it was my job to convince PolyGram and everyone to go with the deal, and I failed to do so.'

On the subject of the role of his co-chairman and partner, Powell was loyal to a fault: 'Obviously, Steve was very busy making what turned out to be very important films, so he couldn't devote the time and energy to the process that he probably would have liked to have done. And I am very glad he did devote that energy to *The Crying Game*.'

Woolley suggested that, had he been more available before and during that Christmas, he would have tried to accelerate the PolyGram deal. 'I would have probably uncovered some of the truths about whether this deal would be done if I'd been allowed to rant and rave, but Nik rightly pulled me back.' Looking back, he felt he and Powell had both pushed too hard following tremendous success too early. 'On reflection, the sensible thing would have been to cancel *The Miracle* and *The Pope Must Die*, and drop our level [of activity in 1990] – stop production, cut the staff – but history had taught us that one film that paid off could save Palace.'

On the corporate side, Woolley had long taken the view that 'Nik's other companies' were nothing to do with him. 'That was a stupid, ego thing. Why did I become involved in a big company that had all these other unrelated companies that I wasn't interested in? I undervalued myself as a film person, and overvalued myself as a co-chairman of a bunch of companies that I had no interest in. So, in retrospect, a lot of things came out of this that I've learnt from and that have made me much stronger.'

Woolley believes that PolyGram pulled the rug from beneath Palace on the verge of its biggest year ever. 'We had *Howards End*, *Reservoir Dogs*, *The Player*, and *The Crying Game* coming up. Those four films would have all been hits for us, and there is no doubt in my mind that we'd definitely have turned the corner. It should be in Michael's mind too, because Palace had the best people to handle those films.' However, by the time those films would have reached Palace, it had already signed the co-distribution deal with Mayfair; and, by that stage, Palace simply did not have access to its own money to buy three of those films.

To this day, Michael Kuhn has no regrets about not buying Palace. On the one hand he feels that Powell is 'one of the most talented, resourceful and lovable people in the business. On the other – and this is something I've said to his face – when you've been an independent and had to live hand-to-mouth for so long, you get into a style of management and working that is not compatible with the way a big company deals. It becomes impossible really to have a healthy relationship in that way. With Nik it was too late, he had gone beyond the point when he could change.'

Indeed, despite Powell's and Woolley's obvious talents as film-makers, Kuhn is uncertain whether PolyGram would have brought out their best qualities. Corporate meetings, tight financial controls and line management are all anathema to the Palace school of film-making.

One of Kuhn's earlier acquisitions for PolyGram, Working Title, went on to produce *Four Weddings and a Funeral*, which became the highest-grossing British film ever, amassing £28 million in the UK, and more than $260 million worldwide. PolyGram's record label approach clearly had its merits, but so did the corporation's deep pockets. Film after film had failed or performed modestly for PolyGram prior to *Four Weddings*.

In a final rider to his views on Palace, Kuhn explained, 'You don't make money out of producing films. You make money out of distributing them, and unless you get the distribution right you can't have a chance of making any money. In order to have the distribution right, you need a tremendous amount of capital. Most people don't realise how much capital you need, and therefore get into the situation where however successful they are creatively, they are never successful financially . . . And that is really the story of Palace.'

Without significant development and production backing, nearly all independent film producers do not make enough money to stay in business. Hence the most aspiring and talented companies look for genuine financial partnerships, arguing that it is better to have a small part of something bigger, than a big share of nothing. It is a view that even Powell and Woolley would adopt in their future development and production arrangements.

Despite the gloom of May 1992, Powell and Woolley still had one last trump card to play. *The Crying Game* was to lay the foundation for their rise from the depths of bankruptcy to the forefront of the film world once again.

# CHAPTER FOURTEEN

# Crying
# All the Way
# to the Banks

The forty-fifth Cannes Film Festival during May 1992 came at a cruel time for Powell and Woolley. Powell was prepared to take the full flak in the festival's bars and parties. Armed with an ever-increasing crop of (almost all bad) jokes, Powell got on with the job of selling his and Woolley's new films and apologising to friends whom he felt he had let down. He looked and felt rough, but believed there was no point in hiding.

Woolley could not have behaved more differently to his partner during the first few days of the collapse. Besides attending Cannes meetings for *Backbeat* – the Beatles film almost ready for production – and forthcoming projects such as *Dark Blood*, he tried to avoid meeting people. He still could not quite believe that Palace had not pulled through. His normally voracious appetite for films at Cannes waned, while the conspicuous absence of a Palace film in competition left him dejected and frustrated. JoAnne Sellar, by now the producer on *Dark Blood*, recalled that he 'was really depressed. He didn't want to leave the apartment and he just felt terrible about the whole thing.'

Whether they liked it or not, Palace was caught in the glare of publicity during the festival. One of the favourite topics of conversation was 'How much did they owe?' Putting an accurate figure on Palace's debts, however, was extremely difficult. Inflated

265

stabs in the trade press estimated at between £25 million and £30 million, a wild guestimate. No consolidated set of accounts combining all the companies' financial positions was ever produced during the administration. In Smith & Williamson's summary Statement of Affairs at 7 May 1992 on Palace Video Limited, the largest of the Group's individual trading concerns, some indication of the damage was given. The fixed chargeholders, including Guinness Mahon and Pierson Heldring & Pierson, were owed £4.16 million and PolyGram was owed the £2 million of its short-term loan. A total of £10.7 million was owed to unsecured creditors. Smith & Williamson estimated that Palace Video's debts totalled just over £15 million. The book value of Palace Video's catalogue of films was placed at £8.8 million, but was estimated to realise a paltry £200,000. Once Palace had gone, so too had its major assets.

The reaction to Palace's fall was divided into three broad categories, in Powell's opinion. In the first bracket were top film industry figures like the former Disney executive Jeffrey Katzenberg, the Weinsteins and other Hollywood professionals who were asking Powell and Woolley, 'So what's next guys? Which projects have you got in development?' Hollywood took the typically American attitude that the Palace partners had 'been through the flames and caught fire', as Woolley put it. Now they should be encouraged to come out the other side and get on with making more films. The major studios and leading independents could afford to be encouraging, although it was debatable how much support was really on offer. Powell recalls later having lunch with Katzenberg at Cannes and being unable to get a word in. 'Everything Jeffrey said I'd already read in *Variety*!' Nevertheless, Katzenberg and Miramax were to give Powell and Woolley significant support in the months to come.

The second category of creditors included long-term clients who'd done up to ten years' worth of business with Palace. Yes, they were upset and damaged by that fact that there were significant debts outstanding, but they were also aware of how much Palace money they had seen passing, albeit tardily, through their books over the years. The smaller creditors in this category provoked considerable anguish and shame in Powell. It included the small businesses who were owed sums between £10,000 and £200,000 and were badly affected by Palace's collapse. Mike Ewin, Palace Pictures' stalwart cinema booker, was owed £14,000. Mike Leedham, the designer of so many of their posters and video covers, was owed £48,000, forcing him to let people go in his suddenly struggling business. Phil Symes, such an important part of Palace's PR operation for most of the decade, was owed by his own estimate more than £100,000.

Harbottle & Lewis's John Stutter, who had so bravely represented Palace in its negotiations with PolyGram, was owed more than £45,000 on paper (the true figure reflected more than £100,000). Explaining the loss to his partners at Hanover Square was a deeply unpleasant experience for the brilliant lawyer.

UK producers knew how badly suppliers had been affected during the production of *Waterland* and *The Crying Game*. One film-maker walked into De Lane Lea, the post-production house on Soho's Dean Street, a few weeks after Palace had gone down. She asked, 'Where's the nice girl behind the desk gone?' The answer was an angry: 'We had to let her go because of those bastards at Palace.' What mystified some of the smaller creditors was why Powell had not acted earlier, to cushion the blow to their vulnerable businesses. 'It was nothing in comparison to what Palace owed in total, but Nik never seemed to think of us in that way,' one victim pointed out.

On the other hand, Powell had doggedly believed that Palace would pull through until the company was finally driven into the hands of the administrators. Once that painful process was started, he was in no position to prefer one creditor to another, whatever their size or vulnerability. After 7 May 1992, when Palace was formally placed into administration with Smith & Williamson, he had no control over management and financial matters. Neither Woolley nor Powell was declared personally bankrupt, despite owing more than £1.2 million in personal banking guarantees to Guinness and Pierson. As neither man had assets worth anything like that, the banks preferred to enter into long-term repayment negotiations rather than immediately call in the debt. Palace finally entered liquidation in August 1992, at the point when the administrators could not find buyers for any of the Group's main companies.

The detailed list of ninety-two creditors for Palace Video included some amusing entries: American Express, whose plastic card helped *The Crying Game* into production, was owed £2,719.25; the Groucho Club was owed £158.50; while Branson's Virgin Atlantic Airways was out of pocket by £638.

In 1993, BBC2's *Moving Pictures* made a sixty-minute special on Palace's rise and fall, 'Who's Crying Now?' Only one creditor out of 200 agreed to go on television to say how much he had lost through Palace's collapse. The *Moving Pictures* editor Saskia Barron discovered Christopher Fowler 'very late in the day'. His Soho-based design and trailer company, The Creative Partnership, had lost £100,000 and as a result had to let staff go. The rest of Palace's creditors, according to Barron, shied away from the cameras, most of them saying they did not want their accountants and bankers to know 'how dumb they were for not calling in the debts earlier', or protesting that it does not help 'washing dirty laundry in public'.

True to form, the partners succeeded in dominating 'Who's Crying Now?'; Woolley gave vent to streams of self-justification. When asked about his views on the pain inflicted on Palace's outstanding creditors, he bluntly replied: 'I'm not going to go and tie a cross on my back and carry it up a mountain.' Asked a year later if he still felt that way, Woolley explained that a lot of businesses in the UK film industry made considerable and consistent amounts of money out of Palace's thriving decade of business. 'Some people got their fingers burnt, so it's unfortunate, but that's part of the epicentre of business.' A financier who had dealt with Palace concurred with Woolley's view. 'There's a good proportion of those creditors who are the architects of their own problems,' he remarked. 'They buried their heads in the sand. I won't say they had it coming to them, but they should have been aware of what was going on.' Fowler too conceded, 'At the end of the day, being in this business is tantamount to being raped from behind. Unless you accept that possibility, you shouldn't be in the film industry.' The film industry is a cyclical business, as dependent on daily cash flow as the Palace Group had been. Ironically, The Creative Partnership went on to design the new logo for Scala and still works closely with Powell and Woolley.

The third category of people owed money consisted of individuals who had not done regular business with Palace, and had little personal relationship with either of the partners. Among this group were found Powell's and Woolley's most vociferous detractors. The most glaring example occurred at Cannes 1992, where the international gossip chain made Wardour Street's rumours pale into insignificance.

Hamish McAlpine, the wealthy son of Robert McAlpine, ran Metro Tartan, a rival independent film distribution operation. That May, he decided to design and print 250 T-shirts to distribute around Cannes. The front of the shirts read 'WHAT ABOUT THE CREDITORS?'. On the back was the Palace Logo with the words 'PALACE RIP 1992' and 'WHO'S CRYING NOW?'

Meanwhile, the corporate bosses at the public relations firm Rogers & Cowan were grilling Symes about the Palace debt. When Symes initially confronted Woolley and Powell (who was still asking him to write and issue press releases) about his staff obligations in a meeting at the Groucho Club, Powell explained there was a deal in the offing.

A few weeks later at Cannes, with the staff situation still unresolved, Symes had another lengthy meeting with Powell. Despite high emotion, nothing was resolved, so Powell told Symes he would get back to him, this time with Woolley. When the three men met that evening, Symes once again pleaded with them: what should he do about his six staff, employed specifically to service Palace? Woolley promptly said:

'Phil, you've just got to let them go.'

'What? Are you telling me that I should let these loyal staff go tomorrow?' asked Symes.

'Fire them, that's life,' Woolley replied.

Woolley's ruthless, single-minded approach was invaluable when it came to exploiting Palace's final film, *The Crying Game*, and the new development deal with PolyGram. One of the administrators recalls bumping into Woolley at Wardour Mews after most of the Palace staff had left. He had never met the Palace co-chairman before, and asked the pony-tailed producer, 'Who the hell are you? Do you realise you shouldn't be making phone calls?' Completely undeterred, Woolley explained himself, and proceeded to reel off all the projects and films his new company, then named Matawa, was involved in. Clearly the depression was lifting already, as he began to focus his energies on making the most of Jordan's *The Crying Game*.

After the first assembly of *The Crying Game* had been screened to Powell, Woolley, Myer and other key individuals in early 1992, Jordan had quietly approached Powell to ascertain his executive producer's reaction. Jordan had leaned gently towards Powell and whispered intensely, 'What do you think, Nik? What do you think?'

'Argh . . . well, Neil, I think we've got another *Mona Lisa*. If things go well, we could do as much business as she did, and we'll be up there in America,' Powell had told the anxious Irishman. Jordan had been heartened, but then, Powell had said much the same thing about *The Big Man*.

Woolley was delighted with the film and felt it stood an excellent chance of being selected for the Cannes Film Festival's official competition that May. Given the financial problems during those long winter months, *The Crying Game's* acceptance into competition at Cannes took on a greater importance than it might otherwise have done. Gilles Jacob, the director of the Cannes Film Festival for seventeen years, had already seen a rough cut, and liked it. He had asked to see a screening in Paris when the film was completed.

Elizabeth Karlsen, co-producer of *The Crying Game*, had just given birth to her and Woolley's first child, Edith, that January. A fluent French speaker, Karlsen flew to Paris with a print of *The Crying Game* and to campaign for the film by meeting Jacob.

Karlsen, armed with two large, heavy 35mm print cans and a six-week-old baby still being breast-fed, asked her mother to come with her to help with the journey. When they got to Paris, it transpired that Heathrow's luggage-loaders had left the prints off the flight. Karlsen rang London and succeeded in getting the prints on the next Heathrow–Paris flight. When they arrived, she had to rush directly to the screening rooms, set the film up, and then walk the streets of Paris with her screaming baby, who was innocently compounding Karlsen's nervous plight because she was not breast-feeding properly.

Eventually, she was called into Jacob's splendid office on the rue du Faubourg, from which the veteran film politician has gracefully controlled the world's biggest film festival for the past two decades. Tall, greying and impeccably well dressed, Jacob waited for the hassled Karlsen to settle in her seat before gently starting to talk.

'I'm sorry to disappoint you, Elizabeth, but there is something which is a little bit too Anglo-Saxon about the film. Neil is a wonderful scriptwriter, and it's a great script, but it has some problems,' Jacob said ominously, explaining that the first third of the film was very different from the rest of the film. The seven-strong jury had turned it down by four votes to three.

When Karlsen relayed the news to Woolley, he was bitterly upset. He rang Jacob, pleading that he and Jordan should be allowed to make a few changes and to show it to the jury again. 'If you still say no, then fine, I won't insist any more.'

It was unusual for Jacob to see a film three times, but he had always like Woolley and considered him a good producer. 'Okay, Stephen, we will see it one more time,' Jacob consented.

A trimmed version of the film was sent back to Paris. Once again the jury was split down the middle. Jacob pointed out that Stephen Rea's role was very interesting, and gently argued for the film's acceptance; but he was outvoted, leaving the grand old man in a difficult position. 'I could still say I would take the film,' he explained later. 'I have done it before, and I will do it again. But I respected the vote. Democracy was the reason for *The Crying Game* not being selected for Cannes.'

Having benefited so much from the hype and glory of Cannes in previous years, 1992 was not Powell's and Woolley's festival. To rub salt into their wounds, *Waterland*, which was up for selection in a sidebar event, Directors' Fortnight, was also rejected that spring.

A major IRA bombing campaign was launched on the British mainland in late October 1992. London pubs were thinly populated as the tabloids beat an anti-Irish drum. *The Crying Game* – named after the 1964 Dave Berry song later covered by Boy George – had a new title due to Jordan's desire to avoid war connotations. Unfortunately, the film happened to be released the same week as the IRA struck. Although *The Crying Game* met with generally favourable and supportive reviews, British critics could not help playing up the film's Irish politics. Despite a plea by Woolley not to give the ending away, the *Financial Times*'s critic Nigel Andrews even revealed the Jaye Davidson sex-swap.

Having to deal with the fallout of the Palace Group finally going into liquidation that August was absorbing most of Powell's time during these months. As well as helping the administrators sort through the tangled mess, Powell put tremendous efforts into helping his former staff find new jobs in other companies. Far from the bitchy suggestion that 'Nik was telling ex-Palace staffers how to claim social security,' as one detractor claimed, Powell was writing recommendations and making new jobs for his old staff a priority.

It was hardly surprising, given the demands made on him, that *The Crying Game*'s executive producer found out too late that Mayfair – the sole UK distributor now that Palace had gone – was planning to distribute the film all over the country after just a few weeks in London. Rows broke out between Mayfair and Powell, who was livid about the release plans. He felt the film needed to be discovered slowly, and required much more subtle marketing than a *Scandal* or an *Absolute Beginners*-style launch. A difficult but unique film like *The Crying Game* was only going to work once a decent word-of-mouth had been established by a long 'platform' run in London. Only then would the multiplex cinemas feel confident about supporting the film and keeping it on screens.

Ironically, PolyGram's marketeers agreed with Powell, and had hoped to keep the initial London release modest and slow-burning.

Mayfair's Hogarth, however, believed that *The Crying Game* needed to be seen across the country and on a large number of screens if it was to make an impact. Indeed, he was so confident about the film's popular appeal that he went ahead and booked *The Crying Game* into multiplex cinemas across the UK without consulting Powell and PolyGram. Such a move would have been fine for a Hollywood or mainstream British film, but general cinema-goers were unlikely to flock to a complex Irish drama with no major stars.

Despite relatively helpful press, Hogarth's well-intentioned support of the film backfired badly. Word-of-mouth on the film had not taken off strongly enough in London to help the release around Britain. As Powell explained, 'It was booked into multiplex cinemas up and down the country, and it completely collapsed. There was no audience for the film.' As the former Palace co-chair had learnt to his expense many times over the previous decade, it needs only one thing to go wrong in a film's distribution and the rest counts for nothing.

The film fizzled out after a few weeks, and by Christmas having taken little more than £300,000, *The Crying Game* was dead in the UK.

Miramax was not a cash-rich company in the middle of 1992. Despite its success at picking foreign language Oscar winners, including, between 1988 and 1991, *Pelle the Conqueror, Cinema Paradiso, Journey Of Hope,* and *Mediterraneo,* the American independent film distributor was having a rough ride. The Weinstein brothers had been trying to raise money with a stock offering, but offers were low due to the deep recession raging through Wall Street. They later denied a cash crisis, but their competitors had the brothers lined up in their spiteful sights.

In one of the most sneering articles ever printed about film-makers, the co-chairmen were described as 'the hateful, blubbery, slobbish brothers'. The two-page piece, published by *Spy* magazine in June 1992, and headlined 'Miramax, Miramax on the Wall, Who's the Sleaziest of Them All?', recorded a host of unhappy former collaborators' views on the brothers. 'This is one company I will never, ever, ever do business with again,' said one producer, 'These are bad people, these are bullies.'

PolyGram's Michael Kuhn was amused to discover how the brothers went about cutting back expenses. Kuhn went to see Harvey Weinstein at the Beverly Hills Hotel, one of the most ritzy hotels in Los Angeles and a frequent haunt of the stars. He went up to Harvey's room, which turned out to be a splendid corner suite, only to hear Harvey deliver a speech about how he was having to cut costs and was sacking staff. Kuhn, amazed at this performance, asked,

'Harvey, if that's the case, how come you are in this huge corner suite?'

'Well, I only pay a single room rate for it.'

'How on earth do you manage that? I can never get anything like that on this floor,' Kuhn responded.

'It's because I spend so much money here!'

For all its financial problems, real and imagined, Miramax was still very much in business. Despite the brothers' concerns about Jordan's film prior to production, once it was completed they were extremely interested in buying the American rights. Woolley and Powell, mindful of the high level of deferred fees on the film which were still unpaid and determined to attract a serious sale price, had asked Jordan's American agent, Jeff Berg, to set up six or seven screenings for the major Hollywood studios and buyers in late February that year. Berg, head of ICM and one of the most powerful executives in Hollywood, wooed the heads of the studios, including Sony, Universal, Paramount and Disney, partly as a way of starting some good word-of-mouth on the film, but also angling for a serious price.

Brandon Tartikoff, then head of Paramount Pictures, saw the film in his office on video. Woolley rang him up a few days later, to ask him what he thought. 'Well, yes, Steve, it's . . . er . . . Yeah, I liked it. But I didn't really understand the ending.' Woolley was somewhat taken aback. It turned out that at the very moment when the camera had panned down Jaye Davidson's body to reveal his true sex, Tartikoff had been called away for a phone call.

The final bidding was between Sony Picture Classics and Miramax, a battle that Berg and Woolley prolonged from March until the Cannes Film Festival. After his stubborn rejection of a script a year and a half earlier, Harvey Weinstein was now bowled over by Jordan's completed film and, in particular, by Davidson's remarkable performance. Just before Cannes, Bob Weinstein flew into London to see the film his brother was raving about. 'Bob just flipped,' Woolley recalled. 'His trip to London really sealed it. They both sensed something was there and were both very excited.'

An offer of $1.5 million was accepted, but before the deal could go through, certain accounts had to be settled. Miramax was forced by British Screen, a co-investor in *The Crying Game*, to settle some outstanding monies due from its previous films released by Miramax in North America. Jordan was less than thrilled by the news of who the buyer was. From his point of view, Miramax had not supported the release of *The Miracle* and the director was nervous of Harvey 'Scissorhands' 's tendency to edit films for their American release. Weinstein had quipped with Woolley about *The Crying Game*'s final cut, saying, 'You can tell Neil that I won't even cut one frame of it.' But Jordan was not taking any chances. He insisted that it was written into his contract that Miramax could not change or alter the movie.

By autumn 1992, the Weinsteins had started to throw their considerable weight behind *The Crying Game*. They saw the film as an event rather than just another picture. Special private screenings were held in New York, to which luminaries such as Robert Altman, Paul Schrader and Robert De Niro were invited. Screenings in LA included U2 as guests and were hosted by Hollywood producing guru Frank Marshall. At Christmas, even the former super-agent Mike Ovitz of Creative Artists Agency joined in, holding a screening in Aspen over the holiday, which was attended by Kurt Russell, Goldie Hawn and Barry Levinson.

An inspired marketing campaign was built around Jordan's gender-jolt, which the Weinstein brothers succeeded in keeping under wraps on the festival circuit and in the US press reviews. Having been turned down at Cannes and Venice, *The Crying Game* played at the Telluride Film Festival in September, and went on to win fine notices at the Toronto and New York Film Festivals that autumn. Audiences were given a letter from Jordan, Woolley and Miramax, urging them to keep the twist in the plot a secret, and at many festival screenings Jordan and Woolley made personal pleas before the screening, asking the audience to keep quiet about Jaye's gender.

Unlike certain of their British counterparts, the American critics and festival audiences played ball. US prints and trailers spun the line: 'The movie everyone is talking about, but no one is giving away its secrets.' Harvey Weinstein deliberately chose a poster which had little to do with the central point of the film. The picture – of Miranda Richardson holding a gun – was not dissimilar to Palace's earlier *Nikita* poster, and brilliantly avoided the film's potentially offputting political themes. 'Harvey had more ideas in five minutes on the release of a movie than the rest of the American distributors have in a year,' Myer noted. Every copy line, poster colour and trailer was checked obsessively, while every journalist's and critic's reaction was monitored by Miramax staff. High awareness of the film was what the Weinsteins needed for they were convinced that the public, if they could be persuaded to buy a ticket to the film, would not be disappointed. Miramax started the release slowly on just six cinema screens in New York and Los Angeles and soon attracted packed houses and a growing aura around the film. During these first few weeks, Harvey Weinstein would enter cinemas after screenings and ask an unsuspecting viewer, 'What happens in this movie? What's the big secret?' People would turn round and dismiss him, snapping, 'See it yourself. I'm not gonna ruin it for you.'

Meanwhile, the US press started to draw attention to the film. *Entertainment Weekly* ran a cover story on 12 February 1993, with a picture of Stephen Rea with his finger over his lips. The six-page special pointed out that the film's secret plot twist was now the hottest topic in town. At the New York Film Critics' Circle dinner, where both Jordan and Miranda Richardson won prizes, director Jonathan Demme *(The Silence of the Lambs)* took the podium and told the audience: 'I love that even here, the secret of *The Crying Game* is being honoured. Is there anyone here who *hasn't* seen it?'

During *The Crying Game*'s impressive opening run, Miramax had taken an unusual step which would ultimately have enormous impact on their profits from the film and its distribution. In order to take on the expensive risk of hundreds of prints and more advertising, Harvey had to prove to his own backers that his share of the American profits was correspondingly strong. The money was not going to be available to him unless he could get a huge share of the copyright to the film. Harvey, together with Peter Hoffman (a former executive with the high-spending Hollywood independent Carolco Pictures, responsible for films such as *Terminator 2: Judgment Day* and *Cliffhanger*), whom Miramax had taken on as a financial consultant, flew round Europe, meeting all the film's investors in an effort to buy their shares in the North American rights. Given the complexity of the original deal that financed *The Crying Game*, Harvey had to chase a paper trail for first and second charges and rights that would cost more than $25,000 in air fares before the two men had even started to renegotiate the deal.

Weinstein's and Hoffman's most important port of call was Channel 4. Prior to the making of the film, Channel 4's director of acquisitions Colin Leventhal had had great difficulty in dovetailing the Eurotrustees' deal with Channel 4's investment in the film. In the end, Channel 4 had taken a first place position (meaning that eventual profits would be paid to the channel first) in North American rights, from which it was planning to recoup the majority of its money. Now Miramax was offering $1 million to go into the film's central collection account – the trust account where all monies paid into the film were held – if they could buy outright the film's US copyright. Channel 4 wanted $2.5 million to go into the account. In the end, Michael Grade became involved in the negotiations and came up with an idea to protect the broadcaster's position: Miramax would buy the North American copyright for $1 million but should *The Crying Game*'s American revenues exceed $40 million, Channel

4 would start to share a significant proportion of the monies. Some hope, Leventhal thought to himself.

At this point in *The Crying Game*'s American run, the film had done well but taken no more than $13 million at the box office. 'To be honest, it was inconceivable that the film was going to do more than forty million dollars. Inconceivable,' Leventhal stressed.

By the time Grade's inventive proposal reached an irritated Miramax, Harvey had already flown back to New York. Bob Weinstein and Hoffman called a meeting at the St James's Club in Mayfair. Miramax's problem was that it was not just a case of getting Channel 4 to sign off the new arrangement. In order for the deal to go through, British Screen, Powell, Woolley, and certain key banks and investors, including Berliner Bank, all had to agree to the new terms of Channel 4's deal with Miramax. After much arbitration, Miramax agreed to the Grade-inspired Channel 4 profit participation deal, while Jordan held out for a separate and better deal.

At about four o'clock on a grey winter afternoon on 17 February 1993, a nervous, chain-smoking Stephen Woolley received a phone call from Bob Weinstein in Los Angeles. The Oscar nominations were being announced live on American television news, and an excited Weinstein wanted to pass on the results. The staff crowded round Woolley, cheering as each *Crying Game* nomination boomed down the phone line, relayed by a euphoric Weinstein.

As the five Oscar nominations including Best Picture, Best Direction, Best Original Screenplay, Best Actor, and Best Supporting Actor, tallied up, Amanda Posey, a young former Palace employee who happened to have come into the office that afternoon, raided the office fridge to bring out some champagne that had been chilled just in case things turned out well. By coincidence, others connected to the film, including Paul Cowan, Redmond Morris and Jordan himself dropped into the office. Woolley and Jordan were suddenly handling six telephone lines, deluged by press enquiries, while Weinstein was proudly proclaiming to Powell that *The Crying Game* might even reach $30 million in the US.

An impromptu party at Soho's Groucho Club was set up that same evening, attended by Woolley, Powell, Jordan and Miranda Richardson, along with any friends and crew they could lay their hands on. A roar erupted half-way through the merriment when it was discovered that a further nomination, for Best Editor, had been overlooked and was added to the five-strong clutch.

A buzz of excitement flew round the offices of Powell's and Woolley's new film company, Scala Productions. The news spread that anyone who paid for their own air tickets could come to the Oscar party. They would have to stay with friends or crash at the former Palace's office-cum-apartment just off Sunset Boulevard, which was now run by Scala. Tickets were booked, and plans were made to arrive in Los Angeles a few days before the big event. The special spirit even got to Powell, who bought a plane ticket for Wendy Broom, his personal assistant.

Angela Morrison and Broom were the last to join *The Crying Game* gang on the Friday night prior to the Monday night Academy event. 'We had this big mad dinner at a French restaurant in LA,' Broom recalled. 'Everyone was there, and the Sky TV team covering the event had just finished shooting the whole dinner scene. Everyone was in a great party mood. By the time Nik stood up and asked Steve's permission to mention all the people who weren't so high on the credits list, we were all incredibly drunk.

"I'd like to thank you all . . . John, Pete, Wendy, Michael . . . Angela, Amanda . . . all of you worked really hard on this film, and I just want to say thank you," Powell waxed lyrically.

"Oh, God, Nik, that's enough. Please, enough," Woolley smiled with embarrassment.'

The celebration went on. That Saturday night, *Scandal* director Michael Caton-Jones held a big party at his home in Beverly Hills, initially just for the film's main crew and stars, but soon all the Brits who had flown over were there. On Sunday, the Spirit Awards took place in a white tent on Santa Monica's beach, and *The Crying Game* was awarded the Best Independent Film prize.

Elizabeth Karlsen, co-producer on the film and Woolley's wife, had come out to LA with their baby girl and her mother. They all bought new dresses in Beverly Hills, and Woolley had a flash Romeo Gigli suit fitted (partly paid for by Miramax), although at the last minute he opted for the 'lucky suit' he'd worn at previous successful award ceremonies. They were staying at The Sunset Marquis Hotel's exclusive villa with Jordan and his partner, also paid for by Miramax. Powell joined them later.

Powell, who was eager to strike up some new business deals in Hollywood on the back of *The Crying Game*'s success, had nevertheless invited his two younger children, the then nine-year-old Jack, and eleven-year-old Amie. He had arranged to take Amie to the Oscars as his date for the evening, and she had also bought a new dress for the occasion. Unlike Woolley, Powell thought a new suit was rather extravagant, and although he bought some new black shoes for the ceremony, he forgot to take them to LA.

Even Jaye Davidson, who by now was thoroughly disenchanted with doing press interviews for the film and had decided against any further acting, was persuaded by Woolley to come out for the event. For a Best Supporting *Actor* nominee, he made a self-consciously low-key arrival with his friend on 28 March, the day before the ceremony. By now, the first-timer was fed up with being hounded by the London tabloids, who had been belting out headlines like: 'Will Jaye wear a dress to the Oscars?'

Prior to the Oscar nominations and just following the new Miramax deal, *The Crying Game* had taken a very promising $16 million after twelve weeks in American cinemas, which was more than any previous Palace production had earned. Fortunately, most of the big films from the Hollywood studios that winter were box office failures, including *Chaplin*, *Toys* and *Hoffa*. Miramax executives lined up an additional 500 cinema screens just as the Oscar nominations were announced on 17 February, and the film went on to take a further $5.2 million that weekend. It marked a box-office rise of 400 per cent on the previous week, and turned *The Crying Game* from an outsider into a much-trumpeted Oscar underdog. Polls by Miramax showed that at least half the new audiences would have seen the film without the Oscar nomination bonus, but the coincidence of timing was hugely rewarding. The press too went into a tailspin of hype as the Oscar race gathered pace. Every talk-show host and radio disc jockey was constantly making quips about the film without giving the game away.

One week before the Oscars on 29 March, *The Crying Game* had already taken $40 million across America. Even before Jordan won his Oscar that night, Woolley and Powell were busy using the film's success to help their new Scala Productions. In Woolley's case, the film's success for Jordan was an additional bonus. Warner Brothers had made a commitment to make *Interview with the Vampire*, and Jordan was asking for his British producer to join the now expanding studio production.

On the morning of 29 March 1993, the Las Vegas bookmakers placed *The Crying Game* at 6–5 favourite for Best Picture, in front of Clint Eastwood's *Unforgiven*. Interviewed by a reporter from *Empire* magazine that morning, an excited Woolley for once felt optimistic. 'I know a lot of the fringe people are voting for us, because it's struck a blow for independent cinema . . . taking $40 million means that [the Academy member's] limo drivers have seen it. We're going to take $50 million on this film even if all we pick up at the end of the Oscars is the bill for the wine and the car hire. We've made the most money for any independent film release in America.'

Twelve hours later, Neil Jordan was walking through the Dorothy Chandler Pavilion to collect his Oscar for Best Original Screenplay. Despite having been warned not to stick his finger in his ear if he made it to the podium – the director's typical nervous reaction when speaking in public – the index finger rose towards his head as he searched for the words to thank his collaborators.

The Best Picture Award is always the last. Woolley had worked himself up into such a state that he was temporarily desperate *not* to win. To face all those people around the world was going to be too much. In the end, Eastwood won it for *Unforgiven* – the film Woolley had most wanted to win if *The Crying Game* did not.

During the post-awards dinner, Amie Powell walked straight up to Jack Nicholson and requested his autograph to go alongside the previously cornered Eastwood.

'Please Mr Nicholson, can I have your autograph?' she asked firmly.

Nicholson, surrounded by minders and wearing dark glasses, gave Powell the impression that his daughter was about to have her head bitten off. He need not have worried. Nicholson missed a beat, checked the eleven-year-old Amie Powell over, and replied: 'Since you're young . . . beautiful . . . and a woman, sure!'

Powell's two children had a memorable Oscar trip, visiting Disneyland courtesy of Harvey Weinstein. On previous trips, Jack had been banned from ordering any hotel extras by his taciturn father. This time he discovered that Harvey was footing the bill: ice-creams, chocolate bars, milkshakes and pizzas winged their way up to his room.

As far as Woolley was concerned, despite all the effort and mountains of money thrown at it, the official Oscar party suffered from the same disease as the award ceremony: four out of five people there were fed up. Since all his and Powell's staff, friends and the film's crew who had made it to the event were watching the ceremony in a big room at Chasens, a smart restaurant and club in Beverly Hills hired by Miramax, he decided to join them.

Two big TV screens had been stuck in the corners of the party room, and once the Academy Awards had got underway, the atmosphere soon resembled a Liverpool away game at Manchester United. The tense and excited crowd was euphoric when Jordan won. When Woolley appeared a couple of hours later, they pounced on him, and, to his horror, carried him seated on a chair round the room. Miramax's executive guests looked on in shock as the party turned into anarchy.

Later, Woolley and Jordan went to Stephen Rea's hotel room and drank until the morning, while Jordan's daughter fell asleep with the Oscar statuette cradled in her arms.

While Woolley and Powell were delighted at *The Crying Game*'s success, some residents of Wardour Street whipped up rumours about the two men making money from the Miramax deal, whilst leaving the crew unpaid. The truth was far removed from the gossip mill version. Given that the UK release had fared badly, and the only European distributors to do well were those who released the film after the American campaign, *The Crying Game* offered slim pickings outside North America. Even in America and Canada, contrary to the popular perception that the Miramax brothers had become multi-millionaires by Oscar-time, the cost of the film's release was enormous.

The figures proved again how tough the film industry is for producers, investors and distributors. By the end of *The Crying Game*'s North American release, the film had taken $63 million at the box office. Miramax's share of that take as distributors could be estimated at around thirty per cent, leaving them with around $19 million. The huge cost of the film's prints and advertising campaign, along with the Oscar race, would have been a minimum of $15 million, leaving perhaps $4 million before its own distribution commission. The company had paid $1.5 million for the film initially, plus an additional $1 million when it took over the North American copyright. So despite taking a tremendous risk, the theatrical release of *The Crying Game* would not have made Miramax a real profit by the middle of 1993.

However, the company controlled the video rights and pay-TV (ie. subscription) rights for North America, and made handsome profits on those ancillary outlets. In fact, so handsome that Miramax was finally bought by Disney for a sum estimated to be between $60 million and $80 million, making Bob and Harvey Weinstein multi-millionaires. According to sources, the deal included five-year employment contracts for the brothers, $20 million of Disney stock options, and $25 million in operating capital. Disney also took over all of Miramax's debts. Struck so soon after *The Crying Game*'s triumph, Miramax's marriage to Disney again proved that perception is all in the film industry. The American 'wide boys' of independent film, on the back of their British counterparts' last film, succeeded in selling out to the Establishment.

Contrary to Wardour Street's inaccurate carping, by autumn

1993 everyone who had worked on *The Crying Game* had been paid in full. The only exceptions, of course, were Woolley and Powell as producers. Their profits were already spoken for by PolyGram and a clutch of banks.

CHAPTER FIFTEEN

# The
# Phoenix
# Effect

On a sunny day during the Cannes Film Festival in May 1993, Powell collapsed from an epileptic fit at the Majestic Hotel. Foaming at the mouth and bleeding from a gash to his eye, Powell was quickly hauled on to his back. His mouth was yanked open by Harvey Weinstein, who yelled for a doctor from the fast-gathering crowd. An American medic pushed his way forward and then stopped, looking at Weinstein in astonishment.

'Hey, aren't you Harvey Weinstein, the guy who did *The Crying Game*?' the doctor gushed idiotically.

'Yeargh,' Weinstein shot back, pointing to Powell convulsing in the hotel lobby. 'Meet one of the producers . . .'

Powell was rushed to a local hospital for stitches and bandages while his friends played the event and subsequent black eye down, explaining that 'Nik just fell over . . .' Soho's bitchy gossip mill was again set in motion, maliciously twisting Powell's black eye into an apocryphal story centring on a supposed fight in the Groucho Club between Powell and an unnamed assailant allegedly still owed money from *The Crying Game*.

Powell had been at his lowest ebb in the year following Palace's collapse. He had taken the weight of the failure on his shoulders, feeling remorse and responsibility for his closest friends and colleagues. That first Christmas after the liquidation, Phil Living-stone, Powell's old Sussex University friend, bumped into him in the Groucho Club. He was shocked at Powell's beer-soaked, depressed state. 'I mean, Nik gets pissed but I'd never seen him in his cups,' Livingstone recalled. While the subsequent Cannes 1993 story was grossly unfair, Powell did tend to find himself in humiliating late-night scrapes during those bleak months.

Allan McKeown, Powell's former partner in The TV Sales Company, held a party for his thriving SelecTV at the Groucho Club at Christmas 1993. He had not seen Powell for eighteen months, when Nik had helpfully sold him Palace's share in The TV Sales Company for £1 in a bid to keep him clear of Palace's problems. The two had plenty to talk about.

'Allan, this has been the worst year of my life,' Powell groaned. 'It's strange, because I think we've made the best film we've ever done.'

McKeown made a supportive stab at being positive. 'Well, Nik, you're still standing. You'll start all over again, you're that kind of guy. And anyway, what does it all matter? You've still got that great girl Sandie. She's smashing, absolutely gorgeous.'

Powell's face tightened. 'Argh . . . actually, Sandie's gone.'

Woolley and Karlsen also came face-to-face with some of the realities of going bankrupt. The threat of the bailiffs and the bleak images of Palace's collapse were a recurring nightmare, Karlsen recalled. At least Karlsen's modest home in Fulham – where the couple lived – had been in her name long before she met Woolley, giving them some sense of security on the home front. That was not to be underestimated, given that Powell was going through a painful separation with Shaw and living in a bedsit.

Woolley was single-minded during these months. He continued to throw himself into new Scala projects, and was determined to avoid the backbiting on Wardour Street. It was not the producer's nature to sit back and cry. Nor was he inclined to confront the discomfort the damage done to smaller suppliers. One small creative businessman remembers how difficult it was to get Woolley to face them: 'It was as if he'd rather look at a cigarette butt on the ground than look me in the face,' remarked the creditor.

Powell's candour, most notable at the creditors' meeting held at the Langham Hilton Hotel in August 1992, was better appreciated. He was direct and straightforward, prepared to stand up and take the flak. Woolley, in New Orleans on an *Interview with the Vampire* recce, was unable to attend the meeting. This infuriated some of Palace's former collaborators. Patrick Cassavetti felt that, although Powell had become so blinded by his problems that he had made some 'terrible mistakes', for Woolley to suggest later that he had had little to do with most of the Palace Group, arguing on television that they had been 'all Nik's companies', was an unforgivable betrayal.

The question of whether Powell and Woolley were fit to be directors of a new company was raised by certain creditors both at the August meeting and afterwards in Soho clubs and pubs. They were also upset by what administrators call 'The Phoenix Effect', the rise of a new company so soon after the old one has gone into receivership. However, in August 1992, when Smith & Williamson came to file its confidential report to the Department of Trade and Industry on the Palace Group's liquidation, a source confirmed that no complaint or negative recommendation was lodged under the Company Directors' Disqualification Act. 'Frankly, there was no intention to try to defraud the creditors,' said the source. 'They made all the efforts they could within their limited capacity to do the right thing. Why should they be penalised for going ahead and trying to make a living?'

Armed with the PolyGram development and overhead deal, making a living was exactly what both men set out to do. Unlike many business partners who split up after a failure, both men assumed their future was together. After all, they were still friends, and their teamwork would help both of them to deal with the disaster behind them. A drive towards new film production (and production only), became the determining force in Powell's and Woolley's new lives. Despite their decade of experience and the olive branch from PolyGram, their rise from the ashes of Palace was far from a foregone conclusion.

During the late autumn of 1993, the two new co-chairmen of Scala Productions encountered a serious twist of misfortune. *Dark Blood*, produced by JoAnne Sellar, was proving a horrendous shoot, stuck 300 miles south of Salt Lake City, Utah, and being steadily poisoned by a feud between its director and star. Tempers had grown so heated between the Dutch-born director George Sluizer and Australian actress Judy Davis that Powell had to fly out before principal photography began. He called a meeting between Sellar, Sluizer, Davis, Jonathan Pryce and River Phoenix on his arrival in an attempt to calm things down.

'It was basically a clash between two control freaks and the people caught in the middle were Pryce, River, the producers and the crew,' Powell explained. 'It was an abrasive meeting, and all of us probably wanted to dive under the table. River was very good in it, wise beyond his years . . .' However, the meeting solved nothing and the atmosphere remained as rancid as before.

The following night, after rehearsals, Powell and the twenty-three-year-old Phoenix, who had dyed his hair black for the part, drove back to the local bar. Phoenix, who had already completed thirteen feature films and picked up an Oscar nomination for Sidney Lumet's *Running On Empty* nearly five years previously, was well practised at film-shoot fall-out. He too was finding the location filming difficult, but the young star appeared calm and collected about the problems. Over a beer, Powell told Phoenix in a fatherly fashion. 'Don't ever lose that wisdom, whatever happens, River.'

Six weeks later, Sellar called Powell in Spain on a Sunday afternoon: 'Nik, hold on to your seat.' On hearing those words, Powell immediately thought that an earthquake had erupted, and then made the more likely assumption that either Davis had flown back to Australia or Sluizer had returned to Amsterdam. He was bored of hearing about personal politics on the set of *Dark Blood*, but Sellar continued, 'River died last last night.'

While Phoenix had been on location in Utah, neither the director nor the actor's fellow stars had seen him take any hard-core drugs. However, on moving back into his hotel in Los Angeles, he had returned to his Hollywood diet. On Saturday 30 October, Phoenix had met his girlfriend, actress Samantha Mathis, his brother Leaf, and some other friends. They had made their way to the Viper Room nightclub by midnight, where River was seen bumping into tables and acting strangely. He was due to join Johnny Depp on stage for a jamming session, but before he was called had started to vomit all over himself. His friends led him, shuddering, to the toilets to clean him up and throw water over him. By now it was one a.m. on 31 October.

He returned to the table, but started another fit of seizures and was taken outside. As he lay on the pavement shaking, his eyes rolling towards the back of his head, his brother called for an ambulance. After about ten minutes of flailing, River passed out, and went completely still. He was pronounced dead less than an hour later in hospital. Cocaine and valium were found in lethal quantities in his body.

A cast and crew meeting was called by Sellar and Sluizer and, under Powell's instructions, the production's employees were put on minimum notice. The problem facing the film's producers was that it was too far into the shoot to cast a new lead, and too emotionally complex a story to use digital technology (as was later used on *The Crow* following Brandon Lee's death). The Phoenix situation left them with little option but to close the film down. Scala and the other co-investors in the film agreed to file for an insurance claim of nearly $6 million plus interest after the American distributors, New Line, confirmed that they would not accept a recasting. Ironically, the insurance settlement was held up when the accounts office was heavily damaged by the Los Angeles earthquake in January 1994, which led Powell to ask the insurers if they had disaster insurance.

*Dark Blood* had taken four years to reach production, originally developed by Sluizer and writer Jim Barton and adopted by Sellar while Palace was still a going concern. The film had demanded tremendous emotional and physical commitment from Sluizer and Sellar in particular. Sluizer initially experienced a similar shock to a parent who had lost a child. 'River had that kind of charisma which made you like him, love him and care for him, so the first thing I felt was devastation.' It was only later that the film-maker started to feel angry. As he put it, 'I felt cheated. I felt like this was four years of my life River had killed at the same time.'

Phoenix's unexpected departure also impacted heavily on a major Hollywood project, *Interview with the Vampire*, which was based on Anne Rice's bestseller. Phoenix was set to star as the interviewer in the film which was to be produced by music billionaire David Geffen for Warner Brothers on a $28 million budget. Phoenix apparently was not thrilled at the prospect, telling American *Premiere* just before his death that he did not like vampires much. 'I find them full of shit, frankly. It's good they cast me as the interviewer in the sense that I can be pessimistic.'

Woolley's involvement in *Interview* came about in a roundabout manner. Around Christmas 1992, Jenne Casarotto, Neil Jordan's British agent, had rung a senior executive at Geffen Pictures and insisted that she go out and rent a tape of *The Company of Wolves*. She realised that Jordan was a natural choice to direct the Anne Rice adaptation. She could only hope that the producer would conveniently forget that *High Spirits* and *We're No Angels* were ever made. The plan worked well, and the timing was perfect. Talks about the script and prospective film coincided with the box-office rise and hype of *The Crying Game* in America, making Jordan an increasingly good prospect from both Geffen's and Warner Brothers' point of view.

Geffen had been developing *Interview* for more than a decade. Fraught with difficulties, Rice's book was proving impossible to adapt for the big screen. Although the novel was written by Rice in 1976, Jordan had never read the book. Nevertheless, when Geffen sent the film-maker a version of the screenplay, Jordan pretended that he had read the novel. He finally got round to reading it on his way to France for a *Crying Game* publicity tour. 'As soon as I had read the novel, I could see the whole movie,' Jordan said. The only problem was whether the Irish film-maker could avoid the Hollywood interference he had suffered on his previous American projects. Fortunately, Geffen was happy with the proposal that *Interview* be independently produced, and so too, amazingly, were

Warner Brothers. Jordan was encouraged to go and write a new draft screenplay based on Rice's book and her own script.

Crucially for Woolley, Geffen was also keen to take on a producing partner for the large-scale film. At Jordan's suggestion and with Geffen's approval, Woolley was signed up to produce the biggest film of his career. Suddenly the irrepressible producer was back in the limelight, riding on the back of *The Crying Game* with a cheek that startled Wardour Street. As he later said, 'Obviously, as the producer of *The Crying Game*, people want to meet you.' Yet Woolley had worked at his relationship with Jordan for more than ten years. He had coaxed, sympathised and cajoled the saturnine Irishman through five feature films since *The Company of Wolves*, so a Hollywood blockbuster seemed an appropriate reward. Due to Geffen's ownership of the project, Scala was not directly involved in the production, a fact of which certain Palace's creditors were unaware. They found it extraordinary that within months of Palace going into liquidation, Woolley was set to collect a healthy Hollywood production fee, estimated at over half a million dollars.

Casting *Interview* proved a considerable challenge. After Daniel Day-Lewis turned down the part of vampire Lestat, Rice stirred a media feeding frenzy by publicly criticising the casting of Tom Cruise in the role. In an interview with the *Los Angeles Times*'s Calendar section of Sunday 22 August, 1993, Rice slammed the decision, claiming that Cruise 'is no more my vampire Lestat than Edward G. Robinson is Rhett Butler . . . [He] should do himself a favour and withdraw.' Warner Brothers, Geffen, Jordan and Woolley closed ranks. Anne Rice could say what she liked, but they were paying their man $15 million in the belief that Cruise's acting ability and star status would help *Interview* become a major hit around the world.

Woolley was on *Interview*'s Orleans shoot on 1 November 1993 when Karlsen rang him at seven a.m., explaining that she had just seen the news and River Phoenix had died. 'That's crazy . . . it's a mistake,' Woolley stammered.

'No, Stephen, it's on the television. Turn your TV on.'

Within the hour, the phone calls started to deluge Woolley's hotel room. Sellar rang; Phoenix's agent rang; the actor's mother called him. Then the faxes started. Virtually all Hollywood's agents were sending their condolences in a couple of lines, while some – doing their clients no good at all – were even sending a list for consideration as the new Interviewer. 'River wasn't even cold, you know,' Woolley said. 'He was still warm. That was very odd, very nasty.' The producers soon replaced Phoenix with Christian Slater, who joined the cast of Cruise, Brad Pitt, Antonio Banderas, Stephen Rea and Kirsten Dunst, and the film was back on the road. Slater donated his entire fee to two of Phoenix's favourite charities, Earth Save in Santa Cruz, and Earth Trust in Malibu.

For Woolley, the whole experience of working on a blockbuster-sized movie with a Hollywood studio committed to its investment was 'a very, very pleasurable experience. The world of independent film-making is highly stressful and highly risky, and I very much take on the creative stress of a film as well as sharing the financial stress with Nik,' Woolley explained. '*Interview* was a lot to take on, but it was great to have David [Geffen] supporting it, and constantly saying how terrific the dailies looked. You don't trust anyone in the independent world, because there's so much doubt and insecurity . . . In the final analysis, when you're making something as big as *Interview*, there is an appropriate marketing machine waiting for it. The Warner Brothers' machine would have been useless for *The Crying Game*, it wouldn't have known what to do with such a specialised movie. So the whole experience was a wonderful challenge and in a way far less stressful.'

By the time *Interview* was released in late 1994, the budget had risen to a little more than $70 million, a typically inflated budget with a huge star like Cruise on board. An enormous advertising campaign was launched, and by the time the film had completed its North American run, it had grossed just over $105 million. The film went on to take a further $110 million in the rest of the world, before any video, subscription-TV and television rights had been exploited. Cruise was so delighted with his experience on *Interview* that he sent the film's key participants a personally embossed leather-bound photo-file, thanking them for their efforts.

Jordan had made a Hollywood hit, and Woolley was right there behind him. *Interview* laid the way for a potential sequel, *Vampire Lestat*, but the first, prized knock-on effect of *Interview* was that Warner Brothers decided to back a film about Michael Collins, the Irish terrorist-cum-statesman, to be directed by Jordan and produced by Woolley. The $30 million picture was shot in Ireland during the summer and autumn of 1995. It starred Liam Neeson as Collins, with Julia Roberts as Kitty Kiernan, the girl Collins planned to marry before he was assassinated by his former comrades at the age of thirty-one. When Woolley saw the early screenings of the film in October 1995, he stated that *Michael Collins* 'is the best film Neil has ever made'.

At a London Film Festival party on the South Bank in November 1993, Powell and his stunning new blonde-haired Austrian girlfriend Erika Trefenthaler were celebrating a development loan awarded to Scala Productions by a European Union Film subsidy body, the European Script Fund. Powell was notably happier than after the previous funding round, when Palace had been rejected. On hearing that news, he had called the fund and sworn down the phone for twenty minutes. This time, Powell was on typical tasteless form, joking with European film financiers, and holding his pocket open 'for donations' due to the problems *Dark Blood* was facing with its insurance claim.

Phoenix's death was not Scala's only nightmare. Their other big feature project, Iain Softley's *Backbeat* – about Stuart Sutcliffe, the fifth Beatle, who died before the band found fame – was facing a potentially serious problem. The story running round the industry was that one night, only days after *Dark Blood* had been aborted, somebody had broken into Bucks Film Laboratories just outside London, where the negatives of *Backbeat* were being stored, and had removed some roles of negative, known as 'lab roles' in the trade. According to the Soho rumour, a rival lab, still owed money as a result of Palace's collapse, had taken their revenge. Those not owed money or directly affected by Palace's demise the previous year were sympathetic to Scala's situation. If part of the film really had been destroyed, re-editing the damaged celluloid from out-takes was every producer's, director's or editor's nightmare.

According to Finola Dwyer, the producer of *Backbeat* (alongside Woolley), Bucks had informed Scala that they could not find two roles of negatives but were sure they would turn up. 'Because we were running up against deadlines, we had to give Bucks a cut-off point to find the missing negative. Iain [Softley] and I put a plan into action in case the negative didn't turn up. We viewed all the "No Good" takes that had been pulled and were extremely lucky in that these gave us eighty per cent of what we needed. Fortunately, we only had to shoot some very simple setups at the eleventh hour.'

The pressure on the delivery of Softley's debut feature was growing. The film's distributors were primed to see the film in London prior to the Milan-based MIFED Film Market in late October. Although the film was not due to be delivered until Christmas, they were eager to see it that autumn. Based on strong test screenings, the distributors, as well as Virgin, which was doing the album release worldwide, were keen to get the film into the cinemas as quickly as possible.

*Backbeat* had a very positive screening at the Sundance Film Festival in Utah in January 1994, and was instantly embraced by the Hollywood film community as a brave and innovative work. The film finally made it to the cinemas in March, and despite receiving good reviews but a poor commercial reception in the US, Softley's debut performed well for PolyGram in the UK. It was known that Michael Kuhn was particularly pleased with *Backbeat*, telling Dwyer and others that the film provided PolyGram with a certain credibility at a point when the fledging film company really needed it.

Producing and completing a film proved to the outside world that Powell and Woolley were back in business. Both men's resilience and their determination to prove that they could still access the money and the talent to make films of significance was not to be underestimated. *Backbeat*'s impact was important both psychologically and financially to the partners.

Dwyer continues to work closely with Powell, Woolley and

Karlsen on new films. The film also contributed to the rise of a new Hollywood star, Stephen Dorff; while Ian Hart (who played John Lennon) has subsequently enjoyed a meteoric rise. Moreover, a Powell–Woolley project had, once again, launched the career of a young, talented director, Iain Softley.

After a crisis-laden start, Scala Productions gradually acquired characteristics that distinguished it from Palace. A sense of order and clarity stemmed from the company's concentration on production. The mess created by the by-products of distribution – posters, video cassettes, boxes, etc – was conspicuously absent from Scala's new offices on Soho's Brewer Street. Even Scala's initial handful of employees was surprised by the perceptible change, watching with interest to see how the new company would develop.

Powell had not made the move from Wardour Mews easy, however. He had attempted to insist that every box, pencil and paper clip should be packed up and taken with them. Karlsen had lost her temper yelling, 'Nik, why do you want to make the new office just like the old one?' Wendy Broom, Powell's loyal assistant for so long, had raised her eyes in despair when faced with organising the files which were to be boxed and moved to the new offices.

'Don't throw any of those old boxes away, Wendy,' Powell had instructed. The heaps of paraphernalia and papers dated back to his Virgin days. 'It was as almost as if Nik didn't want to get rid of anything in case it was going to be used as evidence for us later,' Broom said. Powell later explained that he had removed the paperwork to keep hold of Palace films' records, which otherwise would have been destroyed in the move.

Scala's overhead expenditure was watched by the eagle eye of PolyGram's accountants. The paperwork expended to satisfy PolyGram regarding the costs for cleaners, heating and paper served to highlight the cultural difference of which Michael Kuhn had been so wary. Perhaps predictably, the deal with PolyGram was not renewed after its first year, so in spring 1993 Powell and Woolley began the search for a suitable investor who could help them consolidate and create some stability. Lengthy talks were held with

Miramax, which by now was a fully owned subsidiary of Disney. After many months, a substantial long-term first-look deal was signed, which gave Miramax the first option to invest in Scala's extensive slate of films.

In mid-1994, Chrysalis Group PLC, the media and entertainment group, announced the setting up of Chrysalis Films. The publicly quoted company committed itself to investing over four years, up to £4 million, in a serious of development and production deals. One of its first investments, announced in November 1994, was the acquisition of a forty-nine per cent shareholding in Scala Productions. The new Scala deal also included a working capital facility to enable Woolley and Powell to continue to produce films when they did not have money coming in from other sources. By late 1995, Scala had approximately fifteen films in development. Under the agreement, Woolley is permitted to make films for other production companies, an arrangement not all Chrysalis consultants agreed with. Certain individuals suggested that Woolley was being allowed too much freedom, but when a variation of the deal was put forward which penalised Woolley's considerable production fees every time he worked outside the Chrysalis deal, it was rejected.

When the Scala deal was put to the Chrysalis board that autumn, a veteran industry accountant asked the people around the table if they had considered what it might mean to the rest of the industry to be seen to back Powell and Woolley. He warbled on about creditors and banking debts, before he was interrupted by a senior member of the Chrysalis board. The bearded, greying man asked in his inimitable persuasive style: 'Haven't you heard of *The Crying Game*? Nik and Steve have just made one of the most successful films ever. We've no option but to do this deal.'

The board member was David Puttnam.

The question that many people, even those close to Powell and Woolley, continue to ask themselves is how long will they stay together. Even before the Oscar ceremony in March 1993, Woolley's career was starting to take off in Hollywood. In the early spring he had received the Producers' Guild of America award for 'Producer of the Year', a rare achievement for a British film-maker. While the American industry had long been aware of Woolley's talents, the award signalled the far-reaching impact *The Crying Game* had had on Hollywood. Powell would later advise young up-and-coming film-makers to 'always take care to get the right credit'. The difference between 'producer' and 'executive producer' had never seemed great to Powell until *The Crying Game* took off. Industry collaborators reflected at the time how unfair it was that 'Steve should take all the glory, after the work Nik put into the financing of that film.'

The Producer's award was a personal triumph for Woolley, and the ceremony allowed him to thank an old friend. Back in his days running The Other Cinema, Howard Koch – the veteran Holly-wood producer and former manager of Frank Sinatra – rang up to find out when he was playing *The Untouchables* and *Untainted Youth*, films he had directed. Woolley invited him to come along and introduce them. After a lively ten minutes, Woolley and Koch spent the rest of the evening chatting in the bar, talking about movies. Koch was impressed by Woolley's encyclopedic knowledge of film, telling him, 'Guys like you should be in the movies!'

A few years later during the LA screening of *The Company of Wolves*, a lonely Woolley wondered who he could call in Hollywood. He tried Koch at Paramount, and left a message saying he had rung. The two men never got to speak.

Four years later, Michael Caton-Jones decided he needed a particular version of Frank Sinatra's 'Witchcraft' for *Scandal*. Woolley wrote to Koch, reminding him that it was ten years since they had that all-night cinema talk in London and, by the way, could he help with the soundtrack? A few days later, the phone rang.

'It was eight years and four months ago!' Koch laughed. 'And by the way, why didn't you ring back? The soundtrack for *Witchcraft* is yours!' Woolley went into Paramount and spent an entire day talking about the old days of moviemaking.

On the night of the Producer's award, five years later, it was hardly surprising that Woolley said in his acceptance speech, 'There is one person I have to thank . . .' Unfortunately, Koch himself had once again missed the producer, unable to attend the awards ceremony. It was nevertheless a fitting moment, epitomising everything the producer had wanted Palace and his life to be about.

The awards kept coming, helping the partners' rehabilitation grow more secure each month. In December 1993, Powell and Woolley won the European equivalent of an Oscar – a Felix – for the European Achievement of the Year as a result of their efforts in making *The Crying Game*. During that same week, in Berlin, Powell was given a glowing introduction by a top producer at a European film school masterclass. Powell replied 'I don't think you really want to be like me: I'm bankrupt, going through a divorce, and living in a bedsit.'

Woolley's creative energy and extreme ambition have kindled in him a burning desire to become a very powerful film-maker. He dreams of creating a body of work that will retain its significance when people look back over the years and consider his contribution to cinema. 'In the year 2030, someone will sit down and watch *Scandal*. It's a great way of looking back into what the world was like then.'

Having spent so long hammering away at the British film Establishment, Woolley has now joined its ranks. He acts as co-vice-chairman of BAFTA, and recently instigated a new short film festival – separate from the big spring BAFTA ceremony – in an effort to showcase new, young talent. Some of his energies are now passionately focused on 'creating a continuum, a way for the fabric of the new to keep moving forwards'. He is delighted that his experience can benefit younger film-makers. Far from removing himself from their hungry clutches, Woolley makes a point of regularly meeting new talent.

The producer talks about his envy of David Puttnam's opportunity in the mid-eighties to run a Hollywood studio. He has always felt the pull of the Hollywood dream, suggesting that if ever offered the chance to become a studio chief, he would consider it very seriously. Woolley certainly has no intention of going down in history as 'Neil Jordan's producer'.

The relationship between Woolley and Jordan shows the fundamentally different viewpoints between the 'artist–creator' and the 'producer–maker'. One supposedly enjoys a unique talent, while the other helps that talent work to its best potential. Woolley believes films are about creative vision, but also about teamwork and a shared spirit.

It is not inconceivable that Stephen Woolley will direct his own films at some point. Few film producers understand as much as he does about the history, content and changing shape of film-making. In less guarded moments, Woolley has described himself as a frustrated writer, but the opportunity to direct will become increasingly available as his career progresses.

For a young screenwriter or director, Woolley is a hero. To listen to the producer's reaction to the script, the casting, the music, the production values of their film inspires them to strive for greater heights. His energy, single-mindedness and obsession to get films made has served a host of talents and also helped spawn a new generation of writers, directors and producers in the UK.

For Powell, the future is less clear. While Woolley can now concentrate exclusively on film-making without the chore of co-chairing a business empire, Powell has no obvious *modus operandi*. His maverick ways both endear him to and frustrate those who work with him, but he will always be happier selling films on the Croisette at Cannes than sitting in a corporate office. As Michael Kuhn pointed out, it is too late for Powell to change his habits.

Operating as Scala's executive producer on its film projects demands considerably less of him that running the former Palace Group. Why he does not fully produce his own films is unclear, but the reason may lie in his continuing insecurity about the creative side of the industry. Having encouraged Woolley to develop his natural instinct and considerable skills in those areas for so long, Powell seems unsure about his own talent.

On the larger scale, since Powell's dreams of an independently run and controlled film empire crashed, the opportunity to attract and develop new business will remain limited for a while. Nobody understands better than Powell the importance of long-term relationships in the film business. His concern to repay the banks the personal guarantees dating back to that black Christmas of 1992 was seen as admirable by Guinness Mahon and Pierson, Heldring & Pierson. (The latter, incidentally, has now withdrawn from independent film production financing as a result of its losses in the late eighties and early nineties.) Powell's concern to make sure that 'everything's all right with the banks' was most apparent when the Chrysalis deal was completed in such a way as to allow a large sum (approximately £400,000) to be instantly transferred to the banks as the first significant repayment of the £1.25 million personal guarantee.

The ambitious Mega Corporation concept of 1982 was not to be. Nevertheless, over the past decade, Powell has helped to raise more than $150 million towards British film production. It is a record that Richard Branson deeply admires. 'There's a thin dividing line between success and failure in any business. People don't realise that, according to my reckoning, only around five per cent of all companies that start actually see it all the way through. One has to take one's hat off to Nik and Steve. They had great fun and created some brave films and survived against the odds for a long time.'

Branson is acutely aware of the dangers inherent in film production, for his own film interests came close to ruining Virgin when payment of $6 million due for *1984* was withheld for months by an American distributor. 'If it hadn't come, that would have been the end of Virgin,' Branson recalls. 'You have to be a top-one-hundred company to feel completely secure, especially if you enjoy a challenge.'

Branson also stressed, contrary to some of Powell's detractors, that 'Nik is a great friend, a very good dad, and a loyal partner. He always looks for the positive in people.'

People in the film business who do not know Powell well frequently ask how honest he is. 'Nik is honest,' Branson confirmed, and then, laughing, added the classic qualifier, 'As honest as any businessman can be on occasions.'

There is no question that the British film industry – having paid for Palace's weaknesses – now misses many of Palace's strengths. What was achievable during the 1980s, however, may no longer be possible or applicable in the 1990s. Bigger financial pockets and stronger control over the final link in the chain – the cinemas themselves – are required if an independent company is to thrive into the next century. It is ironic that Branson's Virgin Entertainment has now bought up the MGM chain of cinemas for nearly £200 million, and plans to re-enter film distribution as a result of the acquisition.

The record shows that Palace Video was a unique and profitable film and video distribution operation. The company's outstandingly talented staff, guerrilla marketing tactics and ability to reach the public with so few resources were fundamental in changing the wider industry. Without the drain from other companies and Palace's own productions (only an occasional source of hits), Palace Pictures and Palace Video would have been profitable concerns today.

Powell's diversification into other cash-generating media businesses certainly fuelled the Group's expansion and, despite its inevitable stress, probably served to prolong its survival until bad luck and a vicious recession took their toll. Far from lining his own pockets or building a nest egg for the future, Powell initially invested his own time and money in an effort to help young and talented film-makers realise their dreams.

However, the film industry is designed to crush the weak. The few successful film-makers, executives and millionaires who have survived have done so only by being prepared to crush more cruelly and quickly than their opponents. Despite his bark, Powell is probably too selfless and emotional to bite hard when it really counts. Whatever Wardour Street might think, his Achilles' heel is his vulnerability and obsession with doing the right thing. As one Hollywood wag recently said, 'Being a nice person in the film industry is an oxymoron.' Nevertheless, at present, Powell is effectively running one of the most successful independent production companies in the UK, and in 1994 he and Woolley were placed at number two in the *Screen International* 'Power 100'.

Woolley has had plenty of opportunities to leave his new roost.

He could have set up an independent deal with a Hollywood studio and left Powell behind a long time ago. Observers and former Palace staff are surprised that the partners are still together, and aware that Woolley now holds more cards than Powell. Powell is philosophical about Woolley's work in Hollywood, arguing that it is good for Scala to have a co-chairman with such a high profile. Woolley feels that to leave his partner would be a betrayal after all those years spent building Palace. So they are likely to remain together, albeit with Woolley increasingly drawn to Hollywood.

Powell now focuses more attention on Europe, attending markets and festivals across the continent. Although still brusque and hurried, he works at a more gentle pace, and often gives hugely amusing and informed teaching sessions to young, up-and-coming film-makers with such a generosity of spirit that nobody would guess he had lost everything a few years previously – if he did not tell them in his opening line.

The Scala office on Soho's Brewer Street is a long, wide, open-plan room. A stuffed wolf greets you at the entrance, but this office is not the jungle of Wardour Mews. The filing cabinets neatly divide the tables and phones, and the atmosphere is one of cleanliness and organised purposefulness.

The one exception is Powell's work area, a squared-off cul-de-sac furnished with two sofas so old that when you sit on them a puff of dust flies up around you. (Powell now insists that they have clean, new covers.) The old Palace coffee cups are scattered around his table and shelves, while the memorabilia of photos, film posters and awards adorns the walls. Powell is in the offices more often than not. Woolley is invariably away.

The two characters remain omnipresent in the film world and instinctively talk of their future in emotional rather than practical terms. Like Fitzgerald's Gatsby, Nik Powell and Stephen Woolley 'believe in the green light, the orgastic future . . . it eluded them once, but that's no matter – tomorrow they will run faster.'

# Where Are They Now?

Many of the Palace's former employees and associates enjoy considerable business and creative influence in the film industry today.

**Martyn Auty**, the former head of Palace Television and producer of *Woman at War*, has moved on to produce successful feature films, including Sandy Johnson's *Soul Survivors* in 1995. He is unlikely to return to Poland again.

**Daniel Battsek** is now one of the most powerful film executives in Europe, having left Palace in February 1993 to head up Buena Vista UK, the first part of a new Walt Disney distribution operation for the whole of Europe. As one former Palace employee put it, 'I realised just how successful Daniel had become when I saw him emerge from a stretch limo dressed in a designer suit, wearing dark glasses, and talking into a mobile phone as he entered a cinema for a Disney screening.' Battsek is now European Acquisitions Director, Vice President; Managing Director UK, Buena Vista International.

**Joe Boyd**, executive producer of *Scandal*, has produced records for such groups as Pink Floyd, REM, 10,000 Maniacs, Richard Thomson and Fairport Convention. He had already produced one film besides *Scandal* – the 1974 rock documentary, *Jimi Hendrix*. Boyd is now a director of leading independent Rykodisc, where he runs his own Hannibal record label.

**Wendy Broom**, Nik Powell's personal assistant, finally left Scala Productions in late 1995 to become a production co-ordinator on independent films.

**Chris Brown** now works in Australia as a film producer. Although unavailable to be interviewed for this book, he told the author that he 'still has chronic nightmares about being on the set of *Siesta*, trying to explain why the crew's money hasn't turned up!'

**Sue Bruce-Smith** left Palace in 1986 to head up the British Film Institute's film sales operation. She moved to the BBC in 1993, and currently holds the position of Business Manager, Feature Films.

**Patrick Cassavetti** has continued to work as a film producer, making films such as *Talk Of Angels* and *Emma*, both set for release in 1996.

**Michael Caton-Jones** moved on to direct *Memphis Belle* (1990); *Doc Hollywood* (1991); *This Boy's Life* (1993) and *Rob Roy* (1995). He is directing Michael Thomas's screenplay of *B Monkey* in 1996, which is being produced by Stephen Woolley and Colin Vaines. He currently lives just outside Dublin, explaining that his move from Hollywood to Ireland was a case of finding some balance. 'At least the Irish have two chips on their shoulders, 'cos those fucking Scots have just got one fucking huge one!'

**Chris Craib** worked as consultant for Goldcrest (the resurrected version) after Palace collapsed, and has now built up a small independent consultancy to the film industry.

**Jaye Davidson** went back on the dole after starring in *The Crying Game*. He was doing odd jobs, modelling round London, when the producers of the $55 million Hollywood picture *Stargate* sent a courier to his home with a message that read: 'If you're interested in this film, phone this man.' Davidson decided he couldn't be bothered to play an Egyptian sun god in a Hollywood sci-fi flick, so he told the producers at two a.m. down the phone: 'All right, I'll do it for a million dollars.' He was told to phone back in an hour. When he did, the producers said, 'Yeah, we'll give you a million dollars.' *Stargate* was Davidson's second film, and his second hit.

**Finola Dwyer** followed up *Backbeat* with a co-executive producer's credit on Angela Pope's *The Hollow Reed*. She is currently developing a David Mamet project, *The Duchess of Malfi*; and *The Dead Heart*, a screenplay by Michael Thomas from the novel by Douglas Kennedy, to be made with Scala.

**Angie Errigo** moved on from PSA to full-time journalism and film criticism in the early 1990s. She now reviews for *Empire* and *Premiere* magazines among others, and is an energetic radio broadcaster. She is very, very happy not being in PR.

**Michael Garland** joined Katy McGuinness's The Good Film Company when he left London in 1992. He moved on from there in early 1995 to produce Mary McGuckian's *This Is The Sea*, his first full producing credit.

**Peter Hitchen** wrote an open letter to the film industry in September 1995, explaining that he was leaving Barclays Bank Soho Square to set up his own business in TV, film and multimedia. Part of the reason for his departure, he explained, was due to the 'growing opportunities ... especially in the area of production finance which cannot and perhaps should not be met within the context of a commercial clearing bank relationship'.

**Premila Hoon** has remained in charge of the entertainment banking department at Guinness Mahon, where she has overseen the financing of a large number of independent films.

**Bob Hoskins** capitalised on his success in *Mona Lisa* with *Who Framed Roger Rabbit?* in 1988. Since then he has had mixed fortunes, including a lead part in *Super Mario Bros.* The film turned out to be one of the most expensive independent disappointments of the 1990s. Hoskins has also pursued his directing interests, with *The Raggedy Rawney* (1987) and *The Rainbow* (1994).

**Norman Humphrey** works as an independent management consultant, offering 'specialist strategic and practical financial advice to a portfolio of corporate clients within the entertainment sector'.

**Angie Hunt**, one of Palace's early video marketing stars, now works in America, writing soap operas.

**John Hurt** went from *Scandal* to the sets of three films in 1990: *The Field*, *Frankenstein Unbound* and *Romeo–Juliet*. Other recent films include *King Ralph, Resident Alien, I Dreamt I Woke Up, Dark at Noon* and *Lapse of Memory*. He has recently played the lead in *Saigon Baby*, a BBC film made in 1995, and a role in *The Darkening*, a high-technology interactive film to be released in 1996.

**Robert Jones** found he had acquired something of a reputation from his ten years at Palace. He went on to write PolyGram's UK business plan before the company moved into film distribution, and made numerous acquisitions for them, including *Reservoir Dogs* and *Shallow Grave*. Now an independent producer, he has played a role in four films, including the 1995 hit, *The Usual Suspects*, starring Stephen Baldwin and Gabriel Byrne.

**Neil Jordan** quickly succeeded in adding a Hollywood box office hit, *Interview with the Vampire*, to his best original screenplay Oscar for *The*

*Crying Game*. He published a novel, *Sunrise With Sea Monster*, in 1994, and directed his own screenplay, *Michael Collins*, in 1995.

**Elizabeth Karlsen** produced (with Olivia Stewart) Terence Davies's *The Neon Bible* and Angela Pope's *The Hollow Reed* in 1995.

**Tony Kelly** is now a senior management partner in two private companies: QED Media Solutions and On Demand Management.

**David Leland** went on from directing *The Big Man* to write screenplays for Warner Brothers, The Kennedy/Marshall Company, Paramount, Disney's Hollywood Pictures and Fox 2000. He is expected to return to directing in 1996.

**Katy McGuinness** returned to her native Dublin after completing post-production on *Waterland*, where she set up an independent production company, The Good Film Company. Its first film was Barry Devlin's *All Things Bright and Beautiful*, made for the BBC's Screen Two series. Her second film was Valerie Jalongo's *Spaghetti Show*, produced in 1995.

**Robert Mitchell** joined Daniel Battsek at Buena Vista International (UK) as executive marketing director. He helped his former Palace colleague build a sales and marketing team. Together, the two men have enjoyed a meteoric run of success, releasing films such as Quentin Tarantino's *Pulp Fiction*, *The Lion King*, *Muriel's Wedding*, *Cool Runnings* and *Pocahontas*.

**Angela Morrison** was one of the few Palace employees to move across to Scala Productions, where she continued to work as an entertainment lawyer. A year later, she was appointed Head of Business Affairs at Working Title, the fully-owned subsidiary of PolyGram Filmed Entertainment. One of her abiding memories of Nik Powell was the moment when she offered a Dutch banker her new Scala Productions business card. Powell swiftly intervened, saying, 'Don't give him that! He already knows you. Those things cost money!'

**Liam Neeson** shrugged off *The Big Man*'s problems, rising to international stardom via his title role in Steven Spielberg's *Schindler's List* in 1993. He plays the lead role in Neil Jordan's *Michael Collins*, due for release in 1996.

**Irving Rappaport** was last seen touring the United States performing the part of Joseph in *I was Jesus's Dad*, a one-man show written by John Dowie. It is rumoured that he is to produce a filmed version of *I was an Alien Sex God* – the cult hit of the 1995 Edinburgh Festival.

**JoAnne Sellar**, undeterred by the collapse of *Dark Blood* following the death of River Phoenix, went on to produce Clive Barker's *Lord of Illusions* in 1994. She is currently working in Los Angeles on a range of feature film projects.

**Anne Sheehan** left her Palace/Scala position as Financial Controller – Productions, at the end of July 1992, joining the BBC's financial planning department. She is now a top management accountant at the BBC, responsible for single drama and BBC films.

**Richard Stanley** fought a very personal and high-profile battle over the editing and release of *Dust Devil*, one of Palace's last productions. The film was finally released as a 'director's cut' on video. Following that disagreement, he went on to direct *The Island of Dr Moreau*, based on his own screenplay. The film went into production in Australia on 5 August 1995, starring Marlon Brando and Val Kilmer. Three days later, Stanley was abruptly taken off the film, following protracted rows with Kilmer. Stanley subsequently joined an idiosyncratic group called the Ferals, a commune in Southern Australia, and is yet to return to film-making.

**Phil Symes** and his company PSA parted from Rogers & Cowan in October 1994. Symes set up a new company Warren Cowan/Phil Symes & Associates in November 1994. The Soho Square-based company remains very active in film PR and marketing.

**Michael Thomas** co-wrote Iain Softley's *Backbeat*, which he followed up by writing a script, *Tom Mix and Pancho Villa*, to be directed by Tony Scott. He wrote the screenplay for *B. Monkey*, which went into production in early 1996; and *West With The Night*, set to go into production at the end of 1996, starring Julia Ormond. He is also working on a Finola Dwyer project he likes to call *Fuck Me Dead* [*The Dead Heart*].

**Paul Webster** moved into production with great success, producing such hit films as *Drop Dead Fred*, starring Rik Mayall. In an ironic circular move, Webster was appointed Vice President of Miramax Film productions in 1995.

**Bob and Harvey Weinstein** remain conspicuous and busy running the Disney-owned Miramax Films. They enjoyed a huge hit with Quentin Tarantino's *Pulp Fiction* in 1994, but the duo are tipped to move across at some point to Dreamworks SKG, the new Steven Spielberg–Jeffrey Katzenberg–David Geffen Hollywood studio launched in 1995. The Weinstein brothers refused to be interviewed for this book, despite two letters, five faxes, numerous phone messages, and personal requests from Powell and Woolley. During the Cannes Film Festival 1994, the author made an effort to interview Harvey Weinstein, and met him on the steps of the Carlton Hotel, where he asked, 'Could you spare some time this year to talk about Palace?' Harvey retorted: 'I know exactly who you are. Fuck off and get outta here!' Three days later, the author confronted the mogul in the lobby of the Majestic Hotel. Weinstein gave a deep sigh, and said: 'Hey, it's nothing personal. It's just that those two guys worked *so* hard for *so* long. I just don't wanna see anyone knock them!'

# PALACE'S PRINCIPAL
# DISTRIBUTION CREDITS
# (UK theatrical and video)

|  | *Title* | *Director* |
|---|---|---|
| Theatrical Credits | *Angel* (1982) | Neil Jordan |
|  | *Bloody Kids* (1982) | Stephen Frears |
|  | *Pixote* (1982) | Hector Babenco |
|  | *Querelle* (1982) | Rainer Werner Fassbinder |
|  | *Diva* (1983) | Jean-Jacques Beineix |
|  | *Evil Dead* (1983) | Sam Raimi |
|  | *Merry Christmas Mr Lawrence* (1983) | Nagisa Oshima |
|  | *Stop Making Sense* (1984) | Jonathan Demme |
|  | *Blood Simple* (1984) | Joel and Ethan Coen |
|  | *Nightmare on Elm Street* (series, 1984–) | Wes Craven |
|  | *Paris Texas* (1984) | Wim Wenders |
|  | *Element of Crime* (1984) | Lars von Trier |
|  | *Kiss of the Spider Woman* (1985) | Hector Babenco |
|  | *The Hit* (1985) | Stephen Frears |
|  | *Insignificance* (1985) | Nicholas Roeg |
|  | *Nine ½ Weeks* (1985) | Adrian Lyne |
|  | *River's Edge* (1986) | Tim Hunter |
|  | *Down by Law* (1986) | Jim Jarmusch |
|  | *Sid and Nancy* (1986) | Alex Cox |
|  | *Wish You Were Here* (1986) | David Leland |
|  | *Prick Up Your Ears* (1987) | Stephen Frears |
|  | *Slam Dance* (1987) | Wayne Wang |
|  | *Red Sorghum* (1987) | Zhang Yimou |
|  | *The Year My Voice Broke* (1987) | John Duigan |
|  | *Sammy and Rosie Get Laid* (1987) | Stephen Frears |

## The Egos Have Landed

| | |
|---|---|
| *A World Apart* (1987) | Chris Menges |
| *High Hopes* (1988) | Mike Leigh |
| *Drowning By Numbers* (1988) | Peter Greenaway |
| *My Left Foot* (1989) | Jim Sheridan |
| *Mystery Train* (1989) | Jim Jarmusch |
| *Cinema Paradiso* (1990) | Guiseppe Tornatore |
| *The Cook, The Thief, His Wife and Her Lover* (1989) | Peter Greenaway |
| *Monsieur Hire (1989)* | Patrice Leconte |
| *The Sheltering Sky* (1990) | Bernardo Bertolucci |
| *When Harry Met Sally* (1990) | Rob Reiner |
| *The Grifters* (1990) | Stephen Frears |
| *Mr and Mrs Bridge* (1990) | James Ivory |
| *Wild at Heart* (1990) | David Lynch |
| *Edward II* (1991) | Derek Jarman |
| *Life is Sweet* (1991) | Mike Leigh |
| *Riff Raff* (1991) | Ken Loach |
| *Prospero's Books* (1991) | Peter Greenaway |
| *Whore* (1991) | Ken Russell |
| *Nikita* (1991) | Luc Besson |
| *Shattered* (1991) | Wolfgang Petersen |
| *The Hairdresser's Husband* (1992) | Patrice Leconte |

| | *Title* | *Director* |
|---|---|---|
| Video only/Credits | The John Cassavetes catalogue | |
| | The Rainer Werner Fassbinder catalogue | |
| | The John Waters catalogue | |
| | The Werner Herzog catalogue | |
| | *La Dolce Vita* (1960) | Federico Fellini |
| | *The Tempest* (1979) | Derek Jarman |
| | *Mephisto* (1981) | Istvan Szabo |
| | *Fitzcarraldo* (1982) | Werner Herzog |
| | *The Snowman* (1982) | Dianne Jackson |
| | *The Making of Thriller* (1984) | John Landis |
| | *A Zed and Two Noughts* (1985) | Peter Greenaway |
| | *She's Gotta Have It* (1986) | Spike Lee |
| | *Jean De Florette* (1986) | Claude Berri |
| | *Manon Des Sources* (1986) | Claude Berri |

# Bibliography

Martyn Auty & Nick Roddick (Editors), *British Cinema Now*, British Film Institute, London, 1985.

John Boorman, *Money into Light*, Faber & Faber, London, 1985.

John Boorman and Walter Donohue (Editors), *Projections 3*, Faber & Faber, London, 1994.

Mick Brown, *Richard Branson*, Headline, London, 1988, 1992.

Peter Chippendale & Suzanne Franks, *Dished! The Rise and Fall of British Satellite Broadcasting*, Simon & Schuster, London, 1991.

Andrew Davidson, *Under The Hammer*, William Heinemann, London, 1992.

Tom Dewe Mathews, *Censored*, Chatto & Windus, London, 1994.

Jake Eberts and Terry Ilott, *My Indecision Is Final: The Rise and Fall of Goldcrest Films*, Faber & Faber, London, 1990.

Tim Jackson, *Virgin King: Inside Richard Branson's Business Empire*, HarperCollins, London, 1994.

Ephraim Katz, *The Film Encyclopedia* (second edition), HarperCollins, New York, 1994.

Christine Keeler, *Scandal!* Xanadu, London, 1989.

Tom Milne (Editor), *The Time Out Film Guide*, Penguin Books, London, 1993.

James Park, *Learning to Dream: The New British Cinema*, Faber & Faber, London, 1984.

Julia Phillips, *You'll Never Eat Lunch In This Town Again*, Signet, New York, 1992.

Brian J. Robb, *River Phoenix: A Short Life*, Plexus, London, 1994, 1995.

Sandie Shaw, *The World at my Feet: A Personal Adventure*, HarperCollins, London, 1991.

Alexander Walker, *National Heroes: British Cinema in the Seventies and Eighties*, Harrap, London, 1985.

Rona Wheaton, *Forever Young, Untimely Deaths in the Screen World*, Warner Books, London, 1994.

Andrew Yule, *David Puttnam: The Story So Far*, Sphere Books, London, 1989.

Andrew Yule, *Hollywood A Go-Go: The True Story of The Cannon Film Empire*, Sphere Books, London, 1987.

# Index

Figures in **bold** refer to the *Where are they now?* section.

313

# Index